A DIFFERENT GOSPEL

A
*D*IFFERENT
GOSPEL

UPDATED EDITION

D. R. McConnell

Foreword by Hank Hanegraaff
Author of *Christianity In Crisis*

HENDRICKSON
PUBLISHERS

A Different Gospel: Updated Edition
Copyright © 1988, 1995 by Hendrickson Publishers, Inc.
P. O. Box 3473
Peabody, Massachusetts 01961-3473
Printed in the United States of America.

ISBN 978-1-56563 132-8

Fourth printing updated edition — October 2007

Library of Congress Cataloging-in-Publication Data

McConnell, D. R.
    A different gospel: biblical and historical insights into the
Word of Faith movement / Dan R. McConnell. — Updated ed.
        p.   cm.
    Revision of thesis (master's—Oral Roberts University, 1982)
originally submitted under title: The Kenyon connection.
    Includes bibliographical references (p.).
    ISBN 1-56563-132-3
    1. Faith movement (Hagin)—Controversial literature.
2. Hagin, Kenneth E., 1917– . 3. Kenyon, Essek William,
1867–1948. I. Title
    BR1643.5.M329   1995
    289.9—dc20
                                                94-49586
                                                    CIP

Table of Contents

Preface to the Original Edition

This study is an expanded and updated version of my master's thesis, "The Kenyon Connection: A Theological and Historical Analysis of the Cultic Origins of the Faith Movement," which was submitted to the faculty of the School of Theology at Oral Roberts University in 1982. Since that thesis was completed, much new historical information about the origins of the Faith movement has come to light, most of which has confirmed my original thesis concerning its "connection" to the metaphysical cults. The theological analysis demonstrating the cultic parallels between the Faith theology and metaphysics has been greatly expanded in this study and, I hope, clarified. I have endeavored to write for the church, both clergy and laity, and I have tried to make simplicity, not profundity, my guiding principle.

With a few notable exceptions, the Faith movement has not been the object of scholarly historical research. Dr. Charles Farah and Dr. Gordon Fee have provided able biblical and theological critiques of the movement, but its historical origins were not within their areas of interest. Other critiques, though well-meaning, have shed far more heat than light. Bruce Barron's *The Health and Wealth Gospel* (IVP, 1987) contains pertinent biographical information on some of the key players of the movement, but offers little regarding its historical background. Clearly a strong need exists for a definitive history to be written of the Faith movement.

One would suspect, therefore, that what follows is an attempt to provide that history. That is not the case. I have included much historical information about the Faith movement in this work, but it in no way constitutes a neutral historical treatise. Although I believe that I have treated the historical evidence in a fair fashion and that my findings will bear the scrutiny of historiographical analysis, I must admit that my intent is not merely to report this information in the placid manner of a professional historian. I have used my historical findings as the basis of a theological polemic against the Faith theology, something a true historian would never do. I have chosen to do so because I believe that, because of its cultic origins, the Faith theology represents a serious threat to the theological orthodoxy and spiritual orthopraxy of the independent charismatic movement. I do not, therefore, want to give the slightest pretense of wanting just to write history.

There are many people I now want to acknowledge and thank for their help in the researching and writing of this book. In expressing my gratitude to those mentioned here, I do not want to imply that they would necessarily agree with all or any of its contents, for which I am solely responsible.

Several university staff and faculty members have gone far beyond the call of duty in their assistance. I would mention Karen Robinson, former director of the Holy Spirit Research Center at ORU, in this regard. The library and archives staff of Barrington College, which is now merged with Gordon College, aided the writer in obtaining materials about Kenyon available nowhere else. Howard Ferrin, former chancellor of Barrington College, was particularly helpful in sharing his insights about Kenyon, who founded Barrington under the name of Bethel Bible Institute. Also, special thanks go to John Coffee and Richard Wentworth for their input about Kenyon's alma mater, Emerson College, now contained in their book, *A Century of Eloquence: The History of Emerson College, 1880–1980.*

Several personal interviews were crucial to this paper. Kenyon's daughter, Ruth Kenyon Houseworth, answered relentless questions about her father, always with clarity, accuracy and, most of all, patience. John Osteen, Fred Price, and Charles Capps took time out of their busy schedules to answer some tough questions about their movement. John Kennington and Ern Baxter provided invaluable information from their personal reminiscences about Kenyon, particularly about his background in metaphysics.

I would like to thank the editorial staff of Hendrickson Publishers for its patience and support, particularly Patrick Alexander, who has endured much in helping a first-time author. I trust that his confidence in this work will not be disappointed. Finally, I want to thank my wife, Wendy, who in my absence did double duty with our four children, and who in my presence listened with grace to my incessant rambling about this book. Het is eindelijk klaar gekomen, en ik hou van je!

D. R. M.
Tulsa, Oklahoma
October 1987

Foreword
by Hank Hanegraaff

In my book *Christianity in Crisis* I pointed out that some of the most scholarly rebuttals of the Faith Movement have come from within the ranks of the charismatic movement. Notable examples include Walter Martin, Gordon Fee, and Charles Farah. None is more noteworthy however than Dan McConnell. From his perspective as a former adjunct professor of theology at Oral Roberts University, he has critiqued Faith theology in a profound and persuasive fashion.

As a confirmed advocate of the charismatic renewal, McConnell writes,

> I would no more reject charismatic renewal than I would reject the Holy Spirit who gave it (see below, p. xxii).

> Nevertheless, it must be admitted that, with a few notable exceptions, the Faith Movement has enjoyed increasing acceptance by charismatics (see below, p. xxiii).

> Although most people assume that the Faith theology is a product of the Pentecostal and charismatic movements, this assumption is not historically accurate. . . . The Faith movement can be traced historically to cultic sources (see below, p. xxiv).

While Faith teachers have been able to cleverly disguise themselves as charismatics, it would be a grave error to equate the Faith movement with the charismatic renewal. Some of today's clearest thinkers and keenest theologians are charismatic Christians. Men like Chuck Smith, pastor of Calvary Chapel of Costa Mesa, California, and founder of one of the largest and most effective Christian movements in modern-day history; Elliot Miller, editor of the *Christian Research Journal* and author of *A Crash Course on the New Age Movement,* and George Carey, respected theologian and archbishop of Canterbury.

McConnell demonstrates that both the "roots and fruits" of Faith theology are decidedly metaphysical rather than charismatic. With irrefutable documentation he traces the historical development and heretical doctrines of Faith theology to such cults as Religious Science, Christian Science, and the Unity School of Christianity.

E. W. Kenyon, the real father of the modern-day Faith movement, "majored" in metaphysics. McConnell provides ample documentation that Kenneth Hagin, referred to by *Charisma* magazine as "the granddaddy of the Faith teachers" and the "father of the Faith movement" in reality plagiarized Kenyon. Hagin's theological perversions were in turn proliferated through men like Fredrick Price and Kenneth Copeland, who is today dubbed by *Time* magazine as the chief exponent of Faith theology.

While the Faith movement is undeniably cultic, it should be pointed out that *there are many sincere, born-again believers within the movement.* I cannot overemphasize this crucial point. These believers, for the most part, seem to be wholly unaware of the movement's cultic theology. We must therefore take care to judge the *theology* of the Faith movement rather than those being seduced by it.

For the most part, charismatics and noncharismatics are unified when it comes to the essentials of the historic Christian faith—such as the meaning of faith, the nature of God, and the person and work of Jesus Christ. Their differences, on the other hand, involve nonessential Christian doctrine—primarily dealing with issues surrounding the perpetuity of spiritual gifts. And while we may vigorously debate such secondary matters within the faith, we must never divide over them.

Not so, however, when it comes to the Faith movement; there we must draw the line. The Faith movement has systematically subverted the very essence of Christianity so as to present us with a counterfeit Christ and a counterfeit Christianity. Therefore standing against the theology of the Faith movement does not *divide*; rather, it *unites* believers.

I have become both weary and wary of those who use the perversions of the Faith movement to drive a wedge between charismatic and noncharismatic Christians. Frankly, this is both counterproductive and divisive, for the Faith movement is not charismatic; it is cultic.

The crisis currently faced by Christianity—in the form of the Faith movement—does not center upon ongoing dialogues and debates among charismatic and noncharismatic believers. Rather, it involves a life-and-death struggle between orthodoxy and heresy—between the kingdom of Christ and the kingdom of the cults.

With penetrating analysis and painstaking attention to detail, Dan McConnell unmasks Faith theology to reveal its cultic identity and to refute its false teachings. He is to be commended for providing an able defense and a potent antidote against a growing cancer feeding on the Body of Christ.

The apostle Paul warned the Christians in Galatia to guard against those preaching a different gospel—a "gospel" contrary to what was proclaimed by Christ and the apostles (Gal. 1:6–9). With so many religious beliefs, philosophies, and teachings circulating today, we must be even more diligent to observe Paul's admonition and heed his words. "Watch your life and doctrine closely," he told young Timothy. "Persevere in them, because if you do, you will save both yourself and your hearers" (1 Tim. 4:16).

Introduction: Charismatics at the Crossroads

I am amazed that you are so quickly deserting Him who called you by the grace of Christ, for a different gospel; which is really not another; only there are some who are disturbing you, and want to distort the gospel of Christ. But even though we, or an angel from heaven, should preach to you a gospel contrary to that which we have preached to you, let him be accursed. As we have said before, so I say again now, if any man is preaching to you a gospel contrary to that which you received, let him be accursed.

—Apostle Paul, Galatians 1:6–9,
NASB

Error, indeed, is never set forth in its naked deformity, lest, being thus exposed, it should at once be detected. But it is craftily decked out in an attractive dress, so as, by its outward form, to make it appear to the inexperienced (ridiculous as the expression may seem) more true than truth itself.

—Irenaeus, *Against Heresies* 1:2

After the Lord Jesus ascended to heaven, the gospel he had entrusted to the church was quickly perverted. Paul warned of "a different gospel" in approximately A.D. 55, a mere 20 to 25 years after the resurrection of Jesus. In Galatians, Paul expresses amazement that the "distortion" of the gospel had taken place so "quickly."[1] He also expresses anger that false teachers in the church were "hindering" and "disturbing" it with false doctrine (Gal. 5:7–12). The Galatians were in danger of "being severed from Christ" and "falling from grace" as the result of listening to these "teachers" (Gal. 5:4).

If the church in Galatia were the only example of this phenomenon, then perhaps it could be dismissed as an isolated incident. There are, however, numerous examples in the New Testament of this bitter conflict with false doctrine. Paul also warned the church of Ephesus that soon after his departure, "savage wolves will come in among you, not sparing the flock; and from among your own selves men will arise, speaking perverse things, to draw away

the disciples after them" (Acts 20:29, 30). These predators were all
the more dangerous because they had infiltrated the Christian community and were doing their damage from within. Through their
false teaching, they were attempting to lure sheep from the flock so
as to prey upon them in isolation. The churches in Rome, Corinth,
Colossae, Thessalonica, Philippi, Crete, and the Diaspora all show
additional evidence of the struggle with false doctrine. We often
think of the first-century church in very idealistic terms. But had it
not been for these "different gospels," the New Testament as we
know it today would never have been written.

Sadly, the struggle with false doctrine did not end with the
writing of the New Testament. History attests to numerous "different
gospels," and from the first century on these gospels have found a
ready market in the church. The true and orthodox gospel of Jesus
Christ has always had to compete with false doctrine for the hearts
and minds of believers. In fact, it has often been said that "the
history of theology is in large part a history of heresies."[2] In other
words, the struggle between heresy and orthodoxy has taken place
in every century of church history. Each new generation of church
leadership has had "to exhort in sound doctrine and to refute those
who contradict" (Tit. 1:9). We can thank God that we have centuries
of historical orthodoxy to fall back on in this struggle, but the
struggle itself continues.

This is no less true today. The twentieth-century Christian is
faced with a plethora, a virtual "legion" of gospels. All of these are
garbed in the most alluring of dress and call to the believer in the
most seductive of whispers. As quoted above, Irenaeus, the great
second-century defender of the faith against the heresy of gnosticism, warned that error is never put forward in a manner that ex-
poses its grotesque deformities. Instead, it is packaged in outward
adornment so appealing that it appears "more true than truth itself."
The tremendous appeal of heresy is that it *looks* and *sounds* like the
real thing! Consequently, the demarcation between heresy and orthodoxy is rarely clear cut. The most dangerous heresies lie in the
gray area, a shadowy place of both light and darkness. These "different gospels" may vary in the particular doctrinal error they propagate, but all heresies have one thing in common: their threat to the
church is directly proportionate to the degree in which they appear
orthodox. The most dangerous of lies is not the bald-faced lie, for
that is easily detected and rejected. A half-truth always does far more
damage than a bald-faced lie.

Not only do different gospels *look* like the real thing, they *sound* like it as well. Another great defender of the faith, Walter Martin, "cult-buster" par excellence, says this of the ability of cults to mimic the gospel of Jesus:

> The student of cultism then, must be prepared to scale the language barrier of terminology. First, he must recognize that it does exist, and second, he must acknowledge the very real fact that unless terms are defined . . . the semantic jungle which the cults have created will envelop him, making difficult, if not impossible, a proper contrast between the teachings of the cults and those of orthodox Christianity.[3]

The most successful cults in the U.S. today use the same terminology, the same phraseology, and the same proof-texts as evangelical Christians. Dialogue with people trapped in these cults is all but impossible because both sides use the very same terms with radically different meanings. Until terms are defined, any differentiation between cultic teachings and orthodox Christianity is an exercise in futility, which is precisely what the cultist wants. Those who preach different gospels want their deception to sound like such a perfect recording of the orthodox gospel that the believer is left scratching his head wondering "Is it live? . . . Or is it Memorex?"

Walter Martin's warning against the "semantic jungle" through which the cults attempt to envelop the believer with confusing terminology should not be heard as just a warning against blatant cults "out there somewhere." It is a strange curiosity that those Christians who are most adamant that ours is the generation that will see the Lord's return—and the end-time deception and apostasy associated with his return—look for signs of this deception *outside* the church, in such conspiracies as the New Age movement, and in such cults as Mormonism, Jehovah's Witnesses, and Christian Science. Admittedly, these movements pose potential threats to the church, but perhaps we would do better to look for the deception of the end-times where Jesus and the New Testament predicted it would occur: *within* the church, within groups that call themselves "Christian" but which actually preach a different gospel.

In speaking of the possibility that sincere believers could be deceived into believing a different gospel, we are not referring to the legitimate doctrinal differences that exist among Christians. What Paul was referring to in Gal. 1:6–9 was much more than that. This different gospel was not just "another" organic variety of the same gospel; the meaning of the Greek words indicates that it was an alien gospel that was of an altogether different kind.[4] One need look no further for evidence of the absolute difference between the Pauline gospel and the false gospel with which the Galatians were being deceived than to the fact that Paul invokes an anathema, a curse of destruction by God, on any being, human or angelic, who preaches any gospel other than the gospel delivered to him by the Lord Jesus himself.[5] Clearly, to preach or believe a different gospel is an extremely serious matter.

We who count ourselves "charismatics" are at a crossroads. The charismatic renewal has reached a spiritual intersection in its history, and the decisions made by charismatic leadership in the next five years will, I believe, forever determine our place in the annals of church history. Nothing less than the doctrinal orthodoxy of our movement is at stake. Responsible leadership within the charismatic renewal must weigh seriously the evidence presented in this book—and the other books like it that I believe will be forthcoming—and, at whatever cost, lead the renewal on the road of return to the orthodox faith of the Christian church.

I am writing this book as a confirmed, unapologetic advocate of and participant in the charismatic renewal. Furthermore, while I am not a Pentecostal by way of theology, I believe that there is sound, biblical evidence to support many of the practices and experiences of charismatic renewal. Those who interpret this book as a rejection of charismatic renewal interpret it wrongly. I would no more reject charismatic renewal than I would reject the Holy Spirit who gave it.

Nevertheless, there has been, and still is, much that passes for "truth" in the charismatic renewal that I believe deeply grieves the Holy Spirit, who is "the Spirit of truth." I would go so far as to say that many in the present charismatic renewal preach and practice a different gospel. This is a most serious charge and one that is not lightly made. It is rendered all the more serious because those preaching this error are some of the most prominent figures in the charismatic renewal. I am referring to Kenneth Hagin, Kenneth Copeland, and all the other ministers and churches who are a part of what we shall refer to in this book as "the Faith movement."[6] With its "faith-formulas" for health, wealth, and prosperity, the Faith movement has taken the charismatic renewal by storm. No one could seriously question its success. The price tag of its success, however, has been nothing less than the orthodoxy of the charismatic renewal. Those in the Faith movement are now, and have been for years, preaching a different gospel.

One may well ask how this different gospel of the Faith movement escaped the notice of the church. The answer is that it hasn't; at least, not entirely. In the last decade, the Faith theology has been described in various publications as "heresy," "cultic," "gnostic," and "a work of Satan." This book is only the latest in a whole series of publications that have challenged the orthodoxy of the Faith movement; it is neither the first, nor the last, of its kind.

Nevertheless, it must be admitted that, with a few notable exceptions,[7] the Faith movement has enjoyed increasing acceptance by charismatics, and the voices being raised against it are fewer and quieter. The reasons for this growing silence are twofold. First, the church has not seen this gospel for what it is largely because of what Walter Martin calls "the language barrier of terminology." The Faith movement uses so much evangelical and Pentecostal terminology and so many biblical proof-texts that most believers are lulled into a false sense of security as to its orthodoxy.

Second, as even one of its arch-critics has admitted, the Faith gospel is "without question the most attractive message being preached today or, for that matter, in the whole history of the Church."[8] Seldom if ever, has there been a gospel that has promised so much, and demanded so little. The Faith gospel is a message ideally suited to the twentieth-century American Christian. In an age in America characterized by complexity, the Faith gospel gives simple, if not revelational, answers. In an economy fueled by materialism and fired by the ambitions of the "upwardly mobile," the Faith gospel preaches wealth and prosperity. The Faith gospel promises health and long life to a world in which death can come a myriad of different ways. Finally, in an international environment characterized by anarchy, in which terrorists strike at will and nuclear holocaust can come screaming from the sky at any moment, the Faith gospel confers an authority with which the believer can supposedly exercise complete control over his or her own environment. Little wonder that armed with such a gospel the Faith movement has grown to the extent that in the minds of many it is no longer just a *part* of the charismatic movement: it *is* the charismatic movement.

So, what is so bad about this association? What is so "different" about the gospel of the Faith movement? Why are there so many outside the movement who are bitterly outspoken in their opposition? Why are such inflammatory words like "cultic" and "heretical" being used by these opponents to describe the Faith movement? The purpose of this book is to answer these very questions. We shall attempt to prove that both the "roots" and the "fruits" of the Faith movement are those of a different gospel, not the gospel of the Lord Jesus Christ. The charges of cultism and heresy leveled against the Faith movement in the past are not without basis. The Faith movement is cultic because of its roots (its historical origins) and it is heretical because of its fruits (its doctrines and practices).

Although most people assume that the Faith theology is a product of the Pentecostal and charismatic movements, this assumption is not historically accurate. The historical origins of the Faith movement are not primarily Pentecostal or charismatic. The Faith movement can be traced historically to cultic sources. As a result, both its doctrines and practices contain heretical elements. The first part of the book will examine the historical origins of the Faith movement and the second part will critique its theological doctrines. Our analysis of the historical origins of the Faith movement will begin with determining who it is that authored the teachings upon which the movement is founded.

Notes

1. In this context, "quickly" could mean "so soon" after their conversion, or quite possibly, "so rashly" after the first opportunity to desert presented itself. J. B. Lightfoot, *St. Paul's Epistle to the Galatians* (reprint; Peabody, Mass.: Hendrickson, 1981), p. 75.

2. Harold O. J. Brown, *Heresies: The Image of Christ in the Mirror of Heresy and Orthodoxy from the Apostles to the Present* (New York: Doubleday, 1984), p. xxiii.

3. Walter R. Martin, *The Kingdom of the Cults: An Analysis of the Major Cult Systems in the Present Christian Era* (Minneapolis, Minn.: Bethany Fellowship, 1977), p. 18.

4. In the Greek this effect is achieved by the use of two different words to indicate "another." *Allos* means "another of the same kind" or "another in a series," while *heteros* means "another of a different kind" (e.g., "heterosexual"). Although some scholars rightly note that *heteros* and *allos* can be used interchangeably, in this context the difference is apparent. Cf. *Amplified Bible*.

5. Many have interpreted *anathema* to connote the idea of excommunication, but it was actually used of objects, either good or bad, consecrated to God for his use and purposes. *Anathema* could be used of "votive gifts" to the glory of God as in Luke 21:5, or it could be used of an invocation of the curse of God, as in Acts 23:14; Rom. 9:3; 1 Cor. 12:3, 16:22. The destructive element of *anathema* in Galatians is corroborated by the fact that in Gal. 5:12 Paul prays, "Would that those who are troubling you would even mutilate themselves." The word translated by the *NASB* as "mutilate" actually means

"to castrate," as indicated by the *NEB* translation, "As for those agitators, they had better go the whole way and make eunuchs of themselves."

6. The "Faith movement" is also known as "the Word movement" and "the Word of Faith movement" or, by its detractors, as "the Faith-Formula movement" or "the Hyper-Faith movement." Besides Hagin and Copeland, some of the main preachers and authors of the Faith movement are: Ken Hagin, Jr., Gloria Copeland, Fred Price, Jerry Savelle, Charles Capps, Norvel Hayes, John Osteen, Robert Tilton, Lester Sumrall, Ed Dufresne, Charles Cowan, Marilyn Hickey, Ken Stewart, Roy Hicks, Don Gossett, and Buddy Harrison. Until his death on Dec. 8, 1984, Hobart Freeman was regarded as a renegade preacher of the Faith movement who was ostracized for his radical beliefs on healing. More shall be said of Freeman later.

7. In the last two years, there have been three major publications which have critiqued the Faith movement. Two of these are by Dave Hunt: (with T. A. McMahon) *The Seduction of Christianity* (Eugene, Ore.: Harvest House, 1985) and *Beyond Seduction* (Eugene, Ore.: Harvest House, 1987). A third critique is Bruce Barron's *The Health and Wealth Gospel* (Downers Grove, Ill.: InterVarsity, 1987).

8. Charles Farah, *This Cancer Kills: A Critical Analysis of the Roots & Fruits of 'Faith-Formula' Theology* (Portland: Charis Life, 1982), p. 15.

Part 1

A Historical Analysis of the Modern Faith Movement

---

1 The True Father of the Modern Faith Movement

People frequently credit my father, Kenneth E. Hagin, with being the "father" of the so-called faith movement. However, as he points out, it's nothing new; it's just the preaching of the simple ageless gospel. But he has had a great effect on many of the well-known faith ministers of today. Almost every major faith ministry of the United States has been influenced by his ministry.
—Kenneth Hagin, Jr.,
"Trend toward the Faith Movement,"
Charisma (Aug. 1985), 67.

They've [the Faith teachers] all copied from my Dad [E. W. Kenyon]. They've changed it a little bit and added their own touch . . . , but they couldn't change the wording. The Lord gave him [Kenyon] words and phrases. He coined them. They can't put it in any other words . . . It's very difficult for some people to be big enough to give credit to somebody else.
—Ruth Kenyon Houseworth,
taped interview, Lynnwood,
Wash., Feb. 19, 1982.

The Relationship between Kenneth Hagin and E. W. Kenyon

The founding father of the Faith movement is commonly held to be Kenneth Erwin Hagin, the man termed by *Charisma* magazine as "the granddaddy of the Faith teachers,"[1] and "the father of the Faith movement."[2] Delivered with his country Texan accent and a disarming "good ol' boy" charm, Hagin's teachings on faith, healing, and prosperity have been foundational for almost every major minister of the Faith movement.[3] Even the other heavyweights of the Faith movement readily admit that Hagin's teaching and leadership were the key to both their own success and that of the movement.

For instance, the heir apparent to Hagin's throne, Kenneth Copeland, frequently acknowledges Hagin as his spiritual father. Although he briefly attended Oral Roberts University, Copeland

points to Hagin as his mentor, not Roberts. Ken Hagin, Jr., recounts
the beginning of Copeland's relationship with his father this way:

> A poverty-stricken student from Oral Roberts University attended my
> father's Tulsa seminars in the mid '60s and got turned onto the Word of
> God. The student was deeply in debt, but he desperately wanted my
> father's tapes. He offered to trade the title to his car for them. Buddy
> Harrison, my brother-in-law, was managing the ministry then. He took
> one look at the old car and told him, "Just go ahead and take the tapes.
> Bring the money when you can." *So young Kenneth Copeland memo-
> rized those tapes and another great ministry was launched.*[4]

According to recent polls and press, Copeland is now the ex officio
leader of the Faith movement. Nevertheless, at least in spiritual
matters, when Hagin speaks, Copeland still listens.

Frederick K. C. Price, a prominent Faith preacher and founder
of the 14 thousand member Crenshaw Christian Center of Inglewood, California, can make the incredible claim that "Kenneth Hagin
has had the greatest influence upon my life of any living man."[5]
Price received a great deal of help from Hagin in the early days of his
Faith ministry, and Hagin is still a frequent speaker at his church in
California.

Many other ministers of the Faith movement also acknowledge
Hagin as their spiritual father. Charles Capps, who bills himself as "a
Spirit-filled farmer from England, Arkansas," and who speaks at
many national and local Faith conferences, states that "most of my
teaching came from Brother Kenneth Hagin" and that Hagin was
"the greatest influence of my life."[6] Even so prominent a preacher of
charismatic renewal as John Osteen, pastor of the Lakewood Outreach Center, Houston, Texas, gratefully acknowledges Hagin as his
introduction to the Faith movement and proclaims, "I think Brother
Hagin is chosen of God and stands in the forefront of the message
of faith."[7]

Indeed, not only does Kenneth Hagin stand in the forefront, for
many in the Faith movement he is also "the Prophet": the Revelator
of the gospel of faith, health, and wealth. As we will see in chapter 4,
Hagin claims to be the man who first received the "revelation" on
which the Faith movement is based. Even though in popularity and
power the younger Copeland has overtaken his elder Hagin, in the
eyes of his disciples, the man who is referred to as "Dad Hagin" at
Rhema Bible Institute is still the grand old man of Faith.

Not everyone in the Faith movement, however, is willing to
concede to Hagin the role of patriarch and founder. Ruth Kenyon

Houseworth, president of the Kenyon Gospel Publishing Society, Lynnwood, Washington, contends that her father, E. W. Kenyon, who died in 1948, is the man who really deserves the title, "father of the Faith movement." Mrs. Houseworth charges that the 18 books written by her father and published by her society have been pilfered, in both idea and word, by the other preachers of the movement.[8]

Houseworth says of her father's lack of acknowledgment by the Faith movement:

> His first book was printed in 1916, and he had the revelation years before that. These that are coming along now that have been in the ministry for just a few years and claiming that this is something that they are just starting, it makes you laugh a little bit. It is very difficult for some people to be big enough to give credit to somebody else.[9]

Although Mrs. Houseworth is extremely gracious when asked about her father's lack of recognition, she is decidedly not "laughing" about it, not even "a little bit." She feels hurt that the Faith teachers have failed to give credit where credit is due. Moreover, the Kenyon Gospel Publishing Society has been exploited financially by the massive popularity of Hagin (whose first book was not published until 1960), Copeland, et al. Houseworth can no longer afford to publish its newsletter because of what she sees as the injustice done to her father.

The injustice done to Kenyon has not gone unnoticed by others who knew him. For instance, one man who both knew and occasionally ministered with Kenyon, John Kennington, pastor of Emmanuel Temple in Portland, Oregon, says this of his role in the Faith movement:

> Today Kenyon's ideas are in the ascendancy. Via the electronic church or in the printed page I readily recognize not only Kenyon's concepts, but at times I recognize pure plagiarism, for I can almost tell you book, chapter, and page where the material is coming from. Kenyon has become the "father" of the so-called "faith" movement.[10]

Kennington claims that plagiarism of Kenyon's writings is a fairly common occurrence in the charismatic movement. "In fact," he says, "one prominent Pentecostal minister hired a writer or writers to rewrite Kenyon's books and put his name on those books."[11] Because of these many plagiarisms, Kennington agrees with Houseworth that her father is also the father of the Faith movement.

Hagin may have the reputation of being "the granddaddy of the Faith teachers," but in the eyes of Mrs. Houseworth, he is just another young preacher who has "borrowed" her deceased father's writings. Kenyon was 70 years old when Hagin was licensed as an Assemblies of God pastor in 1937 at the age of 20. Hagin himself, however, has gone on record with the claim that he was teaching his message on faith and healing long before he ever heard of E. W. Kenyon.

> Mr. Kenyon went home to be with the Lord in 1948. It was 1950 before I was introduced to his books. A brother in the Lord asked me, "Did you ever read after Dr. Kenyon?" I said, "I've never heard of him." He said, "You preach healing and faith just like he does." He gave me some of Kenyon's books. And he did preach faith and healing just like I do. After all, if someone preaches the new birth, and somebody else preaches the new birth, it has to be the same. Likewise, if you preach faith and healing—and I mean Bible faith and Bible healing—it has to be the same. We may have different words to express it, but if it is according to the word of God, it is the same truth.[12]

Hagin claims that it was not until 1950 that he came into contact with Kenyon, some 17 years after he had gotten "the revelation" that launched his ministry. Any similarities between himself and Kenyon are to be attributed, says Hagin, to the fact that both are merely "using different words to express" what the Bible has to say on "the same truth."[13]

At first glance, this statement may appear a reasonable explanation, but does it account for the amazing similarities between Hagin's writings and Kenyon's? Unfortunately, no, for as this chapter unfolds the reader will be presented with seemingly undeniable evidence that E. W. Kenyon is the true father of the Faith movement, a position which has been unjustly usurped by Kenneth Hagin. As Mrs. Houseworth has testified, the Faith movement in general and Kenneth Hagin in particular have used Kenyon's many books and pamphlets without ever acknowledging that he is the author of their teachings and the founder of their movement.

Hagin's Plagiarism of Kenyon

Hagin, of course, would deny any plagiarism of Kenyon. He maintains that it was not until *after* his discovery of the truths of the Faith gospel that he was introduced to Kenyon's writings. There is reason to believe, however, that he was acquainted with Kenyon earlier than 1950, perhaps much earlier. For example, Hagin remembers reading a book in 1949 with the following quotation: "It seems that God is limited by our prayer life, that He can do nothing for humanity unless someone asks Him to do it. Why this is, I do not know."[14] This quotation comes from E. W. Kenyon's book, *The Two Kinds of Faith*.[15] Even the "revelation" supposedly given to Hagin on his deathbed is described by him with an undocumented and plagiarized quotation from *The Two Kinds of Faith*.[16]

Such confusion over when Hagin read various materials by Kenyon is fairly common. For instance, Hagin says that, in February of 1978, the Lord told him to prepare a teaching seminar on "the name of Jesus." Only after he began his research does Hagin admit that he discovered Kenyon's book, *The Wonderful Name of Jesus*. At his request, Mrs. Houseworth gave Hagin permission to quote from Kenyon's *The Wonderful Name of Jesus*. Hagin's book, *The Name of Jesus*, was first published in 1979. Concerning his indebtedness to Kenyon, Hagin writes:

> At the time [1978], I had one sermon I preached on this wonderful subject, but I had never really taught on it at length. I began to look around to see what I could find written on the subject. For others, you see, have revelations from God. I was amazed how little material there is in print on this subject. The only good book devoted entirely to it that I have found is E. W. Kenyon's *The Wonderful Name of Jesus*. I encourage you to get a copy. It is a marvelous book. It is revelation knowledge. It is the Word of God.[17]

This is one of the few candid, direct acknowledgments of Kenyon to appear in any of Hagin's writings. The problem is that two years prior to 1978, the first date that Hagin admits to having read Kenyon's *The Wonderful Name of Jesus*, he had already copied extensively from this book for an article published in his magazine in 1976.[18] That article never mentions the name of E. W. Kenyon.

Nor is Kenyon mentioned where his words and thoughts appear in numerous other books and articles by Hagin. Whereas Hagin appears to have copied only occasionally from sources other than Kenyon,[19] he has plagiarized Kenyon both repeatedly and extensively. Actually, it would not be overstated to say that the very doctrines that have made Kenneth Hagin and the Faith movement such a distinctive and powerful force within the independent charismatic movement are all plagiarized from E. W. Kenyon. This is a most serious charge and one that will be substantiated by ample evidence. Part 2 of this volume will examine the fact that all of the major thoughts and ideas of Faith theology are taken from Kenyon. At this point in our study, it is sufficient to say that the writings of

Kenneth Hagin are verbally dependent upon Kenyon. The accusa-
tions of plagiarism by Houseworth and Kennington are absolutely
correct. In many instances, Hagin has, indeed, copied word-for-
word without documentation from Kenyon's writings. The following
excerpts of plagiarisms from no less than eight books by E. W. Kenyon are presented as evidence of this charge. This is only a sampling
of such plagiarisms. Many more could be cited.

Kenneth Hagin
The 22nd Psalm gives a graphic
picture of the crucifixion of Jesus—
more vivid than that of John, Matthew or
Mark who witnessed it.

E. W. Kenyon
The twenty-second Psalm gives a graphic
picture of the crucifixion of Jesus. It is
more vivid than that of John, Matthew or
Mark who witnessed it.

He utters the strange words "But
thou art holy." What does that mean? He
is becoming sin. . . . His
parched lips cry, "I am a worm and no
man." He is spiritually dead—the worm.
Jesus died of a ruptured heart. When
it happened, blood from all parts of
His body poured through the rent into
the sack which holds the heart. As the
body cooled, the red corpuscles
coagulated and rose to the top, the white
serum settled to the bottom. When that
Roman spear pierced the sack,
water poured out first, then the
coagulated blood oozed out, rolling
down his side onto the ground. John
bore witness of it. ("Christ our
Substitute," *The Word of Faith* [Mar.,
1975], pp. 1, 4, 5, 7)

But He says the strangest words, "But
thou art holy." What does that mean? He
is becoming sin. Can you hear those
parched lips cry, "I am a worm and no
man"? He is spiritually dead. The worm.
Jesus had died of a ruptured heart. When
that happened, blood from all parts of
the body poured in through the rent, into
the sack that holds the heart. Then as the
body cooled, the red corpuscles
coagulated and rose to the top. The white
serum settled to the bottom. When that
Roman soldier's spear pierced the sack,
water poured out first. Then the
coagulated blood oozed out, rolled
down His side onto the ground, and John
bore witness of it. (*What Happened from
the Cross to the Throne* [Seattle: Kenyon's
Gospel Publishing Society, 1969], 44–45)

What does identification mean?

It means our complete union with Christ.

This gives us the key which unlocks the
great teachings of identification.
Christ became one with us in sin that we
might become one with Him in
righteousness.
He became as we were to the end that we
might become as He is now.
He died to make us live.
He became weak to make us strong.
He suffered shame to give us glory.
He went to hell to take us to heaven.

At once you ask, "What does identi-
    fication mean?"
It means our complete union with Him
in His Substitutionary Sacrifice.
This gives us the key that unlocks the
great teaching of identification.
Christ became one with us in sin, that we
might become one with Him in
righteousness.
He became as we were to the end that we
might become as He is now.
. . . He died to make us live . . .
He became weak to make us strong.
He suffered shame to give us glory.
He went to hell to take us to heaven.

He was condemned to justify us.
He was made sick that healing might be
ours.
("The Resurrection! What it Gives Us . . .
" *The Word of Faith* [Apr., 1977], p. 5)

Here is a picture of Christ
in awful combat with the hosts of
darkness. It gives us a glimpse of the
tremendous victory He won before He
rose from the dead. The
margin of King James reads, "He put off
from Himself the principalities and the
powers." It is quite obvious and evident
that whole demon hosts, when they
had Jesus within their power intended
to swamp Him, to overwhelm Him, and
to hold Him in fearful bondage. But
the cry came forth from the throne of
God that Jesus had met the demands of
Justice, that the sin problem had been
settled, that man's redemption was a fact.
And when that cry reached the dark
regions, Jesus arose and threw back the
host of demons and met Satan in
awful combat.

God has made this investment for the
church. He has made this
deposit on which the church has a right
to draw for her every need. Oh that our
eyes would open, that our souls would
dare to rise in the realm of
omnipotent where that name would
mean to us all that God the Father
intended it to mean! In one sense, this is
practically unexplored table land in
Christian experience. ("The Name of
Jesus: The More Excellent Name," *The
Word of Faith* [Apr., 1976], pp. 4–6)

God's method of physical
healing is spiritual.
It is not mental as Christian Science,
Unity and other metaphysical teachers
claim. Neither is it physical as the
medical world teaches. When man heals,
he must do it either through the mind
or through the physical body.
When God heals He heals through
the human spirit, for God is a Spirit. Life's
greatest forces are spiritual forces. . . .
Love and hate, faith and fear, joy and

He was condemned to justify us.
He was made sick that healing might be
ours.
(*Identification: A Romance in
Redemption* [Seattle: Kenyon's Gospel
Publishing Society, 1968], 6, 7)

The picture here is of Christ . . .
in awful combat with the hosts of
darkness. It gives us a glimpse of the
tremendous battle and victory that Jesus
won before He rose from the dead. The
margin reads: Having put off
from Himself the principalities and
powers." It is evident
that the whole demon host, when they
saw Jesus in their power simply intended
to swamp Him, overwhelm Him, and
they held Him in fearful bondage until
the cry came forth from the throne of
God that Jesus had met the demands of
justice; that the sin problem was
settled and man's redemption was a fact.
When this cry reached the dark
regions, Jesus rose and hurled back the
hosts of darkness, and met Satan in
awful combat.

God has made this investment for the
benefit of the Church: He has made this
deposit on which the Church has a right
to draw for Her every need. Oh, that our
eyes were open; that our souls would
dare rise into the realm of
Omnipotence where the Name would
mean to us all that the Father has
invested in it. . . . This is
practically an unexplored tableland in
Christian experience. (*The Wonderful
Name of Jesus* [Seattle: Kenyon's Gospel
Publishing Society, 1927], 8, 9, 11)

You must have seen as you have studied
this book that healing is spiritual.
It is not mental as Christian Science and
Unity and other metaphysical teachers
claim. Neither is it physical as the
medical world teaches. When man heals,
he must either do it through the mind . . .
or he does it through the physical body
. . . When God heals He heals through
the spirit. We can understand that the
greatest forces in life are spiritual forces.
Love and hate, fear and faith, joy and

peace, are all of the spirit. ("Spirit, Soul,& Body; Part Three: God Heals through the Spirit of Man," *Word of Faith* [Dec., 1977], p. 5)

grief, are all of the spirit. (*Jesus the Healer* [Seattle: Kenyon's Gospel Publishing Society, 1940], p. 90)

The fact that there is enmity between Satan and the woman is seen through woman's history. . . . She has been bought and sold as common chattel. Only where Christianity has reached the heart of the country has woman been elevated above the brute creation. Woman's seed is Christ. Christ was hunted from His babyhood by Satan's seed until finally He was nailed to the cross. From the resurrection of Jesus until this day, the church has been the subject of the bitterest persecution and enmity of the world. "and it . . . shall bruise thy head" (the head of Satan). In Oriental languages "bruising the head" means breaking the lordship of a ruler. "The heel" is the Church in its earth walk. . . . The long ages of persecution of the Church by the seed of Satan are today merely a matter of history. ("Incarnation," *Word of Faith* [Dec., 1978], p. 4)

That is, there will be enmity between Satan and woman. This is proved by woman's history. She has been bought and sold as common chattel. Only where Christianity has reached the hearts of a country has woman ever received any treatment that would lift her above the brute creation. . . . and woman's seed is Christ. Christ was hunted from His babyhood by Satan's seed until finally they nailed him to the cross; and from the resurrection of Jesus until this day, the church has been the subject of the bitterest persecution and enmity of the world. "He shall bruise thy head" —that is, the head of Satan. In all Oriental languages the term "bruise the head" means breaking the lordship of the ruler. "The heel" is the Church in its earth walk. The long ages of persecution of the Church by the seed of Satan are a matter of history. (*The Bible in the Light of Our Redemption* [Seattle: Kenyon's Gospel Publishing Society, 1969], p. 58)

Here in Genesis, God refused to destroy Sodom and Gomorrah until He had talked it over with Abraham, His blood covenant friend. Abraham's prayer is one of the most suggestive and illuminating prayers of the Old Testament. Abraham was taking his place in the covenant. Abraham had, through the covenant, received rights and privileges which we very little understand. The covenant Abraham had just solemnized with Jehovah gave him a legal standing with God. . . . we hear him speaking so plainly . . . "Shall not the judge of all the earth do right?" All through the Old Testament we find men who understood and took their place in the covenant. Joshua could open the Jordan. He could command the sun, moon and stars to stand still in the heavens. Elijah could bring fire out of heaven to consume the altar as well as the sacrifice.

. . . in Gen. 18 when God refused to destroy Sodom and Gomorrah until He had talked it over with His blood covenant friend, Abraham. Abraham's prayer . . . is one of the most illuminating and suggestive prayers in the Old Covenant. . . . Abraham was taking his place in the covenant. Abraham had through the Covenant received rights and privileges that we little understand. The Covenant that Abraham had just solemnized with Jehovah gave him a legal standing with God. We hear him speak so plainly, "Shall not the judge of all the earth do right?" All through the Old Covenant we find men who understood and took their place in the Covenant. Joshua could open the Jordan. He could command the sun, moon and stars to stand still in the heavens. Elijah could bring fire out of heaven to consume the offering as well as the altar.

David's mighty men were utterly shielded from death in time of war as long as they	David's mighty men were utterly shielded from death in their wars. They became supermen as long as they
remembered the covenant. (*Plead Your Case* [Tulsa: Faith Library, 1979], pp. 4–9; cf. pp. 23–32)	remembered the covenant. (*The Two Kinds of Faith* [Seattle: Kenyon's Gospel Publishing Society, 1969], pp. 76–84)
In John 1:4 we get the first intimation of what this life will do for us: "In him was life; and the life was the light of men."	Jesus gave us the first intimation of what this Life would do for man. "In him was life; and the life was the light of men."
There are four different Greek words translated "life" in the New Testament. First, there is *zoe*. Then there is *psuche*. That means natural or human life. *Bios* means manner of life. And	There are four Greek words translated "life" . . . in the New Testament. The first one is *psuche* which means natural, human life. The second is *bios* which means manner of life . . . . The third is
anastrophee means confused behavior. It seems strange that the church has majored on "manner of life" or "behavior" rather than eternal life, which determines in a very large way the manner of life. Receiving eternal life is the most miraculous incident in life. Often we call it conversion or the new birth. Some call it "getting religion," but that's not what it is, really. It is, in reality, God imparting His very nature, substance, and being to our human spirits. (*The God Kind of Life* [Tulsa: Faith Library, 1981], pp. 1–2, 9)	*anastrophee* which . . . means "a confused behavior." It is a strange thing that the Church has majored in "manner of life" or "behavior" rather than Eternal Life which determines in a very large way the "manner of life." Receiving Eternal Life is the most miraculous incident or event in life. It is called conversion, the New Birth and the New Creation. Some have called it "getting religion." It is, in reality, God imparting His very Nature, Substance, and Being to our human spirits. (*Two Kinds of Life* [Seattle: Kenyon's Gospel Publishing Society, 1971], pp. 2–3)
Man is a spirit who possesses a soul and lives in a body. . . . He is in the same class with God. . . . We know that God is a Spirit. And yet [He] took upon Himself a man's body. . . . when God took upon Himself human form, He was no less God than when He didn't have a body. Man, at physical death, leaves his body. Yet he is no less man than he was when he had his body. (*Man of Three Dimensions* [Tulsa: Faith Library, 1973], no page)	Man is a spirit being, he has a soul, and he lives . . . in a body. He is in the same class as God. We know that God is a spirit and He became a man and took on a man's body, and when He did it He was no less God than He was before He took the physical body. . . . Man, at death, leaves his physical body and is no less man than he was when he had his . . . body. (*The Hidden Man* [Seattle: Kenyon's Gospel Publishing Society, 1970], p. 40; *Two Kinds of Faith*, p. 3)

The True Father of the Faith Movement

The primary purpose of revealing Hagin's plagiarisms is to prove his verbal and doctrinal dependency upon Kenyon. This book will offer neither theories as to why Hagin plagiarized Kenyon, nor indictments as to the fact that he did so. When he was once confronted with the plagiarism of another writer, Hagin claimed that the appropriate documentation giving credit to the author was omitted from his book "in error."[20] Because of the number and extent of Hagin's plagiarisms of Kenyon, it seems unlikely that *all* of them are an oversight. But we are more than willing to concede such a possibility, particularly if Hagin were to admit the extent of his dependency upon Kenyon. His honesty in doing so would give credibility to any claim of having plagiarized Kenyon by accident. It would also do much towards righting the injustice done to the Kenyon Gospel Publishing Society.

In admitting that he took his theology from the writings of Kenyon, Hagin would also have to acknowledge that his teaching is of human origins. As we shall see, Hagin claims to have received most of the Faith gospel by divine visitation, visions, and revelation. Much of his reputation as a "prophet" in the Faith movement rests upon these experiences. His reputation and revelation aside, however, it must be said that Hagin's theology has historical roots, and these may be traced directly to Kenyon, whose writings predate Hagin's by more than thirty years. The word-for-word correspondences between Hagin's writings and Kenyon's cannot be attributed to coincidence, nor can they be attributed to a miracle of inspiration by the Holy Spirit. It is inconceivable that the Holy Spirit would inspire Hagin to use another man's words without also informing him as to who first wrote those words. That man was E. W. Kenyon.

In conclusion, it must be admitted that Hagin is the man who single-handedly took Kenyon's teachings and from them forged a movement, the Faith movement. Hagin's influence is omnipresent in Faith circles. His mark is printed indelibly upon his countless disciples, such as Copeland, Price, and Capps. Hagin's son, Ken, Jr., is quite correct in his statement cited earlier that "almost every major faith ministry of the United States has been influenced by his ministry." What Hagin's son does not say is that his father plagiarized the majority of his teaching from E. W. Kenyon. *If this is true, however, then through the person of Kenneth Hagin, E. W. Kenyon's teachings are the foundation of the entire Faith movement.* Hagin was the key player in the early Faith movement. But Kenyon was the author of its major doctrines.

Consequently, we cannot agree that Hagin's leadership thereby merits him the title of "father of the Faith movement." Vladimir

Lenin and Joseph Stalin provided the leadership to transform communism into an international movement, but Karl Marx and Friedrich Engels first taught the doctrines on which communism came to be based. Thus, they are today considered the founding fathers of the Communist movement. Likewise, Hagin was the primary leader of the early Faith movement, but he was not the man who first taught its doctrines and thus was not its founding father. Consequently, we must agree with Ruth Kenyon Houseworth that since her father, E. W. Kenyon, was the man who first authored its teachings, he is, in fact, "the True Father of the Faith movement."

Notes

1. Sherry Andrews, "Kenneth Hagin: Keeping the Faith," *Charisma* (Oct., 1981), p. 24.

2. E. S. Caldwell, "Kenneth Hagin, Sr.: Acknowledged as Father of the Faith Movement," *Charisma* (Aug., 1985), p. 116. It is interesting to note that in a random sampling of *Charisma* readers concerning those ministers who influenced them the most, Kenneth Hagin was third, ranked only behind TV kingpin and presidential aspirant, Pat Robertson, and the heir apparent of the throne of the Faith movement, Kenneth Copeland. Faith preachers Marilyn Hickey and Fred Price were ranked sixth and ninth respectively, and Robert Tilton, John Osteen and Norvel Hayes were in the top 24. The Faith movement was listed as one of the ten "decatrends" of the charismatic movement. See Kenneth Hagin, Jr., "Trend toward the Faith Movement," *Charisma* (Aug., 1985), pp. 67–70.

3. Hagin, Jr., "Trend toward the Faith Movement," p. 67.

4. Ibid.; italics added for emphasis.

5. Fred Price, taped correspondence, Inglewood, Calif., Feb. 18, 1982.

6. Charles Capps, taped correspondence, England, Ark., Feb. 17, 1982.

7. John Osteen, taped phone interview, Pastor of Lakewood Outreach Center, Houston, Tex., Feb. 24, 1982.

8. Ruth Kenyon Houseworth, taped phone interview, Lynnwood, Wash., Feb. 19, 1982.

9. Ibid.

10. John Kennington, "E. W. Kenyon and the Metaphysics of Christian Science," unpublished written statement, Portland, Ore., July 8, 1986.

11. Ibid.

12. Kenneth Hagin, *The Name of Jesus* (Tulsa: Faith Library, 1981), preface

13. Ibid.

14. Kenneth Hagin, *The Art of Intercession* (Tulsa: Faith Library, 1980), p. 1.

15. E. W. Kenyon, *The Two Kinds of Faith: Faith's Secrets Revealed* (Seattle: Kenyon's Gospel Publishing Society, 1942), p. 76.

16. Cf., Hagin's *Six Hindrances to Faith* (Tulsa: Faith Library, [n.d.]) to Kenyon's *Two Kinds of Faith*, p. 67.

17. Hagin, *The Name of Jesus*, preface.

18. Cf., E. W. Kenyon, *The Wonderful Name of Jesus* (Seatle: Kenyon's Gospel Publishing Society, 1927), pp. 8–11, with Kenneth Hagin, "The Name of Jesus: The More Excellent Name," *The Word of Faith* (April, 1976), pp. 4–6.

19. One other author from whom Hagin has explicitly plagiarized is John A. MacMillan. See ch. 4, pp. 67–69.

20. See ch. 4, pp. 69ff.

2 The Cultic Origins of the Faith Movement

When I preach on the mind, it frightens some congregations. They immediately think of Christian Science.

—Kenneth Hagin,
Right and Wrong Thinking
(Tulsa: Faith Library, 1966), pp. 18–19

Discerning men and women have been asking for a new type of Christianity. They do not want a new philosophy or a new metaphysical concept of Christ, but an unveiling of the reality that was seen in Jesus in His earth walk.

—E. W. Kenyon,
The Two Kinds of Life
(Seattle: Kenyon Gospel Publishing Society, 1971), p. 143.

At one time I was a blind follower of E. W. Kenyon. . . . Now with the passing of a little time and with a little more understanding I have come to realize that E. W. Kenyon has simply "baptized" many concepts from Christian Science. In so doing, he became a source for a form of "Pentecostal Christian Science," even though Kenyon himself was not a Pentecostal.

—John Kennington,
"E. W. Kenyon and the Metaphysics of Christian Science,"
unpublished written statement, Portland, Oregon, July 8, 1986.

The preceding chapter offered considerable literary evidence that Kenneth Hagin copied extensively from the writings of E. W. Kenyon. The intent in doing so was to prove that Kenyon, not Hagin, is the true father of the Faith movement. He authored the teachings on which the movement is based. Consequently, Kenyon is the historical root from which the Faith movement grew.

But what are Kenyon's roots? This is a most important question, because anything that influenced Kenyon has undoubtedly also influenced the modern Faith movement. The quotations above would indicate that Kenyon's roots extend into cultic sources, particularly Christian Science. Even Hagin admits that his audiences occasionally fear such cultic association. Their fears are not unjustified. This chapter will offer firsthand evidence that Kenyon's life and ministry were influenced heavily by his personal background in the metaphysical cults. Contrary to popular opinion, Kenyon was not a Pentecostal, nor is the Faith gospel just another Pentecostal perversion.[1] The gospel of the Faith movement is, in fact, a cultic infiltration of the Pentecostal and charismatic movements. Before presenting the evidence for this charge, the relation of the term "cultic" to the Faith movement should be briefly defined.

The Faith Theology:
New Revelation or Heretical Cult?

One scholar recently complained that "defining a cult is far more difficult than is often appreciated."[2] Because of this difficulty and because of the powerful propaganda value of the term "cult," this same scholar has argued that it should be replaced by the more academic phrase, "new religious movements."[3] The words "cult" and "cultic" elicit powerful reactions among conservative Christians, who almost automatically associate cults with gurus, brainwashing, kidnapping, communes, and strange people selling flowers at intersections and airports. This may be a legitimate (albeit somewhat paranoid) connotation of the word "cult," but is not its primary meaning and is certainly not the usage intended in the title of this chapter. It is necessary, therefore, to explain in what sense it is being claimed that the "origins" of the Faith movement are "cultic."

Sociologist and cult specialist Ronald Enroth mentions three approaches in defining the term "cult": (1) the sensational, (2) the sociological, and (3) the theological.[4] The sensational approach focuses on the bizarre and dangerous behaviors of the more extremist cults, such as those mentioned above. It frequently utilizes pejorative language and makes stern value judgments that may or may not be based on fact. It tends to focus on individual cases rather than the cult as a whole. Although cultic research has long been popular among conservative Christians, much of it unfortunately has been of the sensationalized variety. Cultic research can often degenerate into witch-hunting and for this reason there is a growing backlash against it.[5] The sensational approach sells books, but frequently runs roughshod over the truth.

The sociological approach, on the other hand, focuses on the broad cultural, psychological, and organizational aspects of cults. It attempts to describe the cult objectively, without making value judgments. The sociological approach frequently utilizes cultural standards to determine whether a group is a cult. For example, Charles Braden defines "cult" this way:

> By the term "cult" I mean nothing derogatory to any group so classified. A cult, as I define it, is any religious group which differs significantly in some one or more respects as to belief or practice, from those religious groups which are regarded as normative expressions of religion in our total culture.[6]

The advantage of the sociological approach is that its purely descriptive methods are much more scientific than the sensational cult books. Much valuable information about cults may be gained by the sociological approach.

For the purposes of the Christian, however, the sociological approach is not enough. Enroth is correct when he states that "for the Christian the most significant component of a definition of cult is theological in nature."[7] The theological approach focuses on the actual doctrines and practices of the cults, comparing them to those of biblical and historical Christianity. Unlike the sociological approach, it utilizes biblical, rather than cultural, standards. For example, Walter Martin states that

> a cult may be defined as a group of people gathered about a specific person's interpretation of the Bible. . . . From a theological viewpoint, the cults contain not a few major deviations from historic Christianity. Yet paradoxically, they continue to insist that they are entitled to be classified as Christians.[8]

The theological approach differs from the sociological in that it is not just descriptive. It is also comparative and evaluative. It *compares* the teachings of the cults to those of the Bible and *evaluates* whether those in the cults, as Martin puts it, are "entitled to be classified as Christians." This involves value judgments, but hopefully not the pejorative value judgments of the sensational approach. The value judgments of the theological approach differ from those of the sensational in two important respects. First, they are judgments upon the doctrines of the cults, not the people in them. Second, they are based upon objective rather than subjective standards. These standards are the Bible and historical orthodoxy. Thus, a theological approach defines as a cult any group which violates these two standards.[9]

Besides the sensational, sociological, and theological approaches mentioned by Enroth, I contend that there is a fourth approach overlooked by him which is valuable in determining whether a group is cultic. That is the historical approach. A historical approach examines the history of a religious movement, particularly its founder. It is frequently used in conjunction with the theological approach.

The historical approach has two primary objectives in evaluating a cult. First, it examines the validity of the historical claims of the cult or its writings: for example, the Mormon claim that on September 22, 1827, Joseph Smith received golden tablets from the angel Moroni from which he translated the *Book of Mormon*.[10] (Utilizing the historical approach, many such historical claims are found to be fraudulent—including this one by Joseph Smith.[11]) Second, the historical approach attempts to determine whether a new religious group or its founder has any direct historical connection to a preexisting cult, particularly to those which Enroth refers to as "institutional" cults.[12] In a pluralistic society such as ours, "new religious movements" seem to arise on an almost daily basis. Utilizing a theological approach, it may be determined that the theology of a particular group is sub-biblical, even heretical. But often it is not apparent why until the historical background of the new religion is known, especially that of the founder. With a historical approach, one frequently discovers that the founder of the new religion drew upon a variety of non-Christian sources to formulate his or her theological views. For example, a historical investigation of Werner Erhard, founder of the "est" seminars, reveals that he drew heavily upon Scientology, Zen Buddhism, and occult sources in the formulation of his supposedly "non-religious" organization.[13]

In this book we shall utilize two approaches in proving the cultic nature of the Faith movement. First, we will use the historical approach to prove that the founder of the Faith movement, E. W. Kenyon, has a direct historical connection to institutional cults, specifically Christian Science and New Thought metaphysics. Second, we will employ the theological approach to prove that because of Kenyon's historical connection to the metaphysical cults, the modern Faith movement teaches doctrines that are neither biblical nor orthodox. In other words, because the historical root is cultic, the theological fruit is cultic as well.

In describing the origins of the Faith movement as "cultic" we are not saying that the movement itself is a cult, or that all members of the movement are cultists. Neither are we saying that every doctrine of Faith theology is cultic. On the contrary, the overwhelming majority of the members of the Faith movement are sincere, Bible-believing Christians. Much of the doctrine of these Christians is evangelical and certainly within the boundaries of Christian orthodoxy. The Faith movement is not a cult in the sense and to the degree of Mormonism, Jehovah's Witnesses, or Christian Science. No, the Faith movement is not a *cult*, but it is *cultic*, that is, it has certain doctrines and practices that are cultic in thought and histor-ical origin. The fact that much of the Faith movement is evangelical makes it all the more necessary, though painful, to expose and refute its cultic elements.

Before proceeding, it is necessary to define one more contro-versial word to be used in this book. That word is "heresy." Heresy is derived from the Greek word *hairesis*, which is used in the New Testament in three distinct ways. First, it is used in a neutral sense to refer to a clearly definable religious sect or party, such as the Sadducees, the Pharisees, or even the early Christians (Acts 5:17; 15:5; 24:14; 28:22). Second, *hairesis* is used of a faction or schism within the Christian community (1 Cor. 11:19; Gal. 5:20). Third, *hairesis* is used of doctrinal errors introduced into the Christian com-munity by false teachers and prophets. This usage is evident in 2 Pet. 2:1–3.

> But false prophets also arose among the people, just as there will also be false teachers among you, who will secretly introduce *destructive heresies*, even denying the Master who bought them, bringing swift destruction upon themselves. And many will follow their sensuality, and because of them the way of truth will be maligned; and in their greed they will exploit you with false words; their judgment from long ago is not idle, and their destruction is not asleep.

When the words "heresy" and "heretical" are used in this book, this usage, which was prevalent in church history, is also the one intended.[14]

That several doctrines of the Faith theology are heretical does not mean, however, that participants in the movement are neces-sarily heretics. The Roman Catholic Church makes a helpful distinc-tion between "formal" and "material" heresy. Formal heresy is defined as "obstinately adhering to objective heresy out of malice," while material heresy is "adhering to what is objectively heresy with-out realizing that it is such."[15] Formal heresy is willful and conscious and is adequate grounds for excommunication.

> "Material heresy," on the other hand, means holding heretical doc-trines through no fault of one's own, "in good faith," as is the case, e.g.,

> with most persons brought up in heretical surroundings. This consti-
> tutes neither crime nor sin, nor is such a person strictly speaking a
> heretic, since, having never accepted certain doctrines, he cannot
> reject or doubt them.[16]

Just as the overwhelming majority in the Faith movement are ignorant of its cultic origins, so most are also ignorant of the heretical
nature of Faith theology. Their heresy is in the material sense only,
not the formal. Many in the Faith movement have never known
anything else of Christianity but Faith theology. Having never known
orthodoxy in the first place, they hold certain heretical beliefs "in
good faith," not realizing that they have made some rather serious
departures from biblical and historical orthodoxy.

It is debatable whether even the founder of the Faith movement realized that he was preaching cultic and heretical doctrine.
Kenyon did, indeed, perceive the need of the church to be "a new
type of Christianity." He also saw his teachings as supplying this
need. Unfortunately, "the new type of Christianity" advocated by
Kenyon is neither new nor Christian. For the most part, Kenyon's
gospel is, as his friend John Kennington put it, a "Pentecostal Christian Science," a "baptized" version of metaphysics. Kenyon recognized that his theology represented a radical rejection of the
Christianity of his day. But in all likelihood, he also believed his
theology to be a restoration of primitive biblical Christianity. I do
not believe that Kenyon consciously preached heretical doctrine. In
his attempt to help the church compete with the metaphysical cults,
he drew from cultic ideas and practices. His motive was pure, but his
theology was heretical. Like many in the modern Faith movement,
his heresy is probably only material and not formal. But it is heresy
nonetheless.

Some charismatics may ask whether it is possible that Kenyon
received new revelation. This I cannot accept, for two reasons. In the
first place, not only was Kenyon's gospel not a "new type of Christianity," it was not even a "new type of metaphysics." Kenyon taught
the same doctrines of healing, positive confession, and prosperity
that New Thought and Christian Science had been teaching for
decades. In the second place, I do not believe that, in a doctrinal
sense, new revelations occur. Despite the general fascination of
independent charismatics with "new (and the newer the better)
revelations," when it comes to doctrine, I must agree with a former
professor of mine who said, "All that is old may not be gold, but if it
is new, it cannot be true!"

The Origins of Kenyon's Gospel

But a new revelation of Christianity was precisely what Kenyon thought he was teaching. Unlike Hagin, Kenyon never claimed to have seen Jesus or to have visited heaven or hell. Nevertheless, he uses the words "revelation" and "unveiling" to describe his teaching. Some of the subtitles of Kenyon's books illustrate his self-perceptions of their importance to the church and the world. For example, the subtitle of *The Two Kinds of Righteousness* is *The Most Important Message Ever Offered to the Church*; the subtitles to *The Two Kinds of Life* are *The Biological Miracle of the Age* and *The Solution of the Social and Economical Problems Facing the Nation*. At points, Kenyon gives the impression that his message would start the last revival, resulting in the Lord's return.[17]

Kenyon believed that his teaching would create a master-race of Christians:

> When these truths really gain the ascendency in us, they will make us spiritual supermen, masters of demons and disease. . . . It will be the end of weakness and failure. There will be no more struggle for faith, for all things are ours. There will be no more praying for power, for He is in us. . . . In the presence of these tremendous realities, we arise and take our place. We go out and live as supermen indwelt by God.[18]

Through his "Revelation Knowledge," Kenyon hoped to create "supermen," a master-race of Christians no longer bound by "Sense Knowledge" or by demons, disease and poverty. This hope is a central thrust of all Kenyon's writings.

E. W. Kenyon and the Pentecostal Movement

Before examining where this emphasis on "supermen" originates, it might also be enlightening to explain from where it did *not* come. Just as examining the historical roots of Hagin's theology led us to Kenyon, it is important to look at the people, ideas, and influences that shaped Kenyon's theology.

At first glance, it is easy to assume that Kenyon's doctrine of the believer's mastery over all of life's circumstances is merely a radicalized Pentecostalism: a supernaturalism run amok, so to speak. In his book *The Health and Wealth Gospel*, Bruce Barron links the doctrines of healing, positive confession, and prosperity directly to the Pentecostal movement. He does admit that "divine healing can be preached separately from Pentecostalism, and that in fact many of its most persuasive expositors have had no connection with tongue-speaking or the other gifts now associated with the charismatic movement."[19] Nevertheless, as one reads Barron's chapter on "The Roots of the Health & Wealth Gospel" it becomes obvious that he places the Faith theology squarely in the classical Pentecostal tradition. Most of the people cited in that chapter as forerunners of the Faith teachers are either Pentecostals or charismatics.

Barron's historical analysis fails at several major points. First, he severely underestimates Kenyon's role as founding father of the Faith movement. The Faith theology does not, as Barron claims, have multiple sources within Pentecostalism. All of the major doctrines of Hagin, Copeland, et al. have been taken directly from the writings of Kenyon. Second, Barron does not explain why Kenyon's theology differs so radically from that of the Wesleyan-Holiness movement from which the Pentecostal and charismatic movements come.[20] None of the distinctive Wesleyan-Holiness doctrines are present in Kenyon's theology, and many are flatly contradicted by him. Third, Barron fails to distinguish adequately between classical Pentecostalism and the post–World War II healing and charismatic revivals. He tends to blame the former for the excesses of the latter. Classical Pentecostalism rejected many of the doctrines and practices of the healing evangelists. Finally, and most critically, Barron all but ignores another healing movement that predates Pentecostalism by more than fifty years: the metaphysical cults. He assumes that the Wesleyan-Holiness-Pentecostal streams are the only possible sources for the Faith movement's teachings on healing, positive confession, and prosperity. The Faith teachers' views on these topics are much closer in content to the metaphysical cults than to the Holiness-Pentecostal tradition.

Barron also seems to make the common assumption that Kenyon himself was a Pentecostal. Given the fact that Kenyon radically influenced the post–World War II Pentecostal healers, this would appear to be a safe assumption. Nevertheless, it is not a correct one. Despite the widespread view in the Faith movement that Kenyon was a Pentecostal preacher, his daughter insists that he never spoke in tongues and was not a Pentecostal.[21] On occasions, Kenyon was even openly hostile towards the Pentecostal movement.

> The Pentecostal movement, as it is called, reaching out over the country has had much blessing in it for many souls, but I must confess after having studied it carefully and impartially for the last

three years, that there is in it as much destruction as there has been inspiration and instruction.[22]

In his early years Kenyon believed that the "destruction" caused by the Pentecostal movement was due to its experience-oriented nature. In his later ministry, Kenyon appears to have made his peace with the Pentecostals. He frequented the great healing campaigns of such Pentecostal leaders as F. F. Bosworth and Aimee Semple McPherson. His writings were widely read by the post–World War II healing evangelists, such as William Branham, T. L Osborn, and, obviously, Kenneth Hagin. Kenyon's influence on the Healing Revival was massive, yet this has never been fully appreciated by Pentecostal historians.[23]

Yet even at the end of his life Kenyon still rejected the two distinctive doctrines of Pentecostalism: subsequence and initial evidence. He believed that subsequence—the Pentecostal doctrine of Spirit baptism as a second definite work of grace—was "erroneous teaching concerning the Baptism of the Holy Spirit."[24] Kenyon taught that the Baptism of the Holy Spirit occurred at the "New Birth" and that any subsequent experiences with the Spirit are "infillings of the Spirit."[25] Moreover, Kenyon also rejected the Pentecostal doctrine that tongues are the exclusive initial evidence of Spirit baptism.

> Not only does the Scripture fail to teach that tongues is the evidence of the indwelling of the Holy Spirit, but to make tongues the evidence of the Holy Spirit's indwelling would be contrary to the law of God's dealing with the New Creation.[26]

According to his daughter, Kenyon did not encourage Pentecostal gifts in his meetings and they seldom occurred. Kenyon may have taught and practiced divine healing, but he did so as a non-Pentecostal.

The question arises as to where Kenyon does fit into the history of the divine healing movement in America. Kenyon's practice and teaching of divine healing pre-date the Pentecostal movement. Even later in his ministry, similar to his rejection of the Pentecostal doctrine of Spirit baptism, Kenyon also renounced Pentecostal teaching on healing. He felt that the Pentecostal conception of healing was too "Sense Knowledge" oriented.[27]

Admittedly, Kenyon could be historically grouped with the non-Pentecostal healers, such as John Alexander Dowie, Charles Cullis, and a whole host of other participants in the divine healing movement who came from the Wesleyan-Holiness tradition, many of whom later became Pentecostals. Grouping Kenyon with these Wesleyan-Holiness healers would be inaccurate, however, for the same reason that Kenyon cannot be classified a Pentecostal. Kenyon never preached the doctrinal distinctives of the Wesleyan-Holiness movement: the second work of grace, instantaneous sanctification, and sinless perfection.[28] Kenyon is as misplaced in the Wesleyan-Holiness tradition as he is in the Pentecostal tradition.

E. W. Kenyon and the Metaphysical Cults

The question remains as to where Kenyon fits into the divine healing movement in America. As with Hagin, it is unacceptable to claim that the seemingly unique doctrines of Kenyon's healing theology come straight from God. Kenyon, too, was a man of his times, whose ideas and beliefs were heavily influenced by his personality, his culture, his education, and his mentors.

Although his theology *does not* fit into either the Wesleyan-Holiness or the Pentecostal healing streams, there is a healing movement in this country into which Kenyon's theology *does* fit. This divine healing movement is known as "metaphysics" and encompasses such religious groups as Christian Science, New Thought, Unity School of Christianity, and Science of the Mind.[29] In *The Seduction of Christianity*, Hunt and McMahon referred to the Faith movement as "a revival of New Thought."[30] They perceived the obvious parallels of thoughts and ideas of the Faith movement and New Thought metaphysics. There is, however, more than a parallel of ideas between the two movements. Through its founder, E. W. Kenyon, there exists a direct historical linkage between the Faith movement and New Thought metaphysics, a linkage which we shall refer to as "the Kenyon Connection." As the father of the Faith movement, Kenyon introduced cultic, metaphysical ideas into the Faith theology. As the popularizer of Kenyon's Faith theology, Hagin unknowingly incorporated these cultic, metaphysical ideas into the contemporary Faith movement. The Kenyon Connection is the historical documentation of how all of this came about.

The best evidence, whether in a court of law or the crucible of human history, is always firsthand. In seeking to establish the facts of a given case, evidence that comes from an original source, such as a signed confession, is considered the most authoritative. The next best thing to a signed confession would be eyewitnesses who saw the accused commit the crime, or else, heard him admit to it. A final form of evidence would be what is referred to as "circumstantial evidence." Circumstantial evidence is evidence that, while not bearing directly on the fact in dispute, does reveal circumstances, background, or motives from which a judge or jury might infer the occurrence of the fact in dispute.

In evaluating the evidence for the Kenyon Connection, we do not have any *written* confession by Kenyon in which he admits to having formed his theology from cultic sources. But we do have witnesses who heard him make a *verbal* admission of doing so. John Kennington, who as a young preacher knew Kenyon intimately and considered him a mentor, gradually came to realize that Kenyon was teaching cultic doctrine. Kennington recalls the conversation in which he confronted Kenyon with his suspicions.

> One of the things that puzzled me in those days was the similarity between what he [Kenyon] taught and what was taught in Christian Science. We discussed this similarity at that time. And he acknowledged the similarity. I can remember him saying, "All that Christian Science lacks is the blood of Jesus Christ." He was not only very conversant with Christian Science concepts but also with a lot of details of how Christian Science originated. I can hear him yet talk about the philosophical roots of Christian Science and Hegelian thought, or about some international lawyer who on an ocean voyage influenced Mary Baker Eddy. *He admitted that he freely drew the water of his thinking from this well.*[31]

On the basis of conversations such as this one, Kennington concludes that Kenyon's theology, and that of the modern Faith movement, is nothing more than a "Pentecostal Christian Science."

But John Kennington was not the only one who heard Kenyon admit to having been influenced by Christian Science. Ern Baxter, who spent a considerable amount of time with Kenyon in the latter years of his life, believes that Kenyon drew heavily upon cultic metaphysical sources. Baxter states that Kenyon "*undoubtedly was influenced by Mary Baker Eddy.*"

> My major reason for saying that is not just that I would pick that up from the kind of metaphysical things that he said in the name of Christianity, but that visiting in my home on one occasion, as he had done on a number of occasions, we had an afternoon relatively free. He was sitting at a reading spot in my living room where I had some miscellaneous books in a shelf, one of which was Mary Baker Eddy's *Key to the Scriptures,* which I kept there for reference purposes, being vigorously opposed to her whole position from just about every standpoint. But I found him reading it, and I smiled as I

passed by, not wanting to disturb him. I came back 30 or 40 minutes later and he was still reading it. Then I made a comment and *he responded very positively that there was a lot that could be gotten from Mary Baker Eddy.* That alerted me. I can't say it surprised me, but it alerted me to the fact that he probably wasn't formulating his faith positions entirely from sola Scriptura, and that he was influenced by the metaphysicians.[32]

Baxter believes that Kenyon was also "fairly widely read" in Ralph Waldo Emerson and in New England Transcendentalism, the major forerunners of New Thought metaphysics. This transcendental and metaphysical background was the basis of Kenyon's philosophy, which, in Baxter's opinion, controlled the way Kenyon interpreted the Bible. According to Baxter, "Kenyon's roots were not in propositional truth. He did not have biblical propositionalism as the basis of his faith."[33]

The Kenyon Connection does not, however, just rest on the testimony of these two friends of Kenyon. As important as this first-hand evidence is, it is not enough to substantiate so serious a charge as cultism. It must be established that Kenyon's alleged knowledge of the cults influenced his teaching. There must also exist circumstantial evidence supporting Kenyon's involvement with cultic thought, as well as some plausible motive for his doing so. To this evidence we shall now turn.

Notes

1. The most recent book which assumes that the Faith movement is of Pentecostal origins is Bruce Barron's *The Health and Wealth Gospels*, pp. 35–63. Barron's theological critique of the Faith theology is constructive; his historical treatment of the movement, however, is superficial and misguided. Classical Pentecostalism has committed more than its share of doctrinal errors, but the Faith theology is not one of them.

2. Irving Hexham, "Cults," *Evangelical Dictionary of Theology*, ed., Walter A. Elwell (Grand Rapids: Baker, 1984), p. 289.

3. Ibid.

4. Ronald Enroth, "What is a Cult?" in *A Guide to Cults & New Religions*, (Downers Grove, Ill.: InterVarsity, 1983), pp. 12–15.

5. Even conservative scholars fear the growing trend towards government regulation created in part by the sensationalized cultic literature. Some states are enacting anti-conversion laws, supposedly directed only towards the cults, but which "because of their lack of definition . . . are in practice aimed at any form of change of life-style brought about by a religious conversion" (Hexham, p. 289). Such laws could inhibit the evangelistic efforts of all religious groups, including evangelicals and charismatics.

6. Charles Braden, *These Also Believe* (New York: Macmillan, 1960), preface, p. xii.

7. Enroth, "What is a Cult?" p. 15.

8. Martin, *Kingdom*, p. 11.

9. One of the best recent examples of the theological approach is James W. Sire's *Scripture Twisting: 20 Ways the Cults Misread the Bible* (Downers Grove, Ill.: InterVarsity, 1980). Sire defines the term "cult" as "any religious movement that is organizationally distinct and has doctrines and/or practices that contradict those of the Scriptures as interpreted by traditional Christianity as represented by the major Catholic and Protestant denominations, and as expressed in such statements as the Apostles' Creed" (p. 20). Millard Erickson defines cult with both theological and sociological terms: cults are "groups which are heretical in one or more significant respects and which frequently practice strong social control over their members." *Concise Dictionary of Christian Theology* (Grand Rapids: Baker, 1986), p. 40.

10. *The Book of Mormon* (Salt Lake City, Utah: Church of Jesus Christ of Latter-day Saints, 1976), introduction.

11. Harry L. Ropp, *The Mormon Papers* (Downers Grove, Ill.: InterVarsity, 1978); cf. Ed Decker and Dave Hunt, *The God Makers* (Eugene, Ore.: Harvest House, 1984).

12. "Institutional cults are those which have been long-established, if not accepted, in American society, but which have been rejected for biblical reasons by the evangelical community. These would include groups such as Jehovah's Witnesses, Mormons, and Christian Science. Because these cults have been around for such a long time, their ideas have had time to penetrate the religious consciousness of American society. Consequently, they have influenced many outside of their own ranks" (Enroth, "What is a Cult?" p. 23).

13. John Weldon, "est," *A Guide to Cults & New Religions* (Downers Grove, Ill.: InterVarsity, 1983), pp. 77, 86.

14. M. R. W. Farrar, "Heresy," *Evangelical Dictionary of Theology*, p. 508.

15. Karl Rahner and Herbert Vorgrimler, *Dictionary of Theology*, 2nd ed. (New York: Crossroad, 1981), p. 206.

16. *The Oxford Dictionary of the Christian Church*, 2nd ed., ed. F. L. Cross and E. A. Livingstone (New York: Oxford Univ. Press, 1983), p. 639.

17. The belief that the Lord's return is somehow dependent upon their ministry and teaching is not an uncommon conviction among Faith healers. Kenyon writes, "I have a conviction that this is the eleventh hour message, that this is the message for the Church today" (*The Blood Covenant* [Seattle: Kenyon's Gospel Publishing Society, 1969], p. 70). In another book, Kenyon states, "Many believe that this message is a forerunner of a great outpouring of the Holy Spirit with a revival such as the nation has never known. It would be beautiful if it were the ushering in of the last days" (*What Happened from the Cross to the Throne* [Seattle: Kenyon's Gospel Publishing Society, 1945], pp. 9, 10).

18. E. W. Kenyon, *Identification* (Seattle: Kenyon's Gospel Publishing Society, 1968), p. 68.

19. Barron, *The Health and Wealth Gospel*, p. 59.

20. For information on the Wesleyan-Holiness background of the Pentecostal movement, see Vinson Synan's *The Holiness-Pentecostal Movement*

in the United States (Grand Rapids: Eerdmans, 1971), pp. 13–54; cf. Donald Dayton's "From Christian Perfection to the 'Baptism of the Holy Ghost' " (pp. 39–54), and Melvin E. Dieter's "Wesleyan-Holiness Aspects of Pentecostal Origins" (pp. 55–80), *Aspects of Pentecostal-Charismatic Origins*, ed. Vinson Synan (Plainfield, N.J.: Logos, 1975).

21. Houseworth, personal interview. One of Kenyon's later followers, John Kennington, states dogmatically that "Kenyon himself was not a Pentecostal." Another preacher who knew Kenyon, Ern Baxter, maintains, however, that Kenyon confessed to him that he did speak in tongues earlier in his life. Baxter claims that Kenyon subsequently rejected his experience with tongues because it "dragged him into an area of subjective experience that he felt was not in accord with where he apparently was philosophically" (Ern Baxter, taped correspondence, El Cajon, Calif., May 15, 1987). Nevertheless, all parties who knew Kenyon well agree that he was not a Pentecostal theologically, philosophically, and for most of his life, experientially. If he ever did speak in tongues, his subsequent renunciation of the experience illustrates all the more that he is *not* rightly categorized as a Pentecostal.

22. E. W. Kenyon, "False Voices," *Reality* 5 (8, 1908) [n.p.].

23. In 1982, the author had the privilege of a personal conversation with Joseph D. Mattsson-Boze, journalist and long-time leader in the Pentecostal movement. Mattsson-Boze confirmed that Kenyon, though not well-known himself, exercised a considerable influence over the theology of many of the evangelists in the Healing Revival. Another leader in the Healing Revival, Ern Baxter, says that Kenyon was "seldom footnoted, but widely quoted" among the evangelists. "He was widely influential," states Baxter. "Many of the post-War evangelists derived from him" (Baxter, taped correspondence).

24. E. W. Kenyon, *The Bible in the Light of Our Redemption* (Seattle: Kenyon's Gospel Publishing Society, 1969), p. 257.

25. Ibid., pp. 259–61.

26. Ibid., pp. 262–63.

27. Ibid.

28. For the definitive work on the Wesleyan-Holiness roots of the American healing movement, see Paul G. Chappell's "The Divine Healing Movement in America," (Ph.D. dissertation, Drew University, 1983).

29. The term "metaphysics" as used in this book does not refer to the philosophical category of metaphysics. Rather, we shall use the term "metaphysics" to refer to those systems of religious thought which say that all reality and causality in life is "above the physical"; the spiritual realm is the only true reality and is the cause of every effect in the physical realm. Although they vary greatly in belief, most metaphysical systems also teach that man must use his spiritual faculties (his mind) to control and create his own reality.

30. Hunt and McMahon, *The Seduction of Christianity*, pp. 150–54; cf. Hunt, *Beyond Seduction*, pp. 65–66.

31. Kennington, "E. W. Kenyon and the Metaphysics of Christian Science," italics added for emphasis.

32. Baxter, taped correspondence, italics added for emphasis.

33. Ibid.

3 The Kenyon Connection

We cannot ignore the amazing growth of Christian Science, Unity, New Thought and Spiritism. . . . This is libel upon the modern church—it is not only libel but a challenge.

—E. W. Kenyon,
The Wonderful Name of Jesus
(Seattle: Kenyon's Gospel Publishing Society, 1927), pp. 69–70.

An extremely important point needs to be stated here: the doctrines of correct thinking and believing, accompanied by positive confession, with the result of calling a sickness a symptom (denial of reality supported by a Gnostic dualism) are not found in Christian writings until after New Thought and its offsprings had begun to develop them. Therefore, it is not unreasonable to state that the doctrine originated and developed in these cults and was later absorbed by Christians in their quest to develop a healing ministry.

—H. Terris Neuman,
"An Analysis of the Sources of the Charismatic
Teaching of 'Positive Confession,' "
(Unpublished manuscript), p. 43.

In this chapter we shall examine the circumstantial evidence for Kenyon's background in the metaphysical cults. Specifically, we shall scrutinize his life, his education, and his writings for evidence of cultism with the intention of establishing the circumstances and motive of Kenyon's use of cultic doctrine. Kenyon was obviously keenly conscious of Christian Science and New Thought metaphysics. *Our thesis is that in his attempt to help the church respond to the "challenge" of the cults, Kenyon "absorbed" metaphysical concepts in order to restore the healing ministry to the church.* Before we address this thesis directly, a brief recounting of Kenyon's life and ministry is in order.

A Biographical Sketch of Kenyon's Early Life and Ministry

A biography of Kenyon has never been written and his writings contain little autobiographical information. Essek William Kenyon was born on April 24, 1867, in Saratoga County, New York, the fourth son in a family of ten. His father was a logger and his mother was a schoolteacher. When Kenyon entered his teens, his family moved to Amsterdam, New York, a small town near the Canadian border. At age 15, Kenyon began working as a weaver in the carpet mills of Amsterdam. Sometime between the ages of 15 and 19, Kenyon was converted to Christianity, apparently due to the influence of his devout mother. In 1886, at age 19, Kenyon preached his first sermon in the Methodist church of Amsterdam, where he was also ordained a deacon. During these busy years, he also found time to study at the Amsterdam Academy.[1] Although Kenyon never formally graduated from any institution—as with Hagin, all of Kenyon's degrees, including his doctorate, were honorary—he was a zealous, self-educated student, an avid reader, and a life-long advocate of higher education.

In the late 1880s and early 1890s Kenyon attended several educational institutions in New Hampshire. In 1892, he moved to Boston, where he attended several more schools. Boston was a veritable hotbed of religious controversy and cultic activity around the turn of the century. Kenyon's mere presence in Boston would have guaranteed him a broad range of religious exposure. More will be said about this shortly.

As the twentieth century began, Kenyon engaged in a vigorous style of rural evangelism throughout New England and the lower provinces of Canada. This evangelistic work was moderately successful and resulted in the founding of a few Primitive Baptist churches. (At some point, Kenyon had left the Methodist Church to become a non-aligned Baptist.) Kenyon married an older widow, who died not long after their marriage.[2] He soon settled in a home just outside of Spencer, Massachusetts, which he used as a base for his rural evangelism and where he eventually located his school.[3]

As Kenyon traveled in his evangelistic work, he began to receive more and more requests from young people desiring to engage in Bible study. At first, he took as many students as possible into his home. This arrangement soon proved inadequate because Kenyon had neither the facilities nor the time to meet his young students' needs. Around 1900, some friends of Kenyon, John and Susan Marble, donated their farm and buildings to him for the establishment of Bethel Bible Institute.[4] The school opened, faltered, and then reopened around 1904.

From 1900 to 1923, Bethel Bible Institute was supported solely by Kenyon's evangelistic work, income from the farm, and prayer.

Kenyon patterned Bethel after the "faith works" of George Mueller's orphanages and Charles Cullis' hospices. He insisted that Bethel "shall always be kept as a Faith Work" and that "no teacher or head of Department or anyone however connected with the Institution shall ever receive a salary."[5] Bethel's newsletter, *Reality*, records the many financial struggles of the school to maintain its existence through prayer and the donations of its supporters. Like Mueller, Kenyon made it a point never to make his needs known to anyone but God,[6] although at times, *Reality* did publicize the needs of the school.

Kenyon was the driving force behind Bethel and its only superintendent from 1900 to 1923. In 1907, F. S. Bernauer was appointed president of the school so that Kenyon could be free to pursue his ever-widening evangelistic activities. *Reality* records that during this time Kenyon expanded his evangelistic ministry from primarily a rural, localized operation to an urban, national one. In the first decade of the twentieth century, he was very active in the Chicago area and sometimes traveled as far as the West Coast. Kenyon remarried in 1914, this time to a younger woman, Alice Whitney.[7]

In 1923, the first signs of serious trouble between the institution and its founder emerged. The student and faculty ranks of Bethel were seriously depleted by World War I. The best sources available indicate that whereas student enrollment at its height was as high as 100, during the war it dropped as low as 40. Several new personalities became involved with Bethel's trustees resulting in plans to relocate the school in Dudley, Massachusetts. This move entailed a merger with Nichols Academy, a liberal arts school that had closed during the war. In the negotiations surrounding these changes, a controversy of uncertain nature developed. Its result was that Kenyon resigned his duties at Bethel in 1923. According to Howard Ferrin, who became the second superintendent of the school in 1925, "when Kenyon left, there was an absolute disassociation of the school from its founder."[8] Kenyon never wrote Bethel, never returned to visit, and never even inquired about it after he left in 1923.

When Kenyon left, Bethel completed the move from Spencer to Dudley and became the "Dudley Bible Institute and Nichols Academy." Under the leadership of Howard Ferrin, who remained the president for over 40 years, the school eventually moved to Providence, Rhode Island, where it became the "Providence Rhode Island Bible Institute." The school subsequently relocated in Barrington,

Rhode Island, where it became "Barrington College," one of the finest evangelical liberal arts institutions in New England. (Recently, Barrington merged with Gordon College, also a prestigious evangelical liberal arts college.) Although Ferrin tells everybody who will listen, few people realize that Kenyon, not Ferrin, was the founder of this well-known evangelical institution. Thus, probably the noblest of Kenyon's many endeavors ended amidst controversy and failed to grace Kenyon with the recognition he deserved.

In 1923, Kenyon left Bethel for California. He conducted evangelistic meetings in San Jose, Oakland, Berkeley, and many other cities on the West Coast. These meetings gained him a reputation as a dynamic speaker and captivating expositor of the Scriptures. His ministry was interdenominational in scope, although he often frequented Pentecostal circles. Aimee Semple McPherson invited him to speak in her Angelus Temple on several occasions. In 1926, Kenyon assumed the pastorate of an independent Baptist church in Pasadena, California. He later moved to Los Angeles proper and began another church, which prospered under his ministry and soon was drawing crowds of over a thousand. Kenyon moved again in 1931, this time to Seattle, where he founded the New Covenant Baptist Church. In the same year, he began "Kenyon's Church of the Air," one of the pioneer religious radio programs on the Pacific Coast.[9] This radio program became the primary ministry involvement of Kenyon's later life. Many of his books are merely edited transcripts of these radio broadcasts.

Kenyon continued in ministry until his death on March 19, 1948, at the age of 80. Daughter Ruth Kenyon Houseworth's memorial edition of *Kenyon's Herald of Life* newsletter records his death:

> Shortly before his passing, he had a premonition that he would not be here long and he called me and said he felt I was the one to carry on his work. He said, "Ruth, dear, I have a feeling I won't be with you much longer. This work must go on. It is up to you now. You have been looking after it all these years, and with the help of the Lord, I know you can carry on." I promised him I would.[10]

At the time of his death, the circulation of *Kenyon's Herald of Life* was over 20 thousand and he had compiled material for an additional 12 books. Mrs. Houseworth did, in fact, "carry on" her father's work, publishing the newsletter and two more of his books posthumously. The Kenyon's Gospel Publishing Society remains in operation to this day. But as noted earlier, it has not received any significant financial support by way of comparison to that received by Kenneth Hagin Ministries Inc., and the other major ministries of the Faith movement.

The Educational and
Religious Background of Kenyon

One of the mysteries of E. W. Kenyon is how to account for the discrepancies between his theology and his ministry. Early in his ministry Kenyon moved in Methodist circles and late in his life in Pentecostal, but his theology reflects neither. In fact, his theology contradicts both Methodism and Pentecostalism. Even those who knew of Kenyon's cultic ties still have trouble categorizing his theology. Ern Baxter comments,

> His thinking differed widely from Pentecostalism and for that matter a thoroughgoing evangelicalism. He was rather a distinct person. I wouldn't quite know how to categorize him theologically. One would be hard put to give him any theological definition.[11]

Baxter and Kennington are both perplexed by the strange mixture of cultic and biblical thought in Kenyon's theology. Only as one studies Kenyon's background does his eclectic theology begin to make sense.

Kenyon was a man of tremendously diverse educational and religious background. The crucial period of his religious and educational development appears to have taken place during his stay in the city of Boston during the early 1890s. As stated earlier, Kenyon's mere presence in Boston afforded him a wide range of exposure to various metaphysical, Unitarian, and transcendental religious groups. There is ample evidence not only that was he exposed to such groups, but that he also participated in some of them as well.

The first indication of such participation is a reference in one of his articles in *Reality* magazine in which Kenyon admitted to attending regularly the services of Minot J. Savage, one of the outstanding ministers and authors of the Unitarian Church.[12] Savage was the author of the Unitarian catechism and president of the National Unitarian Conference from 1895 to 1899, about the time Kenyon was in Boston.[13] In sitting under Savage's preaching, Kenyon was listening to one of the most powerful architects and expositors of Unitarian thought.

Kenyon's flirtations with Unitarianism are significant for two reasons. First, according to Charles Braden, the transcendental and metaphysical movements arose in reaction to Unitarianism.[14] More than a few Unitarians ended up in some form of New

Thought. In attending a Unitarian church, Kenyon may have been taking the first step in a well-traveled path from Unitarianism to Transcendentalism to New Thought. Second, Unitarianism is, by evangelical standards, heretical. It rejects the bedrock doctrines of orthodoxy: the trinity, the deity of Jesus Christ, his vicarious substitutionary atonement, the fall and depravity of humankind, and eternal punishment. We do not know if during this period Kenyon ever consciously rejected these doctrines or was ever a full-fledged Unitarian. All that is being claimed at this point is that the father of the Faith movement seems to have associated with a religious group that denied the fundamental doctrines of the Christian faith.

Had this been the only such heretical group with which Kenyon associated during his years in Boston, then his Unitarian venture could be written off as a meaningless experiment in religious curiosity. That is simply not the case, however, for in 1892 Kenyon enrolled in the Emerson College of Oratory, an institution that was absolutely inundated with metaphysical, cultic ideas and practices.[15] His enrollment at Emerson betrays a continued involvement with New Thought and Christian Science metaphysics. In order to grasp the significance of Kenyon's involvement with this school, let us now turn our attention to Charles Wesley Emerson, founder of the Emerson College of Oratory.

Charles Wesley Emerson and the Emerson College of Oratory

Charles Wesley Emerson began his religious career as the minister of a Congregationalist church in West Halifax, Vermont in 1860. Emerson subsequently pastored a Universalist church in Northfield, Vermont between 1866 and 1871. In 1871, Emerson was installed as minister of a Unitarian church in Fitchburg, Massachusetts, which he then left in 1875 to study law at Boston University. While pursuing his law studies, Emerson was called by the Unitarian church of Chelsea, Massachusetts, in May of 1877. He continued to study law while pastoring in Chelsea and even added to his course work by enrolling at the Monroe School of Oratory at Boston University.[16] In March of 1878, Emerson's health broke under the strain of his responsibilities and studies, forcing him to take a leave of absence.[17]

After a few months of rest, Emerson delivered some lectures on oratory in Vineland, New Jersey. These lectures earned him a certain notoriety and launched his career as an orator.[18] Emerson's oratory career was aided considerably by a bogus medical school degree obtained from the Eclectic Medical College of Pennsylvania, "which was not a genuine medical school at all, but a diploma mill that sold diplomas en masse to all comers."[19] With the added prestige of his new credentials, "Dr. Emerson" received an appointment to teach at the Monroe School of Oratory.

The Monroe School of Oratory was founded in 1872 by Professor Lewis B. Monroe, "one of the outstanding figures in education in Boston."[20] In 1879, Monroe died. Since he was the primary drawing card of the school, the administration of Boston University decided to close it down that same year. With the help of a few of Monroe's former colleagues, Emerson reorganized the school independently of Boston University and reopened it as the Boston Conservatory of Elocution and Dramatic Art. It was later renamed, with the approval of the widow of Monroe, the Monroe Conservatory of Oratory. Eventually the school became the Emerson College of Oratory in honor of its new drawing card, Charles Emerson.[21]

If Emerson College was simply a school of oratory founded by an Unitarian minister, then Kenyon's attendance there would not be that significant. Certainly it would not justify so intriguing a label as the Kenyon Connection. The historical data, however, indicate that Emerson College was something more than a school of oratory and that Emerson himself was not a typical Unitarian minister. In actuality, during his tenure as president of the college, Emerson was not a Unitarian at all. Having begun his ministry as a Congregationalist, he soon accepted the Unitarian theology, as did a significant number of Congregationalist ministers in the early nineteenth century. Yet very soon even the dogma and rationalism of Unitarianism proved too restraining for so fertile a religious mind as Emerson's.

Charles Emerson was a collector of religions, an eclectic in the truest sense of the word. A long-time admirer of the Transcendentalism of Ralph Waldo Emerson, of whom he was not a relative, Charles Emerson also held to the basic tenets of Spencer's social Darwinism. His religion was a veritable smorgasbord of the sources underlying New Thought metaphysics: Platonism, Swedenborgianism, New England Unitarianism, and Emersonian Transcendentalism. All of these various elements were held together by heavy proof-texting from the Bible and a quasi-Darwinian view of the religious evolution of humanity which ended in man becoming a god.

The importance of evolution to Emerson is no better illustrated than by his own religious pilgrimage. In his 40 years of ministry,

Emerson's theology evolved from Congregationalism, to Universalism, to Unitarianism, to Transcendentalism, to New Thought, and ended, at last, in the most rigid and dogmatic of all metaphysical cults, Christian Science. Emerson joined Christian Science in 1903 and remained involved until his death in 1908.[22] His conversion to Christian Science was the last logical progression in his metaphysical evolution from the orthodox to the cultic.

Simply to document that Emerson was involved with the metaphysical cults is not enough to prove that Emerson College was itself cultic. Yet this is precisely what must be demonstrated. The religious milieu of Kenyon's alma mater is absolutely essential to the Kenyon Connection because the intellectual *environment* of Emerson College undoubtedly influenced Kenyon more than the *person* of Emerson himself. Theoretically, Kenyon could have attended Emerson College without ever speaking to Charles Emerson—although it is unlikely given the small size of the school. But it is virtually impossible that he could have attended an institution without talking, exchanging ideas, and being influenced by somebody there. If Emerson College was a typical institution of higher education, then Kenyon probably interacted with *many* of his professors and classmates, both in and out of the classroom.[23] Thus, the religious environment of Emerson College is a crucial component of the Kenyon Connection.

The Religious Environment of Emerson College

Every institution has a mission. Sometimes this mission is stated officially in writing, and sometimes it is left unwritten. The mission of an institution is its self-understanding and its *raison d'être*. Admittedly, the mission of an institution can, and in the case of religious institutions, usually does, change as time passes and the institution grows. This is certainly true of Emerson College, which today is an altogether different institution from the small college of oratory and metaphysics which Emerson founded and Kenyon attended. For our purposes, however, the mission of Emerson College in its infancy is our central focus. Because of its formative influence on Kenyon, and its indirect influence on the contemporary Faith movement, the founding mission of Emerson College is of particular importance.

Crucial to an understanding of the mission of Emerson College is that its founder considered the very existence of the school to be the work of God. Emerson believed that God was the true founder of the college and that if he did not incorporate religion into his teaching he would be compromising the purposes for which it was founded. Regarding the mission of his college, Emerson often spoke along the following lines:

> I have not built this school. . . . God has built it. . . . If I . . . come on this platform, trusting in Charles Wesley Emerson to teach you, I am a failure. But every single morning as I enter here I lift up my thoughts to God, and say, "God, speak through me in just the ratio that I can be an open channel, and in no other way." . . . *Palsied be the tongue of the teacher who does not lead the student to God.*[24]

Such exhortations to the faculty were quite common. The primary task of the faculty of Emerson College was not just to teach oratory: it was to teach religion. In one of his lectures, Emerson stated, "My friends let us come home: let us feel that this Kingdom of God is right here in this college. It is here and if it is not here, then the college is nothing. For we have built our very technique upon it."[25] Emerson's "technique" of teaching oratory, though for its day not lacking in scientific theory, was of a decidedly religious bent.[26]

Not only did Emerson believe that teachers should lead students to God, he also believed that, upon graduation, his students should do likewise. He admonished them, "Do not forget you are to be missionaries wherever you go." These "missionaries" were not to spread the traditional, orthodox gospel, but rather the gospel according to Charles Emerson. "We are not," stated Emerson to his students, "trying to make you ministers of the Gospel in any, shall I say, denominational sense—but ministers of good news, or real gospel everywhere."[27] As will be shown, the "real gospel" of Emerson College was not that of historical Christian orthodoxy, but rather, that of New Thought metaphysics.

Emerson's attempts to propagate his metaphysical religion did not pass unnoticed either by his students or by his colleagues outside of the college. For example, in praise of the faculty at his graduation in 1896, one student remarked,

> You have taught us not only how to think but what to think. You have taught us not only how to live but what to live. You have broadened our horizons, and made of us larger and better men and women, so that we shall go out from here better equipped to live the Christ life. . . . And this is the best thing, I think, about this institution. It teaches us the way to be Christians. Dr. Emerson is preaching the gospel under the guise of teaching oratory.[28]

The best statement capturing the intensity of the religious environment at Emerson College was that of Charles Mallory, a close friend
of Ralph Waldo Emerson and a frequent guest lecturer at the college.

> Why do you call this a College of Oratory? All people should come here
> whether they intend to do anything in the line of elocution or not. This
> is a school where the philosophy of life is taught. It ought to be called,
> "The First Church of Emerson."[29]

In his enrollment at Emerson College, Kenyon was not, therefore,
merely attending a school of oratory, but rather a "church" that was
"preaching the Gospel under the guise of teaching oratory."

Emerson College and New Thought

The gospel preached at the "The First Church of Emerson" can
be neatly categorized into that broad body of metaphysical teaching known as New Thought. New Thought was the brainchild of
Phineas P. Quimby (1802–66). "Dr. Quimby," as he was called by
patients and friends, though he possessed only a common education, originally healed through secular hypnotism, but later developed a more religio-psychic method. Because it is not a rigid system
of belief, New Thought has come to be the banner under which
numerous metaphysical groups have marched. The most significant of these are the Unity School of Christianity, Divine Science, the
Church of Religious Science, the Home of Truth, the Church of Truth,
the Christ Church League, the Society of the Healing Christ, and the
Christian Assembly. In addition, although she never admitted it, it is
generally agreed by scholars of the metaphysical cults that Mary
Baker Eddy, the founder of Christian Science, was heavily dependent on the writings of P. P. Quimby, by whom she received a healing
and under whom she later studied.

These formal religious groups do not, however, represent the
extent to which New Thought has influenced the church and world.
New Thought ideas form the foundation of a variety of widely read
self-help and success-motivation books. The majority who read
these writings are unaware that they are metaphysical in nature.
Some examples include: Lloyd Douglas's *The Magnificent Obsession*,
Claude Bristol's The *Magic of Believing*, Orison Marden's *He Who
Thinks He Can*, Dale Carnegie's *How to Win Friends and Influence
People*, Norman Peale's *The Power of Positive Thinking*, and
Napolean Hill's *Think and Grow Rich*.

But what are the specific beliefs of New Thought? It is possible to state these beliefs in general terms, but only with the qualification that not every New Thought group would hold to all of the beliefs listed. New Thought is characterized by its diversity of opinion, its liberality towards differences, and, unlike Christian Science, its refusal to systematize its beliefs into formal creeds. The following propositions of the Boston Metaphysical Club are representative of New Thought beliefs during the time of Kenyon's enrollment at Emerson College.[30]

> All primary causes are internal forces. . . .
>
> Mind is primary and causative. . . .
>
> The remedy for all defect and all disorder is metaphysical, beyond the physical, in the realm of causes which are mental and spiritual. . . .
>
> God is immanent, indwelling Spirit, All-Wisdom, All-Goodness, ever-present in the universe.
>
> Therefore evil can have no place in the world as a permanent reality; it is the absence of good. . . .
>
> It [New Thought] would proclaim to man his freedom from the necessity of belief in disease, poverty, and all evil as a part of God's plan. . . .
>
> It stands for the practice of the presence of God reduced to a scientific method; of living a selfless life through union in thought with a power that is Love in action.
>
> It robs death of its sting, though not specifically denying its reality; takes the terror out of disease; crowns life with joy and health and abundance that are the rightful inheritance of every child of God.

One scholar characterized New Thought beliefs this way:

> This purpose and these principles emphasized the immanence of God, the divine nature of man, the immediate availability of God's power to man, the spiritual character of the universe, and the fact that sin, human disorders, and human disease are basically matters of incorrect thinking. . . . Many New Thought groups emphasize Jesus as teacher and healer and proclaim his kingdom as being within a person. . . . New Thought leaders have increasingly stressed material prosperity as one result of New Thought. New Thought implies a kind of monism, or view of the oneness of the world, but it also has strong Gnostic (i.e., dualistic, matter being opposed to spirit) undertones; that is, though New Thought is open to all, spiritual healing and strength of mind and body are available only to those who have the insights and who have been initiated into the movements at some point.[31]

In summary, New Thought was a system of cultic belief that taught that true reality is spiritual, that the spiritual is the cause of all physical effects, and that the human mind through positive mental attitude and positive confession has the power to create its own reality: either health and wealth, or sickness and poverty.

Since New Thought was so eclectic and diverse in nature, and since it was tolerant of all religious belief, many varieties and combinations of metaphysical thought could have thrived under its guise at Emerson College. Nevertheless, the fact that it was the "philosophy of life" taught at Emerson is undeniable. Coffee and Wentworth write:

> Whether Dr. Emerson taught New Thought is not subject to question. It is clear that he did, and that students such as Mary Ann Greely, Class of 1893, found it quite valuable personally as she wrote some years later in the Emerson College Magazine: "We dealt familiarly with the great truths that have now become popular under the name of 'new thought.' "[32]

Kenyon's personal acceptance or rejection of New Thought during his days as a student is not altogether clear, but that he was exposed extensively to its teachings and healing practices at Emerson College is a historical certainty. The mission of the college was to produce graduates who would believe, practice, and preach the New Thought gospel of Charles Emerson.

For instance, one of Kenyon's classmates—and perhaps teachers— eventually became one of the most brilliant articulators and authors of New Thought metaphysics. That man was the inimitable Ralph Waldo Trine (1866–1958), who is characterized by American church historians as "the patriarch of the modern health and harmony tradition"[33] and "the most reputable of New Thought writers."[34] In 1892, at the time of Kenyon's enrollment, Trine was both a student and a teacher of rhetoric at Emerson College.

The exact date of Trine's conversion to New Thought is uncertain, but Coffee and Wentworth claim that "it is quite possible that he first learned of its doctrine from Charles Wesley Emerson."[35] That Trine enrolled as a student at Emerson College, in addition to his faculty position there, would seem to indicate some sort of tutelage under Emerson, either in oratory, in New Thought, or in both. If Trine was converted to New Thought while at Emerson, it would certainly illustrate the point that Kenyon, as one of Trine's classmates, was exposed to New Thought believers who saw it as their duty to convert nonbelievers.

Trine's presence at Emerson College also indicates that the brand of New Thought taught there was of a pure and intense variety. This claim is substantiated by the fact that within three years after leaving Emerson College, Trine wrote *In Tune with the Infinite* (1897), "an almost perfect presentation of New Thought at its best."[36] This book has sold more copies (over 1.5 million) than any other single book by a New Thought writer. It has been translated into 20 languages and its readership extends far beyond New Thought circles into the general public, most of whom never realize that the book is a New Thought publication. The subtitle of *In Tune with the Infinite*, which is *Fulness of Peace, Power and Plenty*, is "a perfect description of the general characteristics of New Thought," known to many as "the religion of peace, power, and plenty."[37] Several of Trine's other books have sold more than a half a million copies. If Kenyon had anything at all to do with his classmate Trine, then he was associated with the most brilliant exponent of New Thought metaphysics of his day—perhaps the most brilliant ever.

In summary, Kenyon did not merely attend a school of oratory at Emerson College, but a school in which both the faculty and student body were heavily involved with the metaphysical cults. Charles Emerson himself was an active participant in the New Thought movement and founded the school to propagate this cultic teaching. The purpose of Emerson College of Oratory according to its founder and many who attended it was not just to teach oratory, nor was it to produce mere orators; rather, its purpose was to teach religion—a philosophy, a way of life—and to produce not only orators, but missionaries of this metaphysical religion. Toward this end, besides Emerson himself, Emerson College had on its faculty some of the best known and most articulate advocates of New Thought.[38] The evidence would also seem to suggest that some of the students and faculty, including the founder and his wife, eventually became converts to Christian Science, a conversion for which their background in New Thought would have well prepared them.[39]

Did Kenyon ever formally convert to New Thought or Christian Science? We do not know. According to his friends, Kenyon freely admitted that he was heavily influenced by metaphysical thought. The historical evidence would also suggest that his time in Boston was one of both exposure to and participation in Unitarianism, New Thought, and Christian Science. A deeper analysis of the impact of Emerson College upon Kenyon's life is hampered somewhat by a lack of biographical sources on his early life and by the fact that Kenyon did not incorporate autobiographical material into his own writings. Consequently, any further evidence that Kenyon's teaching is derived from the metaphysical cults must be gathered from an

analysis of his overall theology and from a study of the various direct
references to these cults in his writings.

References to the Metaphysical Cults
in Kenyon's Writings

The direct statements of Kenyon regarding the metaphysical
cults do not betray any *conscious* acceptance on his part of their
ideas. In fact, in his earlier writings, Kenyon is occasionally hostile
towards these cults, describing them as "hellism" and "devilism."[40]
In 1907, he wrote, "New Thought has failed to satisfy the cry of the
human heart and now it has turned and is feeding upon itself."[41] On
other occasions, Kenyon was milder in his critique of the cults.
Commenting upon the New Thought notion that man could develop
a "divine element" within him to the point of becoming "fit to dwell
with God eternally," Kenyon wrote simply that such a view was "not
true, to put it mildly."[42] (This last critique of New Thought is a bit
ironic, given the fact that Kenyon later taught that just such a "divine
element" existed within man and could, indeed, be developed to the
point of man becoming a god.[43])

In all his various denunciations of the cults, it is significant to
note that Kenyon criticizes only a certain type of cult: those that are
derived from Quimby's metaphysical writings—New Thought,
Christian Science, Unity School of Christianity—and Spiritism, a
cultic and occultic group dedicated to necromancy (i.e., communication with the dead). Kenyon fails to mention any other major cults,
including two that began in his native Northeast: Mormonism and
Jehovah's Witnesses. Apparently, Kenyon's interest in the cultic
extended only to those groups that purported to be a "science"
dedicated to revealing the secret, metaphysical workings of the
spirit realm.

Kenyon's interest in the metaphysical cults was not only exclusive, his knowledge of the origins and teachings of these groups was
extensive. According to one of his close friends, Kenyon "was not
only very conversant with Christian Science concepts but also with
a lot of details of how Christian Science originated."[44] For example,
Kenyon was informed enough about Christian Science origins to
know that it "grew out of Hagel's [*sic*] philosophy" and that Mrs.
Eddy "copied" Hegel.[45] Although his historical analysis might have
been severely overstated, Kenyon's assertion about Eddy's alleged
plagiarism of the German philosopher Friedrich Hegel reflects a

technical knowledge of the origins of Christian Science that extends far beyond the novice level.[46] His knowledge would also seem to indicate more than a casual interest in the beliefs and healing practices of Eddy, who is the only cultist Kenyon ever refers to by name.

In many instances, Kenyon displays an extensive knowledge of what the metaphysical cults do and do not teach.

> Christian Science, Unity, and the other Metaphysical and philosophical teachers of today do not believe that God is a person. They will tell you that He is perfect mind, but He has no location. It is just a great and universal mind which finds its home in every individual. He has no headquarters. It is mind without brain, without a personality. They do not believe in sin as Paul taught in the revelation given to him. They do not believe that Jesus died for our sins, but that He died as a martyr. They do not believe He had a literal Resurrection, a physical resurrection, but as one puts it, "a metaphysical resurrection" (whatever that means). . . . One of them calls Him [Jesus] "the way shower." He is not the wayshower. HE IS THE WAY! Their [the metaphysical cults'] faith in Jesus and their faith in God is, after all, faith in themselves, and what they inherently have within themselves.[47]

In this passage Kenyon appears to be interacting with unnamed metaphysical teachers. He claims not to agree with them, but at this point in our analysis the only intent is to demonstrate that Kenyon possessed an intimate knowledge of New Thought metaphysics. It must be admitted, however, that, at times, Kenyon does attempt on the basis of this knowledge to correct their faulty beliefs. Although some in the Faith movement might claim that Kenyon's efforts to refute certain beliefs of the cults prove that he rejected their beliefs, such a claim is simplistic and does not take into account several other serious considerations.

For example, how does one account for the amazing parallels between Kenyon's teaching and the metaphysical cults? There is evidence that Kenyon himself was aware of such parallels and wanted to dissociate himself from the cults. Kenyon was in the habit, as are many in the Faith movement, of issuing disclaimers as to the obvious similarities between his teaching and the cults. The typical pattern in such instances is to disclaim any similarities with cultic teaching on a particular topic and then proceed to teach exactly what the cults teach. The following are fairly representative of such disclaimers from Kenyon.

> We are not dealing with mysticism, philosophy or metaphysics. We are dealing with realities. . . . we are dealing with the basic laws of man's being, the great spiritual laws that govern the unseen forces of life.[48]

> This is not a new metaphysics or philosophy. This is reality. This is God breaking into the sense realm. This is God imparting His own nature to the human spirit.[49]

> This is not psychology or metaphysics. This is absolute fact. God becomes a part of our very consciousness.[50]

In each of these, Kenyon claims that his teaching is not metaphysical and then immediately follows his disclaimer with a central dogma of metaphysics. For example, when he speaks of "the great spiritual laws that govern the unseen forces of life," he is espousing *deism*, the metaphysical world view that the universe is governed by impersonal, spiritual laws rather than a personal, sovereign God. When Kenyon refers to "God breaking into the sense realm," he is espousing *dualism*, which is the metaphysical view of reality that the spiritual realm and the physical realm are mutually exclusive and even opposed to one another. Finally, when Kenyon refers to "God imparting his own nature to the human spirit" and "God becoming a part of our very consciousness," he is espousing *deification*, which is the metaphysical view that salvation entails man becoming a god (and which, in the quotation cited earlier, he criticizes New Thought for teaching). Although it is not at all clear that Kenyon was doing so intentionally, nevertheless, these types of disclaimers are also the classical ploys of modern day cultists, who use them to confuse and disarm the intellectual defenses of those whom they are indoctrinating into their cult.

Despite such disclaimers, metaphysical ideas and beliefs pervade Kenyon's writings (and through Kenyon, the Faith movement). Occasionally, metaphysical terms surface as well. For example, Kenyon claims:

> There can be scientists in the realm of the spirit as well as in the realm of the Senses. It has always been hard for Sense Knowledge men to accept spiritual things. . . . Sense Knowledge cannot find God and would not know God if it found Him. . . . The spiritual scientist does not deal in theories. He deals in facts. . . . The spiritual scientist has proven there is a God. . . . He has found that man is a spirit being in the class with God, he is Eternal, he originally had an eternal body.[51]

Kenyon's use of the term "spiritual scientist" is a perfect example of his assimilation of New Thought metaphysics into his theology. The formation of a "spiritual science," through which "the realm of the spirit" could be explored and exploited by the human mind in the same way as the physical sciences explore and exploit the physical world, was the primary goal of P. P. Quimby and Mary Baker Eddy.

Well before Kenyon, Quimby wrote that "there are two sciences, one of this world, and the other of the spiritual world."[52] It has been documented that Quimby was the first to use the term "Christian Science" and continued to do so long after Mary Baker Eddy made her claim to it by using it as the name for her own metaphysical system. In describing his theology as "spiritual science" (and in another place, "Spiritology"[53]), Kenyon was espousing the typical metaphysical line that his principles were a science of the spiritual realm and not just another religion.

In closing, we will theorize as to why and how Kenyon assimilated elements of the metaphysical cults into his theology. Regarding why Kenyon was vulnerable to cultic influences, it is necessary to understand his view of the church of his day. Kenyon believed that the rise of the metaphysical cults was due to the unpaid debts of the church, a church torn by the fundamentalist-modernist controversy and rapidly giving way to liberalism in its theology and anti-supernaturalism in its ministry. Having witnessed firsthand at Emerson College the purpose and power of metaphysics to minister to the practical needs of the people, Kenyon indicted the church for its failure to execute its supernatural healing ministry. Around 1927, he wrote,

> We cannot ignore the amazing growth of Christian Science, Unity, New Thought and Spiritism. The people who are flocking to them are not the ignorant masses, but the most cultured and wealthy of the land, and their strongest appeal is the supernatural element of their so-called religions—the testimonies of healing are their strongest asset. We cannot close our eyes to the fact that in many of our cities in the Pacific Coast, Mrs. Eddy has a stronger following today and a larger attendance at her churches than have the old line denominations; and the larger percentage of her followers have at one time been worshipers in the denominations— they have left them because they believe that they are receiving more help from Mrs. Eddy's teaching than from the preachers. They will tell you how they are healed and how they were helped in their spiritual life by this strange cult. This is libel upon the modern church—it is not only libel but a challenge.[54]

Many independent charismatics could well sympathize with Kenyon's critical assessment of the denominational churches, for it was precisely this failure of the denominations to address the needs of the people on a supernatural basis that drove many denominational church members into the ranks of the independent charismatic movement in the first place. According to Kenyon, the ability of Christian Science to apply supernatural means to the healing needs of the masses was the reason for the serious rates of attrition in the denominational churches. The "amazing growth" of the metaphysical cults was "libel" upon the reputation of an impotent church and a "challenge" to the church to fulfill its healing ministry, a ministry that the cults had opportunistically usurped.

The reason that the church failed in its healing ministry was, in Kenyon's estimation, a dangerous antisupernaturalism that had infiltrated the church, reducing its gospel to pious platitudes and ethical demands that were void of the power to deliver and heal.[55] Kenyon believed that the antisupernaturalism of the church was directly related to its low view of Jesus Christ, that is, its failure to appreciate the divine and supernatural aspects of his healing ministry. He says that "we cannot blame . . . the non-conformist cults that are arising everywhere"; Kenyon almost seems to excuse the "extravagances" and "fanaticism" of groups such as Christian Science. The growth of such cults was merely a "protest" of the people against a church that refused to give them what they needed and wanted: "a supernatural religion." Kenyon felt that the people were willing to accept the extremism of the cults "in order that they might get a little touch of the supernatural God."[56] The denominational church possessed only "Sense Knowledge faith"—a faith which, unlike that in the cults, would never look beyond the senses for healing or miracles. "This is the reason why," wrote Kenyon, "some of the modern movements [the cults], which have so much physical demonstration, have challenged the faith of the multitudes."[57]

The "challenge" posed to the church by the metaphysical cults was to provide the people with the supernatural which they craved. Based on his belief that "discerning men and women have been asking for a new type of Christianity," Kenyon attempted to provide a middle-of-the-road alternative to the extremism of the cults and the dead liberalism of the denominations. According to Kenyon, the human spirit longs for the supernatural, but cannot find satisfaction for this longing until it is liberated from "Sense Knowledge" (i.e., empirical knowledge based on the five physical senses), which holds people in bondage and unbelief.

> This new order of Life, this new type of Christianity that has unveiled to us the truth about Sense Knowledge and has made us masters in the name of Jesus over the forces that have held us in bondage all our lives, has become a Living Reality. We now know what makes an atheist an atheist; a modernist, a modernist. We know the why of metaphysics. We understand why men have become philosophers. It is all sense knowledge seeking after something to satisfy a hungry human spirit that is

craving God. These people are all in one class. They are all sense knowledge devotees.[58]

Not only were those who practiced metaphysics in bondage to sense knowledge, but also atheists, modernists, and philosophers (elsewhere Kenyon adds scientists to the "class" of "sense knowledge devotees"). In contrast, those who have transcended the realm of sense knowledge into the realm of *revelation knowledge* (i.e., supernatural knowledge of the spirit realm and its workings as revealed in Kenyon's interpretation of the Bible), are in a "new class of men," the "supermen," the illuminati of Kenyon's "new type of Christianity."[59] Kenyon perceived the church to be in desperate need of his revelation in order to compete with supernatural manifestations of the metaphysical cults.

Kenyon's view of the church helps answer *why* he incorporated metaphysical elements into his theology, but it does not answer *how*. Did he do so knowingly or unknowingly? Several of his friends testify that Kenyon knowingly drew upon cultic sources, even though he himself rejected many of their beliefs. From the references to the cults in his writings, we are able to deduce that Kenyon did so in order to help the church compete with the cults. He wanted to restore supernaturalism to a church that had long since forsaken it.

But how could Kenyon have justified using cultic sources to help the church? Although it is speculative, the following scenario is probably the best answer. Having attended a school that, religiously speaking, drew its inspiration from New Thought and Christian Science, Kenyon was indoctrinated with a cultic view of the supernatural. Since we have no evidence that he outrightly converted to New Thought, it is safer to assume that Kenyon left Emerson with most of his evangelical beliefs intact. In this respect, Emerson College was a more significant influence in what it added to Kenyon's theology than what it took away.

After leaving Emerson, Kenyon began his evangelistic ministry, the outgrowth of which was Bethel Bible Institute. Kenyon was, however, more than a Baptist evangelist. His first newsletter, *Reality*, records numerous teachings and testimonies from Bethel about divine healing, a decidedly non-Baptist practice. The vast majority of these teachings in *Reality* were, nonetheless, fairly conservative and well within the boundaries of evangelical orthodoxy. But as the years passed and his ministry grew, Kenyon became increasingly concerned about the growth of the metaphysical cults because of their supernatural manifestations and practices, and the absence of the same in the denominational churches. Through his writings and radio sermons, Kenyon began to formulate a more radical theology of healing which he believed to be truly Christian, and yet which incorporated the metaphysical practices of divine healing and prosperity, practices for which he felt there were strong biblical precedents.

Because he had no theological background in the more biblically sound healing movements that arose from the Holiness-Pentecostal tradition, in formulating his "new type of Christianity" of healing and prosperity, Kenyon drew from the only background in these areas that he did have: metaphysics. He did not do so because he agreed with everything that the cults taught and practiced, for it is obvious that he did not. In attempting to respond to the cults and offer a Christian alternative to their beliefs and practices, Kenyon did, however, incorporate metaphysics into his theology.

His is a textbook example of a process recurring quite often in church history known as "syncretism," which is the combining of two or more different, even contradictory, religious beliefs in an attempt to formulate one belief system. Syncretism can be intentional, or it can be unintentional. It can be done with malice, or, as in Kenyon's case, it can be done with the intent to help. Although his intent was to help the church, Kenyon's syncretism of cultic ideas resulted in a strange blend of evangelical fundamentalism and New Thought metaphysics. In his attempt to correct one error, Kenyon created another.

That is not to say that Kenyon's writings are lacking in biblical proof-texts and Christian jargon. On the contrary, his writings are an endless series of proof-texts followed by one and two-sentence paragraphs of short, pithy statements about the text in question. Those in the Faith movement who are students of Kenyon would be scandalized by the claim that writings so filled with Scriptures could contain cultic ideas. What they fail to consider is that all of the New Thought and Christian Science writings are similarly filled with biblical proof-texts and Christian jargon. Cultic writers such as Quimby, Eddy, and Trine referred to the Bible constantly. Like Kenyon, they claimed that their metaphysical interpretations were merely the same "spiritual science" that Jesus himself preached and practiced.

In fact, this is precisely what makes Kenyon's syncretism of the various metaphysical cults such a threat to the church. The most successful cults in American church history, including New Thought and all its expressions, are those that make the most use of the Bible and sound the most similar to evangelical Christianity. This is no less true of Kenyon and the Faith movement. The cultic elements in Kenyon's theology are all the more dangerous because of his biblical prooftexting and proximity to evangelicalism. The facade of orthodoxy created by Kenyon's biblical proof-texting and evangelical jargon make the cultic elements in the Faith movement even more dangerous than a blatantly heretical cult, which would have been detected by charismatics long ago. These cultic elements may not constitute the entirety of his theology, but then again, they do not have to in order to do quite a bit of damage. Or, to use St. Paul's analogy, "A little leaven leavens the whole lump of dough" (Gal. 5:9).

The impact of Kenyon's cultic ideas upon the Faith movement classically illustrates the progressive nature of syncretism. Like a little leaven, the cultic elements in Kenyon's early writings were actually quite small, but grew considerably in his later writings. This progression continued in Hagin, who not only retained Kenyon's cultic ideas, but also amplified their importance in the Faith theology. The younger preachers of the Faith movement, such as Copeland, Price, and Tilton, have radicalized Kenyon's teachings even further, particularly his teaching on prosperity. The progressive evolution of cultic thought in the Faith movement is consistent with the nature of syncretism. Jacques Ellul states that

> In the ensuing evolution [of syncretism], it is the mistake or elision, that is, the wrong aspect, that achieves dominance. When there is in theological thinking an element of error . . . some dreg of laxity or syncretism, these are the things that capture attention and become the focus of interest. These are the things that Christian people have retained and prized. These have carried the day, increased in astonishing fashion, corrupted everything else, and gained the loyalty of believers, being adored by them as though they were the truth of God.[60]

Kenyon's legacy in the Faith movement is not the genius of his biblical interpretation, but rather, his syncretism of cultic ideas. It is these ideas—the concepts syncretized from metaphysics, of healing, positive confession, and prosperity—that account for the success of the movement. The sad truth is that the cultic, not the biblical, elements of the Faith theology are the very elements that distinguish it the most, cause its amazing growth, and occupy center stage in the Faith movement. These cultic ideas are widely accepted in the independent charismatic movement and are even proclaimed to be a key to the progressive revelation of God being poured out in the end times. How far Kenyon's syncretism will spread remains to be seen.

Is "Kenyonism," then, a cult in the same fashion and degree as New Thought or Christian Science? This is a difficult question to answer. On the one hand, it must be admitted that Kenyon did not approve of much of the cults' doctrine, particularly their emphasis upon the extrabiblical writings of their founders (e.g., the co-equality in Christian Science of the Bible and Eddy's *Science and Health*). For Kenyon, the books of the New Testament, particularly Paul's epistles, were the only legitimate source of revelation knowledge. On the other hand, as one reads his many books and pamphlets, it is also evident that Kenyon did, indeed, consider his own writings to be a wonderful new interpretation of the Scriptures, a "new type of Christianity," which would bring healing and prosperity to all who possessed his revelation knowledge of the Bible. The problem with Kenyon's revelation of healing and prosperity is its strong, but well-disguised, parallels with metaphysics.[61] Thus, while we do not at all believe that Kenyon's Faith movement in its entirety is a *cult*, we do contend that many of its most distinctive and popular doctrines are *cultic* in historical origin.

The historical origins of the Faith movement are not enough, however, to justify the charge of cultism. That would be an example of theological guilt by mere historical association. To prove cultism requires that it be demonstrated in no uncertain terms that the beliefs and practices of the contemporary Faith movement (not just those of Kenyon) are both cultic and heretical. This we shall do in the second part of the book. It shall be proven that not only are many of the doctrines of the Faith movement cultic in historical origin, they are also heretical in theological content.[62] The Faith movement is cultic not just because of where it comes from, but also because of what it teaches.

Many charismatics would object that a movement that has produced so many healings and miracles could not possibly be heretical. The gospel of the Faith movement does, indeed, produce *results*, but so does the gospel of metaphysics. *Results* can never be the criterion by which the *truth* of an idea is proven. If that were the case, charismatics would have to admit that Mary Baker Eddy is a prophetess and that Christian Science is true gospel. Likewise, the numerous healings and miracles occurring in the Faith movement are not necessarily signs from God that the Faith gospel is the gospel of the New Testament. Charismatics who naively assume that healings vindicate truth are overlooking the fact that almost every major religion and cult the world has ever known has produced healings. For every god there is a religion, and in every religion there are healings.

Granted, the Faith movement does claim to heal "in the name of Jesus," but this proves nothing, for so does New Thought. Both the Faith movement and metaphysical cults incessantly use the name of Jesus. Because of the historical connection between the two, the question that must be raised, however, is whether the Jesus of the Faith movement is the Jesus of the New Testament. The answer to this question that will be given in this book is a decisive *no*. The Jesus of the Faith movement is "another Jesus" (2 Cor. 11:4) and the gospel of the Faith movement is a "different gospel" (Gal. 1:6).

Notes

1. Ruth A. Kenyon [Houseworth], "He is at Rest," *Kenyon's Herald of Life*, 13 (Apr., 1948), p. 1.

2. Houseworth, personal interview.

3. Howard Ferrin, Chancellor of Barrington College, phone interview, Feb. 23, 1982.

4. Francis S. Bernauer, "Bethel Bible Institute: Its Aim, Method, and Outlook," *Reality* 4 (June, 1907), 14.

5. Article 9, "Constitution of Bethel Bible Institute," *Reality* (Apr., 1907), p. 209.

6. Bernauer, "Bethel Bible Institute," p. 17.

7. Houseworth, personal interview.

8. Ferrin, phone interview.

9. Houseworth, personal interview.

10. Houseworth, "He is at Rest," p. 1.

11. Baxter, taped correspondence.

12. E. W. Kenyon, *Reality* 2 (Oct., 1904), p. 4.

13. For more information on Savage, see George Willis Cooke, *Unitarianism in America* (Boston: American Unitarian Assoc., 1902), pp. 196, 274.

14. Charles Braden, *Spirits in Rebellion: The Rise and Development of New Thought* (Dallas: Southern Methodist Univ. Press, 1966), pp. 27–30.

15. Kenyon's attendance of Emerson College in 1892 is a matter of public record and was confirmed to the author by Bob Flemming, the archivist at Emerson (phone interview, May 1, 1986). His attendance at Emerson is also mentioned in the memorial edition of his newsletter (Houseworth, "He is at Rest," p. 1).

16. John M. Coffee, Jr. and Richard L. Wentworth, *A Century of Eloquence: The History of Emerson College, 1880–1890* (Boston: Alternative Publications, 1982), p. 10. Most of the information on Emerson College came from this book and a personal interview with one of its co-authors, Richard Wentworth.

17. The church at Chelsea was Emerson's last pastorate. It is interesting to note that Emerson was replaced at Chelsea by James Henry Wiggins, who was the literary advisor to Mary Baker Eddy, the founder of Christian Science.

18. Ibid., pp. 16, 17.

19. Ibid., pp. 17, 18. The perpetrator of this diploma mill was a man named John Buchanan, a charlatan and self-confessed grave robber, who was eventually imprisoned for his fraud.

20. Ibid., pp. 11–13.

21. Ibid., p. 19. According to Richard Wentworth, as a drawing card, Emerson's appeal was largely to women. Emerson College eventually gained the reputation of being a type of finishing school for girls, even though it was co-educational from its inception. In addition, Wentworth claims that there is reason to believe that Emerson obtained substantial financial gains from the college despite the fact that it had always been a non-profit organization.

22. Emerson's conversion to Christian Science is a matter of public record and may be confirmed by the Christian Science Mother Church, Boston, Mass.

23. One setting where Kenyon surely received religious instruction was during Charles Emerson's Saturday morning lecture series, which was dedicated to his strange mixture of biblical exposition and New Thought metaphysics.

24. Coffee and Wentworth, p. 39; quoting Emerson, "The Human Brain: Its Friend and Foes," *Lectures* (Apr. 28, 1894), pp. 18–19; italics added for emphasis.

25. Coffee and Wentworth, p. 39; quoting Emerson, "The Suggestive Period in Art," *Lectures* (Jan. 30, 1892), p. 74.

26. Emerson's "technique" for teaching oratory involved voice culture, gesture, the evolution of expression, the perfective laws of art, dramatic interpretation, English literature, rhetoric, singing, anatomy, psychology, philosophy, pedagogy, art, aesthetics, and physical culture. This last aspect of physical culture, or training, was of particular importance in the Emerson system and was religious in nature: "train the body to express the sentiments received from the indwelling Spirit of the Most High." Emerson also claimed that his system of physical training cured "all forms of chronic disease." One minister differentiated Emerson's system from calisthenics "in that it works from the spiritual and psychical standpoint, instead of the animal" (Coffee and Wentworth, pp. 49, 52).

27. Ibid., p. 68; quoting Emerson, *Emerson College Magazine* (May, 1897), p. 191.

28. Ibid., p. 64; quoting Albert Armstrong, *Emerson College Magazine* (May, 1896), p. 162.

29. Ibid., p. 68; quoting Charles Mallory, *Emerson College Magazine* (Dec., 1910), p. 108.

30. As quoted in Braden, *Spirits in Rebellion*, pp. 14–18.

31. "New Thought," *Encyclopedia Britannica* (15th ed., 1983), vol. 13, p. 15.

32. Ibid., p. 61; quoting Mary Ann Greely, *Emerson College Magazine* (Dec., 1910), p. 108.

33. Sydney E. Ahlstrom, *A Religious History of the American People* (New Haven: Yale Univ. Press, 1972), p. 1030.

34. Charles W. Ferguson, *The New Books of Revelation: The Inside Story of America's Astounding Religious Cults* (New York: Doubleday Doran and Co., 1928), p. 158.

35. Coffee and Wentworth, p. 59.

36. Braden, *Spirits in Rebellion*, p. 165. Despite the success of his writings, Trine never led the New Thought movement in any organizational sense beyond a few honorary, figurehead positions. Furthermore, Braden claims that "whether he made a practice of healing personally and professionally is not certain. One gets the impression that he made his contribution to the movement chiefly through his books and through lecturing."

37. Ibid.

38. In addition to Trine, another New Thought V.I.P. associated with Emerson was Horatio J. Dresser, who was one of his earliest students and who eventually became a historian of the New Thought movement. Dresser's father, Julius, had been healed by the founder of New Thought, P. P. Quimby, and so Julius and Horatio committed themselves to distributing Quimby's writings, a task which the latter achieved with the publication of *The Quimby Manuscripts* (1921).

39. Besides Charles and Susie Emerson, who converted to Christian Science, several prominent practitioners of Christian Science were associated with Emerson College during Kenyon's enrollment there. Laura Carey attended from 1890 to 1893 and after graduation became a reader of the Bible at the Christian Science Mother Church in Boston (a fact mentioned in Eddy's collected prose works). Carey married a fellow student, Albert Connant, who also graduated in 1893 and who eventually became the organist of the Mother Church. Connant also compiled *The Complete Concordance of the Writings of Mary Baker Eddy*. Another prominent Christian Scientist who attended Emerson between 1893 and 1895 was Irving C. Tomlinson, who converted to Eddy's religion in 1895. Tomlinson was the first lecturer on the Christian Science Board of Leadership and lived in Eddy's home the last two years of her life. Tomlinson's autobiography was entitled *Twelve Years with Mary Baker Eddy* (Coffee and Wentworth, pp. 63, 64).

40. E. W. Kenyon, "Rural Evangelism," *Reality* 1 (Mar., 1904), p. 124.

41. E. W. Kenyon, *Reality* 3 (Feb.–Mar., 1907), p. 184.

42. E. W. Kenyon, *Reality* 2 (Oct., 1904), p. 4.

43. E. W. Kenyon, *The Hidden Man: An Unveiling of the Subconscious Mind* (Seattle: Kenyon's Gospel Publishing Society, 1970), pp. 25–27; cf. Kenyon, *The Two Kinds of Life* (Seattle: Kenyon's Gospel Publishing Society, 1971), p. 82.

44. John Kennington, "E. W. Kenyon and the Metaphysics of Christian Science," p. 1.

45. Kenyon, *The Two Kinds of Righteousness* (Seattle: Kenyon's Gospel Publishing Society, 1942), pp. 5, 9.

46. The source of Kenyon's claim could have been a scholarly, but controversial, book by Walter M. Haushalter, *Mrs. Eddy Purloins from Hegel* (Boston: A. A. Beauchamp, 1936). For a fuller analysis of the relation between Eddy and Hegel, see Charles Braden, *Christian Science Today: Power, Policy, Practice* (Dallas: Southern Methodist Univ. Press, 1958), pp. 32, 33.

47. Kenyon, *The Two Kinds of Faith*, pp. 17–18.

48. Kenyon, *Hidden Man*, p. 35.

49. Ibid., p. 74.

50. Ibid., p. 137.

51. Kenyon, *The Two Kinds of Knowledge* (Seattle: Kenyon's Gospel Publishing Society, 1942), pp. 34, 35.

52. Horatio Dresser, *The Quimby Manuscripts* (Seacacus, N.J.: Citadel, 1980), p. 195. In his efforts to establish the same "science" of healing that Jesus was attempting, Quimby fancied himself as a warrior combatting the "error" of the ignorance of metaphysical science, an ignorance which was the ultimate cause of disease. He wrote, "Now I stand alone on this rock [his metaphysical science], fighting the errors of this world, and establishing the Science of Life by my works. What is my mode of warfare? With the axe of truth, I strike at the root of every tree of error and hew it down, so that there shall not be one error in man showing itself in the form of disease. My knowledge is my wisdom and is not matter or opinion. It decomposes the thoughts . . . and produces an idea clear from the error that makes a person unhappy or diseased. You see that I have something to reason about, and this something is eternal life, which is in Science, and is what Jesus tried to establish" (Ibid., pp. 242–43).

53. Kenyon, *Hidden Man*, p. 94; Kenyon claimed that his "Spiritology" would be the "new psychology" which would enable man "to study psychology and get to know himself in Reality." (It should be pointed out that "Reality" as Kenyon uses it is a term often used in New Thought and Christian Science to refer to the spiritual realm and truths that were hidden by the sensations of physical reality, which was not reality at all, but was considered "error," the opposite of metaphysical reality. *Reality* was also the name of Kenyon's first newsletter.)

54. Kenyon, *Wonderful Name of Jesus*, pp. 69, 70.

55. E. W. Kenyon, "The Crisis," *Reality* 7 (May, 1904), pp. 133–34.

56. Kenyon, *Wonderful Name of Jesus*, p. 70.

57. Kenyon, *Two Kinds of Righteousness*, p. 15.

58. Kenyon, *Hidden Man*, p. 214.

59. Ibid., pp. 193, 201.

60. Jacques Ellul, *The Subversion of Christianity* (Grand Rapids: Eerdmans, 1986), p. 20.

61. In the second part of the book, a detailed analysis of the cultic elements of the Faith theology will be presented. Suffice to say at this point that the cultic parallels between metaphysics and the Faith theology are: positive mental attitude, positive confession, prosperity, deification, deism, pantheism, and the denial of physical symptoms.

62. Historically, the label "heresy" has been reserved for gross error involving the godhead or the person and work of Christ. Although the Faith movement engages in many practices of healing that I regard as sub-biblical and even dangerous, I am not referring to these as heretical. The heresy of the Faith movement is its denial of the sovereignty and personhood of God, its subversion of the full deity of Jesus Christ, and its implicit rejection of Christ's blood atonement. Its doctrines of deification and dualism are also highly questionable.

4 The Role of Kenneth Hagin in the Faith Movement

Some of us, like Paul, stand in more than one office. Often we'll weave in and out of these offices. Thank God I had the anointing to preach and then the anointing to teach. I spoke in tongues and prophesied, but I never stood in the office of the prophet until 1952. I know exactly when I entered into the ministry of the prophet.

—Kenneth Hagin,
Understanding the Anointing
(Faith Library, 1985), p. 65

An able preacher with a homey and humorous Texas style, Hagin had nevertheless always been more of a student and a teacher than platform performer. He early sensed that the gift of teaching was a more enduring basis for his ministry. . . . While conceding that gifts had their place, he could see the day of the teacher and prophet coming.

—David Edwin Harrell, Jr.,
All Things Are Possible
(Indiana Univ. Press, 1975), pp. 185–86

Although there is little doubt that E. W. Kenyon is its founding father, the contemporary Faith movement is virtually incomprehensible without explicating the role played in it by Kenneth Hagin. Kenyon may have authored the teachings on which the Faith movement is based, but Hagin is the man who fashioned these teachings into the fastest growing movement in charismatic Christendom. All of the major ministers of the Faith movement readily admit Hagin's tutelage. He is universally recognized in the movement as both a teacher and a prophet. This chapter will examine Hagin's role as a teacher/ prophet, particularly in the light of his plagiarism of Kenyon's writings. Before turning to this examination, let us first briefly recount the major events of his early life and ministry.

A Biographical Sketch of
Hagin's Early Life and Ministry

An official biography of Kenneth Hagin has never been written, but his early life and ministry can be reconstructed from the numerous self-references scattered throughout his writings.[1] Kenneth Erwin Hagin was born in McKinney, Texas, on August 20, 1917. Because Hagin was born with a congenital heart defect and weighed less than two pounds at his premature birth, the attending physician gave him up for dead. Hagin was weak and sickly throughout his childhood and in general was not a physically or emotionally healthy child. His unhappiness was compounded when at age six his father deserted his mother. She subsequently suffered a nervous breakdown and, as a result, was suicidal during most of Hagin's early life. Few of Hagin's references to his childhood are positive or nostalgic.

During his adolescence, things went from bad to worse for Hagin. Four months before his sixteenth birthday, his heart condition worsened and he became completely bedfast. For the next 16 months, Hagin was incapacitated, often in state of physical paralysis and mental delirium. Two events occurred during his illness that would forever change his life and ministry. First, Hagin claims that he (literally) "went to hell," not just once, but three successive times, his "inward man rushed out of [his] body" and left it "lying dead, with eyes set and flesh cold."[2] Hagin describes his first descent into hell this way:

> I went down, down, down, until the lights of earth faded away. . . . The further down I went the blacker it became, until it was all blackness. I could not have seen my hand if it had been one inch in front of my eyes. The further down I went, the hotter it was and the more stifling it became. Finally, far down below me I could see lights flickering on the walls of the caverns of the damned. They were caused by the fires of hell. The giant, white-crested orb of flame pulled me, drawing me as a magnet draws metal to itself. *I did not want to go!* I did not walk, but just as metal jumps to the magnet, my spirit was drawn to that place. I could not take my eyes off it. The heat beat me in the face. Many years have now gone by, yet I can see it as clearly as I saw it then. It is just as fresh in my memory as though it happened last night.[3]

This same experience was repeated two more times. After the third descent into hell, Hagin gave his life to Christ and felt that he was ready to die in peace.

Hagin's second life-changing experience as he lay on his death-bed was a "revelation" of the scripture that has become the hallmark of his ministry, Mark 11:23, 24:

> Truly I say to you, whoever says to this mountain, "Be taken up and cast into the sea," and does not doubt in his heart, but believes that what he says is going to happen, it shall be granted him. Therefore I say to you, all things for which you pray and ask, believe that you have received them, and they shall be granted you (NASB).

The revelation of this passage came in two parts to Hagin. The first was on January 1, 1934, and was a profoundly emotional experience. The doctrinal substance of that experience was something less than profound, however, and Hagin was able to express it in one terse sentence; "Here is the principle of faith: believe in your heart, say it with your mouth, and 'he shall have whatsoever he saith.' "[4] Stunned by this new "principle of faith," Hagin began to confess his own healing daily. Nevertheless, healing did not come for eight more months.

In the second week of August 1934, Hagin received the second part of the revelation of Mark 11:23, 24.

> In this moment, I saw exactly what that verse in Mark 11:24 meant. Until then I was going to wait till I was actually healed. I was looking at my body and testing my heartbeat to see if I had been healed. But I saw that the verse says that you have to believe when you pray. The *having* comes after the *believing*. I had been reversing it. I was trying to *have* first and then *believe*. . . . "I see it. I see it," I said with joy. "I see what I've got to do, Lord. I've got to believe that my paralysis is gone while I'm still lying here on this bed, and while my heart is not beating right. I've got to believe that my paralysis is gone while I'm still lying here flat on my back and helpless."[5]

Hagin began to thank God for his healing in spite of the fact that he was still seemingly paralyzed. After 10 minutes of such confession, Hagin claims that the Holy Spirit spoke to him and said, "You believe that you are healed. If you are healed, then you should be up and out of that bed." Hagin then pushed himself up and holding on to various stationary objects succeeded in circling the room. He practiced thus for several days and then asked for clothes to join his family for breakfast.[6] Although he would experience periodic symptoms for years afterward, Hagin was apparently healed from his terminal illness.[7]

After his graduation from high school, he began his ministry as a young preacher at a local community church in Roland, Texas about eight miles from McKinney. Although primarily Baptist in background, Hagin's ministry at this church was hardly Baptist in content: it was often accompanied by divine visitations of "the glory cloud" under which Hagin's face shone like that of an angel and his faculties were entirely suspended while he preached.[8] In 1937, Hagin began to frequent Pentecostal circles, not because he wanted to speak in tongues—a practice which until this point in his life he found distasteful—but rather, because the Full Gospel churches were the only ones preaching the doctrine of divine healing that he had experienced and in which he believed so ardently. That same year, Hagin received the "baptism of the Holy Spirit" and spoke in tongues.

In 1937, Hagin was licensed as an Assemblies of God minister and pastored various small Assemblies churches in Texas. As a Pentecostal, his ministry grew even more overtly supernatural. In addition to the glory cloud and his preaching in a state of suspended animation, Hagin describes meetings in which one woman was levitated in mid-air while dancing, and another woman was frozen bodily in a cataleptic trance for 8 hours and 40 minutes.[9] Healings were frequent and even "resurrections of the dead" purportedly occurred in Hagin's pastoral ministry.[10]

Despite such tremendous events, Hagin is now rather negative about his early pastoral ministry and considers it a failure for which he needed divine forgiveness. The major reason that Hagin regrets his years as a pastor is that he did not have "the anointing" or calling to be one.[11] Hagin spent 3 years as a Baptist evangelist (1934–37) and 12 years as an Assemblies of God pastor (1937–49). He preached his final pastoral sermon in Van, Texas, in the second week of February, 1949.

At this point, Hagin entered the intensely competitive and sometimes strange world of the post–World War II Healing Revival (ca. 1947–58). Although he retained his ministerial papers with the Assemblies and did not form his own evangelistic association until 1962, Hagin began to minister in the circles of such independent healing evangelists as William Branham, Oral Roberts, A. A. Allen, Jack Coe, and T. L. Osborn. He also associated himself, as did most of the healing evangelists of that period, with Gordon Lindsay, whose *Voice of Healing* magazine was the official periodical of the Healing Revival. This move towards a more itinerant, revivalistic methodology was to be, according to a vision of Jesus granted to Hagin, the "first phase" of his ministry, the one to which God had called him in the first place: the office of the prophet and teacher. As already noted, Hagin's contribution to the Healing Revival was not so much as a healer or platform performer—for in these activities he was considerably outclassed by the likes of Branham, Roberts, and Allen—but rather, in his role as a prophetic teacher or, better yet, a teaching prophet.

Kenneth Hagin: Prophet and Teacher of Faith

Hagin claims that his teaching ministry began at three o'clock on a Thursday afternoon in 1943. The reason that he is able to know with such pinpoint accuracy is because his teaching is based not only on his expertise in the Scriptures (he claims that he read the New Testament 150 times before he preached his first sermon), but also on an anointing that he received on that day. Until receiving this anointing, Hagin admits that he was hard-pressed even to teach a Sunday school class, much less articulate a theology that has altered the face of the entire charismatic movement. He describes this experience as follows.

> I'd been lying down. I walked across the parsonage living room and into the kitchen for a drink of water. As I was coming back across the living room, right in the middle of the room, something dropped down on me and inside me. It just clicked down on the inside of me like a coin drops inside a pay phone. I stopped dead still. I knew what it was. It was a teaching gift. The anointing to teach had dropped inside me. I said, "Now I can teach."[12]

Although nobody could accuse Hagin of not quoting a sufficient number of biblical proof-texts in his teachings, it must be noted that his anointing as a teacher, just as his anointing as a prophet, is in no way dependent on his formal education or theological training, both of which are minimal. Hagin claims to teach from a higher source, a mystical "anointing" and interpretational principle known in the Faith movement as "revelation knowledge."

Hagin's call to the prophetic office occurred nine years later in 1952 and was no less certain than his call as a teacher. His working definition of a prophet is one who "has visions and revelations, among other things."[13] Although he never specifies what these "other things" are, there can be no doubt that Hagin more than fulfills his own criterion. He claims to have had numerous visions and revelations, to be exact, eight personal visitations of Jesus, and more visionary experiences than can be contained in a single volume.

The first visitation of Jesus experienced by Hagin was more of an out-of-the-body heavenly journey than a mere visitation. In an evangelistic meeting held in Rockwall, Texas, on September 2, 1950, Hagin heard a voice from heaven, saying "Come up hither." Just like the Apostle John on the island of Patmos, Hagin was allowed to see and move into "the spirit realm," where he was caught up to a mountain in heaven just outside the heavenly city. After a relatively brief audience with Jesus—some of his conversations with the Lord last for hours—Hagin was taken by Jesus down into hell (his fourth trip there) for even more instruction. After he had been transported by Jesus back to his meeting, Hagin was immediately caught up again and taken to a destitute wilderness area, where he encountered an apocalyptic horseman who handed him a scroll labeled "War and Destruction." Commanded to "read, in the name of Jesus Christ," Hagin took the scroll from the angel and read of the coming destruction of the cities of America and the last great revival that was to come. Hagin claims that those in his meeting heard him read this scroll. After he finished reading, Hagin was again returned to his meeting.

But the vision was not over even yet. Jesus again took Hagin up into heaven to speak with him about his ministry. Explaining that Hagin's first 15 years as a pastor and evangelist had been in his permissive will only, Jesus told him that he had entered into the "first phase" of his ministry when he left the pastorate and had joined the healing ministry. Nevertheless, during this first phase, said Jesus, "you didn't do what I told you to do. The reason that you didn't is that you doubted it was my Spirit that had spoken to you." Having repented of his unbelief, Hagin began the "second phase" of his ministry, which lasted only eight months, from January to August of 1950, but was the first time that Hagin's ministry entirely pleased Jesus. (It is interesting to note that 1950 was also the year that Hagin insists that he first read any of Kenyon's books.) In this vision of September 1950, Hagin maintains that Jesus told him that he was about to enter the "third phase" of his ministry. If he proved faithful, Jesus would appear to him again to lead him into "the fourth and final phase of [his] ministry."[14]

The times from 1950 to 1959 were survival years for the Hagin ministry. Despite the fact that during these years, Jesus appeared to Hagin seven more times, the historical record indicates that his healing ministry was only minimally successful, at best. By his own admission, these were lean years of growing debts and dwindling crowds.[15] In his sixth vision of Jesus given to him in February of 1959, Hagin found out part of the reason why. On this occasion, Hagin was in the hospital recovering from a dislocated and fractured elbow which he had suffered from a fall in El Paso, Texas. Jesus appeared to him in his hospital room and explained that, once again, he had been walking in the "permissive will of God" only. As a result, Jesus had "permitted Satan" to damage Hagin's arm in order "to arrest his attention" to the fact that he was placing his teaching ministry before his prophetic ministry. The prophetic ministry, Jesus explained, was greater than the teaching ministry and was to be Hagin's primary calling. In order to force him to reprioritize his ministry, God allowed Hagin to suffer an interruption of the divine health that he had enjoyed for 25 years.[16]

The dual office of prophet and teacher is crucial to an understanding of Hagin's role and influence in the Faith movement. By his own admission, he "weaves in and out of these offices," a talent which accounts for much of the current success of his ministry. As a prophet, Hagin communicates revelation that is received by way of divine voice, vision, or visitation. As a teacher, he exposits the Scriptures in a plain and often humorous fashion. When both offices are combined, the result is a ministry that appears utterly supernatural, and yet thoroughly biblical. *Herein lies the genius of Hagin: his followers believe him to be a mystical seer and a biblical scholar at the same time.* Those who would challenge Hagin's prophecies on a mystical basis are rebuked for "rejecting the Word of God" and those who would challenge his teachings on a rational basis are warned "to touch not the Lord's anointed." Within the confines of the Faith movement, Hagin's doctrine is, therefore, impervious to criticism on any plane, whether mystical or rational.

Hagin's Claims of Divine Visitations

The theology of Kenneth Hagin is inexplicable apart from the personal visitations of Jesus that he claims have been granted him. At least three of Hagin's books—*I Believe in Visions, The Ministry of the Prophet*, and *How You Can Be Led by the Spirit of God*—are based, in part or in whole, on divine visitations in which Hagin converses face to face and engages in biblical interpretation with Jesus Christ himself. Hagin describes one such visitation as follows:

> Let me go back . . . to what Jesus said to me in February of 1959 in El Paso, Texas. It was 6:30 in the afternoon. I was sitting up in bed study- ing. My eyes were wide open . . . I heard footsteps. The door to my room was ajar 12 to 14 inches. So I looked to see who was coming into my room. I expected some literal physical person. But as I looked to see who it was, I saw Jesus. It seemed as if the hair on my neck and head stood straight up on end. Chill bumps popped out all over my body. I saw Him. He had on a white robe. He wore Roman sandals. (Jesus has appeared to me eight times. Every time except this time His feet were bare. This time He had on sandals; that's what I had heard.) He seemed to be about 5 feet 11 inches tall. He looked to weigh about 180 pounds. He came through the door and pushed it back almost shut. He walked around the foot of my bed. I followed Him with my eyes—almost spellbound. He took hold of a straight chair and pushed it up close to my bed. Then He sat down on it, folded His hands, and began His conversation by saying, "I said to you night before last in the automo- bile by My Spirit . . . "[17]

Hagin goes on to describe how Jesus instructed him in how to be "led by the Spirit" by means of "the inward witness" such that "open visions" of Jesus (ones in which Jesus appears visibly) would no longer be necessary for guidance.[18] Nevertheless, "open visions" continue to occur in Hagin's ministry.

The visitations of Jesus granted to Hagin are not just for his personal benefit. Hagin is usually instructed to teach the church that which Jesus taught him. For instance, in the appearance of Jesus described above, Hagin recounts,

> Then the Lord said this to me, which is not just for my benefit, but for yours, "If you will learn to follow that inward witness, I will make you rich. . . . I am not opposed to my children being rich. I am opposed to their being covetous." I [Hagin] have followed that inward witness and He has done just what He said He would. He has made me rich.[19]

This is a fairly typical example of how Hagin claims to have formed his theology. The doctrinal "bottom line" of this experience is that Jesus personally taught Hagin how to get rich by means of obeying "the inward witness" and that Hagin, in turn, was to teach this technique to the church.

Hagin claims to have a divine mandate to teach all of his con- cepts of faith to the church.

> The Lord said to me years ago, "I want you to go teach my people faith. I have taught you faith through my Word, and I have permitted you to go through certain experiences. You have learned faith both through my Word and through experience. Now go teach my people faith.

Teach them what I have taught you." I heard a voice from heaven speak those words to me.[20]

Throughout his writings Hagin repeatedly attributes his teaching to visions or voices from Jesus, which he is then instructed to teach to his followers. These experiences are the bedrock of Hagin's authority as a prophet and teacher.

Hagin purportedly receives not just general revelation from Jesus, but precise interpretations of specific verses of the Bible. Frequently, Hagin even argues with Jesus about matters of interpretation. For example, Hagin once complained that something the Lord was teaching him was "really different from anything I ever heard preached or that I ever preached myself" and that such teaching "really upends my theology." The Lord supposedly told Hagin, "Sometimes your theology needs upending."[21]

Sometimes Hagin attempts to "upend" Jesus' theology. When Jesus appeared to him and gave him a formula for success with which "you can write your own ticket with God," Hagin demanded proof from the Bible. Supposedly "Jesus smiled" and gladly obliged.[22] On yet another occasion in which Jesus was trying to convince Hagin that he had the power to command angels, Hagin again demanded scriptural proof, explaining to the Lord, "You know that I'm a real stickler for the Word." Hagin justified his demands on Jesus for biblical evidence by saying, "After all, I wanted to be Scriptural."[23] Hagin's desire to be scriptural produces some heated debates with Jesus. In one vision, the Lord told Hagin a particular doctrinal concept no less than four times and he still would not accept it unless Jesus could give to him not just one biblical proof-text, but several. Hagin reports that

> I told the Lord I didn't care how many times I saw him in visions—He would have to prove this to me by at least three Scriptures out of the New Testament. . . . Jesus smiled sweetly and said He would give me four. I said, "I've read the New Testament 150 times, and many portions of it more than that. If that is in there, I don't know it."[24]

Although his writings contain several debates about biblical interpretation, Hagin does not claim to have ever changed Jesus' mind about the meaning of a particular verse.

From these specific cases, Hagin's general pattern of revelation may be summarized as follows: (1) Jesus appears to Hagin, usually at some point of considerable need in his life; (2) Jesus imparts some new doctrine to Hagin; (3) skeptical at first, Hagin argues with Jesus about the new doctrine and demands proof from the Bible; (4) Jesus provides the proof from the Bible and Hagin is convinced; and (5) Jesus commands Hagin to teach the new doctrine to the church. With slight variations, this same revelatory pattern has occurred eight major times in Hagin's ministry in which Jesus has appeared to him in "an open vision" and innumerable other times in which Jesus has taught him by means of "the inward witness."

Hagin's Threats of Divine Judgments

Given the divine origins of his theology, it is not terribly surprising that Hagin also claims that divine judgment is on everyone who rejects his prophetic teaching. The first example of this judgment occurred early in his ministry. After an incident of supernatural levitation in one of his services, Hagin's own wife, as well as the wife and the brother of the pastor at whose church he was ministering, questioned whether or not the phenomenon was of God. As he was praying the next day, "the word of the Lord" came to Hagin, instructing him to touch all three of them lightly on the forehead with his little finger. When he did this to his wife, "it was as though someone hit her with a ball bat and knocked her flat on her back on the floor."[25] The other two were similarly "slain in the Spirit."[26] The three paralyzed victims were "glued to the floor." When the reasonably concerned pastor tried to help his wife up, he "couldn't even lift her arm off the floor, much less her body." A voice then instructed Hagin to "go kneel by each one. Tell them to try to get up. Then ask them if they acknowledge that what is happening is the power of God." When the three tried to move and found themselves completely immobilized, they, of course, were willing to admit that Hagin's power and ministry were of God. Hagin was then instructed by the voice to "release them" by again touching them with his finger.[27] They had been convinced.

If by obeying the "inner voice," Hagin could accomplish so much with just his little finger, it was inevitable that such prophetic judgments would increase as his ministry grew. In his sixth vision of Jesus in 1959, the Lord told Hagin, "The judgment must begin in the house of God, and if the righteous scarcely be saved, where shall the sinner and the ungodly appear. If the church won't accept this ministry, then they wouldn't accept His Word and He can't help them." Moreover, if a church refused to accept Hagin's ministry, God "would remove their candlestick."[28]

As serious as these consequences are for a church, they are nothing by way of comparison to the judgment pronounced on an individual minister who challenges Hagin's prophethood. Claiming that "if a pastor would not accept this message then judgment would come on him," Hagin writes,

> The Lord said to me, "If I give you a message for an individual, a church, or a pastor and they don't accept it, you will not be responsible. They will be responsible. There will be ministers who don't accept it and will fall dead in the pulpit."[29]

For those who think that such statements by Hagin are idle threats or prophetic hyperbole, listen further to the "prophet":

> I say this with reluctance but this actually happened in one place where I preached. Two weeks from the day that I closed the meeting, the pastor fell dead in the pulpit. When I left that church I left crying. I told the pastor in the next church where I went to hold a meeting, "That man will fall dead in the pulpit." And just a very short time after that he did. *Why? Because he didn't accept the message that God gave me to give him from the Holy Spirit.*[30]

If a minister could suffer such a fate, then what would become of a mere layperson who dared to question Hagin's message? In the original publication of this material, Hagin also warned that "there are going to be lay-members that are going to fall dead in the church, in the last days, like Ananias and Sapphira. They lied to God."[31]

Thus, Kenneth Hagin maintains that much of his theology comes straight from Jesus and that the divine wrath burns against all who oppose his prophetic ministry. His teaching has both a divine source and a divine *sanction*. Before critiquing Hagin's prophethood, we shall recount in more detail the quite human origins of his theology.

The Human Origins of Hagin's Theology

The major historical root of the Faith movement is, of course, E. W. Kenyon. Because of Hagin's success in the ministry, Kenyon's teachings have become the foundational principles of the Faith movement. Moreover, because of the wild success of the Faith movement, Kenyon's teachings are also now widely accepted throughout much of the independent charismatic movement. This means that the root of the major branch of the charismatic movement is cultic in nature. And if the root is cultic, then so must be the fruit. There is no question that many charismatics have derived a type of benefit from the fruit of which they have partaken in the Faith movement. What is in question, however, is the root from which this fruit has come. According to St. Paul, "if the root be holy, the branches are too" (Rom. 11:16). On the contrary, if the root is not holy, then what can we say about the fruit of the Faith movement? A bad root cannot produce good fruit.

Just as Hagin will rarely admit to having a personal theology (that does not come straight from God), so also is it rare that he will admit to his own historical roots. He has repeatedly denied that he plagiarized the overwhelming majority of his theology from Kenyon. Hagin's refusal to acknowledge his indebtedness to Kenyon is accentuated by his openness in speaking of ministers who were of minimal influence in his life and ministry. Hagin is usually candid in acknowledging the secondary influences on his teaching. The overwhelming majority of people he cites were activists in the early Pentecostal movement or post–World War II Healing Revival, most of whom in one way or another were involved directly in the healing ministry.[32] Hagin's citations of these faith-healers are usually limited to a story about their lives and ministries, or a brief quotation from one of their books or sermons. The following is not intended as an exhaustive list but merely a summary.

F. F. Bosworth

Hagin occasionally refers to F. F. Bosworth in his books and on his radio program. Raised in John Alexander Dowie's City of Zion, Bosworth began a healing ministry that spanned two world wars. He was also a pioneer in radio evangelism. Not particularly well-educated or literary by nature, Bosworth's sermons were collected into a book, *Christ the Healer* (Fleming H. Revell, 1973), which is a required text at Hagin's Rhema Bible Training Center. Like Hagin, Bosworth took much of his doctrine from E. W. Kenyon.[33] Bosworth taught Kenyon's emphasis on the centrality of faith and confession in obtaining the benefits of the atonement, such as healing and prosperity.

Smith Wigglesworth

Wigglesworth is consistently cited by Hagin as the personification of faith in action. Because Wigglesworth was illiterate most of his life and, even after he learned to read, never read any book but the Bible, his contribution to the Faith movement consists almost entirely in the inspiration of his biography and an endless series of one-liners preserved from his preaching.

Influences from the Pentecostal Movement and Healing Revival

Hagin is obviously well-schooled in the biographies and teachings of the famous names of the early Pentecostal movement and the post–World War II Healing Revival. Because they were his contemporaries and competitors in the Healing Revival, Hagin was influenced heavily by his peers, many of whom were loosely associated through Gordon Lindsay's *Voice of Healing* magazine: William Branham, Oral Roberts, A. A. Allen, Jack Coe, T. L. Osborn, and others. In addition, although he did not know them personally, he occasionally and casually cites such prominent Pentecostal figures as Ethan Allen, Carrie Judd Montgomery, John G. Lake, Andrew Murray, Aimee Semple McPherson, P. C. Nelson, Charles Price, and Lilian B. Yeomans. In all of these citations, Hagin demonstrates the ability to give credit where credit is due with regard to the sources that he drew on to develop a particular idea.

A different situation exists, however, concerning the writers who were of a more extensive influence upon Hagin. It is a peculiar fact that *those who have influenced Kenneth Hagin the least, he acknowledges the most, and those who have influenced him the most, he fails to acknowledge at all* (at least, he fails to acknowledge that they influenced him while he was forming his theology). What influence from these primary sources he will admit to he will do so only after the fact. In general, it is not unfair to say that the doctrines Hagin claims to have originated, and which have made him a man of considerable importance, are the very doctrines that he has taken from other authors. The overwhelming example of Hagin's practice in this regard is Kenyon, but there are other minor examples as well.

John A. MacMillan

For instance, Dale Simmons, then a graduate student at Oral Roberts University, discovered in 1983 that as much as 75% of one of Hagin's best selling pamphlets, *The Authority of the Believer*, which was first published in 1967 and has gone through 21 printings, was taken word-for-word from a series of articles published in 1932 by

John A. MacMillan under the same title, "The Authority of the Believer." These articles were published in *The Alliance Weekly*, a publication of the Christian and Missionary Alliance Church (CMA), and were later republished in pamphlet form.

When Simmons realized that Hagin had plagiarized MacMillan's work, he immediately contacted H. Robert Cowles, vice-president of the publishing branch of the CMA, Christian Publications. Mr. Cowles, in turn, wrote Kenneth Hagin and confronted him with the plagiarism. In his response to Cowles on Feb. 28, 1984, Hagin claimed that his book, *The Authority of the Believer*, was taken from sermons he had preached on the subject. In these sermons, Hagin claims, "I gave credit to the fact that my teaching was based *in part* [emphasis his] on the book by J. A. MacMillan. This fact was evidently omitted in error when the book was edited." Hagin further claims that an unidentified article in *The Pentecostal Evangel* had prompted his study on the words "power" and "authority" and that "this study and its findings were done before my having read Mr. MacMillan's book."

The evidence against Hagin's claim that he did his study before reading MacMillan's work would seem to suggest otherwise. First, MacMillan wrote his articles in 1932, a year before Kenneth Hagin was saved in 1933, 16 years before Hagin admits to reading MacMillan in 1948, and 35 years before Hagin published his first edition of *The Authority of the Believer* in 1967. Second, as Simmons points out in his analysis, Hagin's dependency upon MacMillan is extensive and massive. In the content of *Authority of the Believer*, Hagin's plagiarism of MacMillan is word-for-word and where it is not word-for-word, it is thought-for-thought.[34] In his letter to Cowles, Hagin offered the following explanation for the amazing similarity between his writing and that of MacMillan.

> I have found through the years that when individuals are speaking on the same subject they will say virtually the same thing. This is because it is the same Spirit that is leading and directing. He will show you things in the same ways and you'll have the same thoughts although you may never have met or read after the other person.[35]

The reader will note that this is virtually the same explanation that Hagin offered when confronted with the word-for-word similarities between his and Kenyon's works. It is a perfect example of the way that Hagin denies that his theology has any historical roots. He admits to studying MacMillan, but he claims that he did so after his own personal study. He further claims that the plagiarisms with which he was confronted by the CMA were not plagiarisms at all, but indeed, were supernatural vindication of the fact that he received his theology from the same Holy Spirit who had inspired MacMillan's writings 35 years before.

As promised to Cowles, Hagin "reedited" *The Authority of the Believer* in 1984, publishing the new edition under the title of *The Believer's Authority*. Even a superficial reading of the new edition, however, reveals that besides a change of wording here and there, the only thing different from the previous edition is the title. Hagin does include in *The Believer's Authority* a foreword in which he pays lip service to the fact that he read MacMillan's work, but as in his letter to the CMA, it is obvious that he still maintains that the book represents his teaching, given by the Holy Spirit, and not somebody else's. In response to Hagin's contention that the Holy Spirit inspired both MacMillan's and Hagin's version of *The Authority of the Believer* three-and-a-half decades apart, Simmons concludes:

> While John MacMillan may have been flattered to know that the Holy Spirit finds him so quotable . . . [Hagin's] excuse seems weak at best. One is certainly justified in asking why Hagin feels it necessary to read any books at all if the Spirit is going to inspire him to "have the same thoughts" as a particular author even though he "may have never met or read after the person." Whatever the case may be one fact is certain, when Hagin received his "inspiration" to write his version of *Authority of the Believer*, the voice that inspired him was that of John A. MacMillan.[36]

Thus, with regards to *Authority of the Believer*, we cannot accept Hagin's explanation that his unacknowledged use of the words and ideas of MacMillan can be explained by the similarity of their subjects, or that the Holy Spirit inspired him to use unknowingly the same words that MacMillan used 35 years before. Without offering any explanations about why he did so, or any moral judgments on the fact that he did so, the only reasonable conclusion that can be drawn from Hagin's unauthorized use of MacMillan is the same conclusion reached regarding Kenyon. Both are plagiarism.

A Critique of Hagin's Prophethood

At this point, it would be very easy to degenerate into a fruitless discussion as to whether Jesus really does appear to Hagin. The truth of the matter is that we shall never know the answer to this question, at least, not definitively. Hagin's visionary experiences of Jesus and journeys to heaven and hell will forever remain a matter of personal conscience between him and God. The most that we can say in defense of such experiences is that (1) the Bible and church history do record visions of Jesus given to various historical personages and (2) these experiences in and of themselves are of a personal, *subjective* nature and will never, this side of judgment day, be proven or disproven by *objective* means. It can no more be proven that Jesus did not appear to Hagin than Hagin can prove that he did. Where we are forced to confront Hagin is not in the legitimacy of these experiences but rather in: (1) the claims that are made for the doctrinal content of these experiences; (2) the impression they leave as to how Hagin does theology; (3) the fear his prophetic threats instill in his followers, and (4) the basic denial of Hagin that his theology cannot be traced historically to E. W. Kenyon.

With regards to doctrinal content, if Jesus were only passing on information for Hagin's private education and use, that would be one thing. It is quite another thing entirely to engage in a public teaching ministry on the basis of such experiences and to use them as a divine stamp of approval on one's doctrine. Obviously, any preacher worth his salt has the conviction that he is in some sense speaking in behalf of God, but to use a supposed appearance of Jesus or threats of divine wrath to coerce an audience into swallowing a teaching "hook, line and sinker" cannot go unchallenged. Thus, even if for the sake of argument we would be willing to concede as legitimate all eight of Hagin's claimed visions of Jesus, the teachings that he received in these divine visitations must bear and pass the tests of biblical examination and historical orthodoxy before they can be accepted by the church. Remember, the Apostle Paul said, "Even though we, *or an angel from heaven*, should preach to you," what is preached must bear the scrutiny of comparison to the apostolic writings, whether it comes from a heavenly being or not. If Paul was willing to submit both himself and angelic messengers to such scrutiny, then so must Hagin.[37]

The fundamental error of Hagin and the Faith movement concerning the Holy Spirit's inspiration of their teaching is a failure to appreciate that even in our highest and holiest moments, we can never claim that everything that we believe and teach is all of God and none of ourselves. The Holy Spirit is not some "hot-line to heaven" by which believers can transcend their own humanity like a snake shedding its skin. Such a concept is totally foreign to the biblical and traditional doctrine of divine inspiration. This concept of inspiration is really much closer to the demoniacal oracles of pagan religions who spoke in uncontrollable, ecstatic outbursts than it is to the Old Testament prophets.

One of the things that distinguished the Hebrew prophets from these oracles is that, for the most part, they spoke their prophecies with full control of their faculties and a heightened sensitivity of their own human frailties and gut-wrenching pathos for what God was saying to his people. Only the most dogmatic of groups in church history have held that a prophet is an "amanuensis" (a dictation or copying machine) of God. Even the inspiration of the Holy Spirit that is so evident in the writing of Scripture did not reduce the biblical writers to mere robots, to "divine dictographs" who were void of their own thoughts, feelings, and desires. Such a view fails to do justice to the humanity of the biblical writers everywhere so apparent in Scripture. When, therefore, Hagin claims to speak under an anointing so heavy that his mental and vocal faculties are in a state of suspended animation, he raises far more questions than he answers concerning the origins of his teaching and does not thereby prove it to be the unvarnished truth.

Furthermore, Hagin's pronounced judgment of God on those who will not receive his ministry instills in his followers the fear of thinking for themselves. One dare not underestimate the effect of such statements upon the laity of the Faith movement. Once Hagin's visions of Jesus are accepted as genuine and as a reliable source of doctrine, the divine judgments pronounced upon those who reject his teaching seem perfectly reasonable claims as well. After all, if God gave the prophet Hagin the revelation, does it not also make sense that God would take care of those who oppose his prophet? Hagin does not make these prophetic threats very often, but then again, given their nature, he should not have to. They remain in print and are frequently cited by his supporters to quiet any dissent.

Although few lay people in the Faith movement need such strong warnings to embrace enthusiastically Hagin's theology, the power of such scare tactics to suppress theological discernment is undeniable. The total effect of Hagin's threats is that he has exalted his theology to a place of hermeneutical mediatorship between the believer and the Word of God. Facing the threat of divine judgment for dissent, Hagin's followers read the Bible through the glasses of Hagin's theology. They see in the Bible what they are taught to see, and little else.

In summary, then, we must say the following. First, Hagin has a theology, whether he will call it that or not. His teaching is not divine; neither is it the "plain and simple Bible truth" that he says it is. Second, Hagin does theology just like the rest of us: right here on planet Earth, not in some superhuman state nor through some hot line to heaven. He is just as subject to all of the personal, social, and cultural influences and sinful biases that all of us have when we approach the Word of God. Third, Hagin's claim to have received his theology straight from Jesus must be vindicated by biblical examination and no pronouncements of divine wrath should be feared or heeded in the process of doing so. Fourth, Hagin's theology has roots, historical roots, that can be traced by any competent historian. The people he studied under, the sermons he heard, the books he read, have all left their influence and imprint on both the "prophet" and his theology. It would be no crime for Hagin to admit all of the above, for in so doing he would only be confessing that he is like the rest of us, that he is, in fact, human.

Notes

1. The best unofficial biographical information on Hagin to date is Dale H. Simmons' master's thesis, "A Theological and Historical Analysis of Kenneth E. Hagin's Claim to be a Prophet," Oral Roberts University, Tulsa, Oklahoma, May, 1985. In this thesis, Simmons offers an able critique of Hagin's theology in addition to his competent biography. All serious students of Hagin and the Faith movement cannot afford to overlook Simmons' work.

2. For the full description of Hagin's out-of-body descent into hell, see his pamphlet, *I Went to Hell* (Tulsa: Faith Library, 1982).

3. Kenneth Hagin, *I Believe in Visions* (Old Tappan, N.J.: Fleming H. Revell, 1972), p. 13.

4. Hagin, *I Believe*, p. 26.

5. Ibid., pp. 27–28.

6. Ibid., pp. 28–30. Hagin's determination to walk as an act of faith and as verification of his confession is known in the Faith movement as "corresponding actions."

7. The exact nature of Hagin's "terminal" illness is not known. Presumably, it was related to his congenital heart defect, but no formal diagnosis was ever made.

8. Kenneth Hagin, *Understanding the Anointing* (Tulsa: Faith Library, 1985), pp. 45, 49; Hagin reports, "The glory cloud still appears quite frequently in our meetings and other services. People have seen it. It comes and fills the room. Sometimes when I am preaching or teaching, it comes in and absolutely blocks everyone from view. Most of the time it just hangs above their heads." The appearance of a "glory cloud" was a common claim among the preachers of the Healing Revival. The divine suspension of Hagin's mental and vocal faculties has also occurred numerous times in his ministry, but has little precedent among the other healing revivalists.

9. Kenneth Hagin, *Why Do People Fall Under the Power?* (Tulsa: Faith Library, 1980), pp. 9–10. Concerning the woman who was levitated in his service, Hagin declares, "God is my witness, my wife is my witness, and each person in that building is my witness, she began to dance right off the end of the altar. She stood in mid-air dancing! Her feet were not touching the floor."

10. In one resurrection account, a prominent member of Hagin's church died and went to heaven. Not willing to release a man who had been a Sunday school superintendent and who gave 20% of his income, Hagin prayed earnestly for the man's life. As the man in question later described it to Hagin, upon his arrival in heaven, he was met by Jesus himself, who told him, "You're going to have to go back." When the man protested that he did not want to go back, Jesus was said to have replied apologetically, "Brother Hagin won't let you come yet." Hagin claims this as an example of the authority of his intercession (see, Kenneth Hagin, *Plead Your Case* [Tulsa: Faith Library, 1979], pp. 16–18).

11. Hagin, *Understanding*, pp. 58–59.

12. Ibid., pp. 52–53.

13. Ibid., p. 65.

14. Hagin, *I Believe*, pp. 45–51. In this vision, Hagin was commissioned by Jesus to lay hands on the sick and heal them. He was also given the ability to discern whether a disease was of demonic origins by a fire that would jump from one of his hands to the other. When this fire or anointing leaves Hagin's hands and enters a person's body, it drives out the disease. Because of the criticism that he had seen those in the healing ministry endure, Hagin begged Jesus to "send somebody else," telling him that "I just want a commonplace ministry" like a "little church to pastor somewhere" (p. 51).

15. Kenneth Hagin, *Godliness is Profitable* (Tulsa: Faith Library, 1982), pp. 15, 16: "I preached faith boldly, bless God, without a dime in my pocket. I preached faith and prosperity boldly with bills stacked up all around me."

16. Hagin, *I Believe*, pp. 93–97.

17. Kenneth Hagin, *How You Can Be Led by the Spirit of God* (Tulsa: Faith Library, 1978), pp. 29, 30.

18. Ibid., pp. 32, 33.

19. Ibid., p. 33.

20. Kenneth Hagin, *Understanding Our Confession* (Tulsa: Faith Library, [n.d.]), p. 23.

21. Hagin, *I Believe*, p. 81.

22. Kenneth Hagin, *How to Write Your Own Ticket with God* (Tulsa: Faith Library, 1979), pp. 5, 20, 21, 32.

23. Hagin, *I Believe*, p. 124.

24. Kenneth Hagin, *The Believer's Authority* (Tulsa: Faith Library, 1985), pp. 30–31.

25. Hagin, *Why Do People Fall*, pp. 11–12.

26. At first glance, the power given to Hagin to paralyze his doubting wife and others appears very similar to the charismatic practice of being "slain in the Spirit" (a.k.a. "falling under the power," "going down," and, by the more gentle, "reposing in the Spirit"). There is, however, a definite coercive and punitive element to this incident with Hagin's wife et al. that is not present in the practice as it generally occurs in charismatic meetings. Sel-

dom, if ever to this writer's knowledge, are the participants in this practice bodily paralyzed. They are neither held down against their will, nor are they immovable; nor does one man have the power to "release" them. In addition, this writer cannot recount seeing or reading that the experience of being slain in the Spirit has ever been used to coerce participants to acknowledge someone's ministry. These prerogatives apparently are exercised only in Hagin's ministry by virtue of his alleged status as a prophet.

27. Ibid.

28. Kenneth Hagin, *The Ministry of a Prophet* (Tulsa: Faith Library, 1984), p. 19.

29. Hagin, *I Believe*, pp. 114–15.

30. Ibid., p. 115; italics added for emphasis.

31. Kenneth Hagin, "God Called Me to the Ministry of a Prophet," *The Voice of Healing* (Apr., 1963), p. 9.

32. The fact that Hagin is a Pentecostal and most of the people who influenced him are Pentecostals is probably what led Bruce Barron to the erroneous conclusion that the Faith movement is an off-shoot of the Pentecostal movement (see *The Health and Wealth Gospel*, chap. 3). Hagin's Pentecostal background has no doubt strongly influenced the contemporary Faith movement, but Kenyon's cultic background still remains predominant.

33. Baxter, taped correspondence. According to Baxter, after Bosworth had "picked up on Kenyon," he took T. L. Osborn under his wings and "immediately introduced him to Kenyon."

34. Dale H. Simmons, "Mimicking MacMillan," Unpublished term paper, Oral Roberts University, Tulsa, Oklahoma, April 23, 1984.

35. Kenneth Hagin, personal correspondence to H. Robert Cowles, Executive Vice-President of Christian Publications, Feb. 28, 1984.

36. Simmons, "Mimicking MacMillan," p. 14.

37. Hagin himself often urges his readers to judge his visions and teachings against Holy Scripture, but because of his supernatural audiences with Jesus and because of what we will call the "touch-not-the-Lord's-anointed" rule, very few in the Faith movement are willing to evaluate critically Hagin's teachings.

5 The Faith Controversy and the Beginning of the Faith Denomination

---

The Faith message has been criticized almost to the point where the wind has been taken out of its sails. Faith teachings have been persecuted by carnal-minded believers. They don't understand what it is to be sons of God, led by the Spirit of God and not led by your senses or feelings.

—Robert Tilton, as quoted by Stephen Strang,
"Robert Tilton Wants You to Be a Success in Life!"
Charisma (July, 1985), 27.

Society will forgive a man anything except informing it of the truth. But often the penalties of a stricken conscience for not bearing witness to the truth outweigh the obvious dangers of retaliation from those rejecting the truth. In such a case, a man must speak out as a witness to the truth, clearly perceiving the madness of such an action, in the probable loss of comfort, security and reputation. It is only when he realizes that it is with the living God with Whom he must deal that he is compelled, however reluctantly, to the task.

Charles Farah, *This Cancer Kills*, p. 3.

Although E. W. Kenyon was undoubtedly the author of the Faith gospel, Kenneth Hagin is the man whose leadership forged the movement that has catapulted Kenyon's doctrines throughout the world. Charismatics look to Hagin not primarily as a healer or miracle worker, but rather, as a teacher and a "prophet" whose ministry can be trusted because of his personal audiences with Jesus and his alleged emphasis on the Bible.[1] However, many in the charismatic movement feel that the Kenyon/Hagin gospel is a gross distortion of the Scriptures, and have opposed it from the very beginning.

The Influence of Kenneth Hagin on the Faith Movement

Although Hagin had been in ministry for years and had participated heavily in the post-war Pentecostal healing movement of the 1950s, his ministry did not begin to blossom until after 1967.[2] As late as 1973, while the Shepherding-Discipleship teaching was still in vogue, his association employed only 19 full-time workers. By the time the Shepherding-Discipleship controversy was over, Hagin's staff had tripled to close to 60. Like some sort of overnight adolescent craze, suddenly authority and discipleship were "out" in the charismatic movement and faith and prosperity were "in." With the exception of the media giants, the prime time televangelists such as Oral Roberts, Pat Robertson, and Jim Bakker, it would be difficult to name a circuit ministry that grew faster in the late 1970s than that of Kenneth Hagin.

Hagin's ministry underwent numerous changes. In 1966, he moved the offices of his association to Tulsa, Oklahoma, and began "Faith Seminar of the Air"—a daily 15-minute radio spot that is syndicated on approximately 180 radio stations in the U.S. and Canada. Feeling the need to provide his radio listeners with practical exercises and study plans in his teaching of the Bible, Hagin formed the Rhema Correspondence Bible School, which since 1974 has taught 15,929 students and presently services 4,935 students. In 1974, Hagin founded Rhema Bible Training Center in Tulsa, which he moved in 1976 to Broken Arrow, a small town just southeast of Tulsa. The charter class of Rhema had only 58 graduates, but by the 1984–85 academic year, the school boasted an enrollment of 1,800 with a graduating class of around 800. Since its inception, Rhema has produced around 6,600 graduates. Hagin's *Word of Faith* magazine is sent to 190 thousand homes monthly and an estimated 20 thousand teaching tapes are distributed by Hagin and Ken Hagin, Jr. each month.[3] His ministry employs 229 people, owns real estate appraised at $20 million, and boasts a mailing list of 200 thousand—to whom were sent 4,217,000 pieces of mail in 1986. His 126 books and pamphlets have sold 33 million copies.[4]

The measure of Hagin's impact on the independent charismatic movement cannot, however, be gauged by either his own ministry or even by that of Rhema Bible Training Center. A veritable army of Rhema graduates have, indeed, gone on to found so-called Word of Faith churches, or to establish successful evangelistic ministries.[5] Nevertheless, these Rhema alumni are relatively insignificant by way of comparison to the ever-widening circle of Hagin imitators—and imitators of the imitators *ad infinitum*—who have turned the Faith movement into a multimillion dollar enterprise.

The most dynamic and ambitious of these is Kenneth Copeland, whose ministry is based in Ft. Worth, Texas, but can be easily described as international in scope. Copeland, claimed by many to be heir apparent to Hagin's throne,[6] is a classic example of the almost apostolic succession that transpires in the Faith movement. For example, Hagin prophetically sanctioned and anointed Copeland, who, in turn, raised up Jerry Savelle, his longtime associate and neighbor in Ft. Worth. The influence of these two men—as well as a whole host of Hagin protégés, such as Fred Price, Charles Capps, and Robert Tilton—and a myriad of other Faith ministers, has propagated Hagin's gospel in a manner analogous to spontaneous combustion.

The Faith Controversy

Just as with the Shepherding-Discipleship movement, it was not until numerous abuses and tragedies had occurred that anybody had the motivation or courage to challenge the Faith movement. In 1979, ORU professor Charles Farah, who from the wings had opposed the abuses of the Shepherding-Discipleship movement, moved to center stage in his opposition of the Faith movement. His book, *From the Pinnacle of the Temple*, though irenic in tone and didactic in intent, characterized the doctrine of the Faith movement as a "faith-formula" that presumed upon the grace and sovereignty of God and that was directly responsible for numerous tragedies and deaths.[7] Farah's book did not name any names, but it was considered highly controversial, and many charismatic bookstores refused to carry it. Characterizing it as a "negative confession," few of the Faith teachers even bothered to read the book, but nevertheless, backhandedly criticized Farah for writing it. For example, Charles Capps stated:

> I haven't read the book so I couldn't comment on it other than what I've heard. . . . Here's a good example for you of head knowledge. Here's a man that is very educated; he's very learned . . . I don't doubt that he's a Christian. He's right in his heart; he's wrong in his head. He's so educated beyond his intellect that he don't [*sic*] know how to control what he's learned. . . . He's put out all revelation knowledge. . . . This is what happens when people get highly educated. . . . But I wouldn't criticize the man. . . . He's a brother in Christ, but he's walking on dangerous territory. He really is. He's bordering on blasphemy. From what I've heard now, but I haven't read the book.[8]

Farah received numerous letters of thanks from those "for whom a faith-formula had not worked"—the book has sold over 40 thousand copies—but from the Faith teachers, he received only the highest of all literary insults: he was ignored.[9]

Farah was not the only scholar ignored by the Faith movement. In the spring of 1979, then Gordon-Conwell professor, Dr. Gordon Fee, himself a member of the Assemblies of God, published a series of articles for *Agora* magazine entitled, "Some Reflections on a Current Disease."[10] Although in part one of this series, entitled "The Cult of Prosperity," Fee cited Oral Roberts, Robert Schuller, Kenneth Hagin, and Kenneth and Gloria Copeland as propagators of the prosperity gospel, it becomes quickly apparent that the Copelands were his primary targets. Fee denounced the Copelands' claim that their teaching on prosperity was "based on the Word, not what we think it says but what it actually says." On the contrary, Fee charged that the Copelands gave everything *but* the plain meaning of the text. After taking them to task on the interpretation of numerous passages, he further stated that "the cult of prosperity thus flies full in the face of the whole New Testament. It is not biblical in any sense."[11] Waxing strong for a scholar, Fee recommended Ronald Sider's *Rich Christians in an Age of Hunger* (InterVarsity, 1977) as a "cure" to the "loathsome disease" of the prosperity cult and concluded by being "so bold and prophetic as to declare that the only alternative to such a 'cure' is the awful judgment of God, which must begin first with the house of God."[12]

The second article in Fee's series is entitled, "The Gospel of Perfect Health."[13] Admitting that he found it more difficult to write on healing than his previous article on prosperity, Fee expressed his fear that he would be interpreted as rejecting divine healing, which he decidedly was not. What he was rejecting, however, was the idea that healing was in the atonement the same way as salvation and the forgiveness of sins. Furthermore, he asserted that the doctrine of healing in the Faith movement was a serious misunderstanding of the eschatology of redemption. God has provided the first fruits of our healing and redemption, but the final and complete healing is the transformation of our fallen bodies, an event that awaits future consummation. Fee concluded his second article by denying that healing was automatically given by God in direct response to the believer's confession and appropriation of the atonement. Contrary to the emphasis in the Faith teaching on God's obligation always to heal upon the confession of faith, Fee stated dogmatically, "God *must* do *nothing!*"

The Faith controversy began to intensify in 1980, with several new anti-faith publications. One of the many tragedies illustrating the potentially disastrous effects of the conception of healing in the Faith movement is that of Wesley Parker, whose story is told in his father Larry's chilling book, *We Let Our Son Die* (Harvest House, 1980). After Wesley had been prayed for by a Faith evangelist, Larry and his wife Lucky decided to withhold insulin from their diabetic son. When Wesley grew ill and went into diabetic coma, the Parkers decided (as they had been taught) that Satan was attempting to deceive them with false symptoms. They continued to confess Wesley's healing until his death in a diabetic coma on August 23, 1973.

Believing that God would raise Wesley from the dead, instead of a funeral, the Parkers conducted "a resurrection service." When no resurrection came, Larry dismissed from the service all those who did not have faith for the miracle. Amazingly, Larry Parker held to his belief in Wesley's resurrection for more than a full year after his death. The Parkers were convicted of child abuse and involuntary manslaughter and each were given a five-year, probated sentence. (The sentence could have been 25 years in a federal penitentiary.) Because of their exemplary lives both before and after the death of their son, and because the judge considered the Parkers good people (just highly misled), the court eventually reversed both verdicts. Whereas Wesley Parker is one of the better-known victims of the doctrine of healing taught in the Faith movement, there are many others, whose stories are just as tragic, and whose deaths were just as senseless.

For sheer volume of death and tragedy, none can match the record of Hobart Freeman, pastor of Faith Assembly, Wilmot, Indiana. Estimates of the number of preventable deaths associated with Faith Assembly itself are as high as 90.[14] The number of deaths nationwide caused by Freeman's teaching on healing is not known.[15] Although he possessed an earned doctorate in Old Testament from Grace Theological Seminary (Winona Lake) and wrote a major scholarly work on the Hebrew prophets, Freeman was also "deeply influenced by healing evangelists like Kenneth Hagin, John Osteen, Kenneth Copeland and T. L. Osborn, along with the writings of E. W. Kenyon."[16] Freeman eventually broke with the other Faith teachers because of his increasingly radical views on medicine, which he rejected *in toto*. True to his own beliefs, Freeman refused medical treatment for an ulcerated leg, which, in the weeks preceding his death, forced him to preach sitting down. Complications set in and

Freeman eventually developed bronchopneumonia, for which he also shunned medical treatment. On December 8, 1984, Freeman died of congestive heart failure, a victim of his own teaching.[17]

Because of abuses and tragedies associated with the Faith movement, on August 19, 1980, the General Presbytery of the Assemblies of God issued an official statement on the Faith movement entitled "The Believer and Positive Confession."[18] This carefully worded, moderate statement attempted "to call attention to these excesses [of the Faith movement] and show how they are in conflict with the Word of God." Attempting to preserve their own longstanding belief in healing and the life of faith, the authors of the Assemblies statement cited biblical passages refuting the central tenets of the Faith message. This statement remains in effect today for all Assemblies churches and ministers.[19]

In all likelihood, had it not been for the events of 1980, Charles Farah almost certainly would have considered his pastoral burden fulfilled and his task done. Being basically a peaceful man burdened for the unity of the body of Christ, however, Farah could not ignore the tremendous controversy that was stirred at his place of employment when in successive semesters Kenneth Copeland and Fred Price brought their gospel of faith, healing, and prosperity to ORU.[20] In November of 1980, Farah used the Society for Pentecostal Studies annual conference being held that year at ORU, as a platform for delivering his paper, "A Critical Analysis: The Roots and Fruits of Faith-Formula Theology." Speaking to a packed house of scholars and students, Farah electrified his audience by calling the Faith teaching "charismatic humanism," "the new gnosticism," and "a burgeoning heresy." News of his paper spread like wildfire in the Christian press. The major evangelical publication, *Christianity Today*, reported that "Farah's paper amounted to a veritable declaration of war on the faith-formula teaching. It will undoubtedly serve as a manifesto for those who oppose the Hagin-Copeland-Price teachings."[21]

Farah's "declaration of war on the faith-formula teaching" quickly escalated into a full-scale armed conflict when in December of 1980, internationally known former Assemblies of God evangelist Jimmy Swaggart published the first of a series of articles under the title of "The Balanced Faith Life." In his first article of the series, Swaggart admitted that "I too have been guilty of preaching some of the errors" of the Faith movement. But he claimed that God had given him a new direction away from what he perceived as the "utopian" claims made for the power of positive confession.[22] In his second article, Swaggart reiterated that "the Faith Life message transformed my life and ministry when I was first exposed to it," but that

> whenever the Church (or a segment of the Church) ferrets out a particular segment of the total teaching of God—even though this teaching is truth within itself—it is in danger of committing heresy. Now people have all kinds of definitions of heresy. Most would probably say heresy is an *extreme* distortion of Christian belief. But in truth, heresy can be a matter of nothing more than a basic truth isolated, and then twisted a little. There is this type of heresy and, I'm afraid, there are areas of popular Christian teaching today *approaching* this distortional heresy.[23]

In both of these articles, Swaggart relates the difficulty of admitting to himself the error of the Faith message he had previously taught. Even though in reality he had espoused a comparatively moderate form of this message, Swaggart describes how he earnestly wrestled with God in prayer over the many abuses and tragedies he had witnessed in the Faith movement. The divine response that Swaggart received in prayer to "Go back to the cross" is a message still relevant to all in the charismatic movement.[24] A careful reading of "The Balanced Faith Life" showed Swaggart to be a man in theological transition. He had not yet broken entirely with the Faith message, but was having serious misgivings about its content and practice.

The transition did not take long to complete. In early 1982, Swaggart published a booklet entitled *Hyper-Faith: A New Gnosticism?* Though he still did not name names, the language and labels he used were much more confrontational and inflammatory. He called the Faith teaching "hyper-faith" (p. 2), "doctrinal error" (p. 4), "a work of Satan" (p. 5), "scientism" (p. 10), "a master race" (p. 19), "legalism" (p. 24), "parasitical" (p. 31), and "a new gnosticism" (pp. 11, 42). This last label, "a new gnosticism," was the central thrust of the booklet and was based on the premise that *gnosis*—esoteric, formulaic knowledge analogous to the ancient heresy of gnosticism—and not biblical knowledge was the real faith of the Faith movement.[25] Swaggart ended his booklet with a confession of error and the warning that "all error [i.e., of Faith teaching] will lead to difficulty and destruction."[26]

Since 1982, the Faith controversy has died down considerably. Gradually, charismatics have learned to accept the Faith teaching and, in many cases, have incorporated part or all of its doctrines. Just as peace seemed to be settling over the charismatic camps, in 1985, yet another searing critique of charismatic theology whipped the entire movement into a frenzied controversy. I am referring, of course, to Dave Hunt's and T. A. McMahon's book, *The Seduction of Christianity* (Harvest House, 1985). This book has engendered much controversy because there is hardly a charismatic minister or ministry left unscathed by it, including those of the Faith movement. Dave Hunt has recently repeated and expanded these charges in *Beyond Seduction* (Harvest House, 1987).

Hunt and McMahon have written a treatise towards which it is virtually impossible to remain neutral. Among charismatics, they are either venerated as prophets, or castigated as witchhunters. The basic thesis of *The Seduction of Christianity* is that the religio-psychic practices within the charismatic movement of positive mental attitude, positive confession, visualization, and inner healing are cultic and occultic in thought and origin. The authors charge that these practices are a "revival of New Thought" and "a new Science of the Mind," both of which are metaphysical cults very similar to Christian Science and Unity School of Christianity.[27] Although many have criticized the content and methodology of *The Seduction of Christianity*[28] with regards to the Faith movement, the thesis of Hunt and McMahon that many charismatic practices are cultic in thought and origin warrants careful examination.

The Faith Denomination

The Faith movement has also emerged as the second major denomination produced by the independent charismatic movement—the first being the Shepherding-Discipleship movement. Like the Shepherding leaders, the Faith teachers vehemently disavow the charge of denominationalism. Nevertheless, the evidence would seem to suggest otherwise, and is even stronger than the evidence that indicates the existence of a Shepherding denomination.

Although at the local level Faith churches are fiercely independent congregations, the formation of a national organization is even now being pursued in the Faith movement. In 1979, Hagin's son-in-law, the Reverend Doyle "Buddy" Harrison, pastor of Faith Christian Fellowship International and president of Harrison House, the major publisher of Faith books, founded the International Convention of Faith Churches and Ministers (ICFCM). The

ICFCM has floundered of late, but its beginnings were impressive, to say the least.

> The Spirit of God spoke in the summer of 1978 and instructed the ministries present to join together. On May 13, 1979 a consolidation of ministries was born in Tulsa, Oklahoma that will propel the Word of God throughout our nation and around the world. Joining together in this historic decision for unity and strength are several world renowned and established ministries in the Word of God.[29]

What "ministries" were present in this "historic decision" is uncertain, but presumably those of the founding officers and trustees, which reads like a *Who's Who?* of the Faith movement: Kenneth Hagin, Sr., Kenneth Hagin, Jr., Kenneth Copeland, Fred Price, John Osteen, Norvel Hayes, Jerry Savelle, Charles Cowan, etc. The mere fact that all of these men were in the same room at one time is significant in and of itself. But when they started using terms like "join together" and "consolidation of ministries," it does not require particularly profound insight to infer that what they were talking about on that day was forming a denomination, whether they called it that or not.

The ICFCM flatly denies this, however, and claims that it is nothing more than "a service bureau" intended to facilitate communication and coordination of common activities of Faith churches and ministers.[30] Nevertheless, the stated purposes and organization of the ICFCM indicate otherwise. Even to be accepted into the ICFCM, a church or minister must be sponsored by a current member of the organization. Presently, there are only about 100 churches with membership in the ICFCM, but there are over 700 ministers, who represent a variety of parachurch ministries, some of which are fairly significant. The constitution and bylaws of the ICFCM depict an organization as structured as any denomination, mandating annual meetings of a board of trustees, an executive board, and various standing committees.

One of the primary purposes of the ICFCM is to organize Faith conferences throughout the U.S. on the international, regional, and district levels. These conferences are primarily for the continuing education of Faith ministers, but the meetings are also open to laypersons. The ministerial meetings of the ICFCM, along with the hundreds of "Believer's Conventions" held yearly are not for *any* ministers or believers, but for *Faith* ministers and believers. Anybody can come, of course, but they should be aware that in so doing they will encounter a doctrinal and ecclesiastical viewpoint as rigid and well-defined as the Baptists, the Methodists, the Presbyterians, or yes, even the Shepherding-Discipleship movement.

Most of the other earmarks of a denomination are present in the Faith movement. The ICFCM intends to provide: (1) a central, national organization responsible for communication and coordination; (2) regional and national conventions; (3) a continuing education system for its ministers; (4) a missionary training board; and (5) an organizational apparatus for placing chaplains in the military. In addition to these staples of the denominational diet, the Faith movement boasts a number of primary and secondary church schools, post-secondary educational institutions (Rhema and like schools), a publishing branch (Harrison House, Tulsa, Okla.) and more parachurch evangelistic associations than you can shake a stick at. In addition, even though the ICFCM does not legally ordain individuals to the ministry, Rhema Bible Training Center does, giving the Faith movement its first noncongregational ordination body.[31] There are countless mainline denominations that do not possess as many institutional bureaucracies and functions as are already in place in the Faith movement.

Although leaders of the Faith movement are vehemently opposed to the concept of denominations, a few admit that organizations like ICFCM might lead to the perception of a denomination among outsiders. One prominent member of the original board of trustees, who asked to remain anonymous and has since resigned from the board, said this concerning the organization: "I never thought it [ICFCM] was the best thing because it shut everybody out. . . . I came out of a structured denomination so I shy away from such things." The ecumenical concern of this man is admirable, but unfortunately, extremely rare in the Faith movement. As will be seen, the concept of faith and "revelation knowledge" results in either "shutting everybody out," or regarding those outside the movement as objects of evangelistic zeal and spiritual patronage.

To date, the ICFCM has been something less than a success in organizing and mobilizing the Faith movement under its own auspices. Because of the very nature of Faith teaching and because Faith preachers demonstrate more than their share of personal ambition, the ICFCM will have a difficult time drawing the thousands of Faith churches and ministries into its orbit. If, however, Hagin, Copeland, and the other stalwarts of the movement were to give it their unqualified support, the ICFCM could come to constitute a congregational confederation of local churches and ministries organized and coordinated by a central, national organization; in other words, it would become, despite all disclaimers and abhorrence of the term, a denomination.

Efforts to Reconcile the Faith Controversy

The first efforts towards restoring unity with the Faith movement began in 1983 and 1984. Ironically, the initial overtures were made by the leaders of the Shepherding-Discipleship movement, who in the 1970s had themselves been the center of considerable controversy. In January of 1984, *New Wine* magazine featured and endorsed Kenneth Copeland, a leader of the Faith movement hitherto a *persona non grata* in Shepherding circles.[32] The Shepherding leaders defended Copeland, claiming that his doctrine, like theirs, was misunderstood and misapplied by followers. Bob Mumford commented,

> One thing all of us have learned through the opposition we have experienced is that when a biblical truth is revealed to us, we cannot cease to preach it because some people misapply it. We feel an identification with Kenneth and those other brothers because of what we have experienced. What they have gone through in teaching the faith message is so analogous to what we have experienced that it's brought a certain sense of camaraderie.[33]

The Shepherding leaders' identification with Copeland was a controversial step of immense proportions, as the subsequent reaction of readers demonstrated.[34]

More formal efforts to reconcile the Faith movement were made in July of 1985 at the first national conference of the "Network of Christian Ministries" (NCM). The Network began two years earlier in July of 1983 through the efforts of Charles Green, Emanuele Cannistraci, and John Gimenez, all three of whom pastor churches not previously associated with either the Shepherding or the Faith movement.[35] The Network was founded

> to be a voice to this generation of the many streams of God's movings and to exchange ideas, helps, and information of vital need to the church today. Although it is not a denomination, NCM gives strength, spiritual direction, and fellowship so badly needed by independent ministries. It provides an identity with a fellowship larger than the local church or ministry.[36]

The more specific purpose of the Network is to provide a code of ethics for its members, producing a unity of ministry which will lead to the evangelization of the world; the reformation of society under the Lordship of Jesus Christ; the restoration of the Church in power, unity, and glory; the full release of ministry resident in the Body—the Church; the maturing of each believer into the stature of Christ; and the practical demonstration of the Love of Christ throughout the Church in all its relationships in all the world.[37]

The first national Network conference in Denver attracted pastors and leaders from many different "streams of ministry," and included Faith leader Kenneth Copeland, and Shepherding leaders Charles Simpson and Bob Mumford. The presence of Mumford and Simpson at the conference suggests that the reconciliation with other charismatics sought by these Shepherding leaders has been achieved, and a full amnesty is being conferred upon them by the Network. In the afterglow of the first Network conference, Kenneth Copeland appeared again in *New Wine*, along with Charles Simpson, John Wimber, and John Gimenez, in a forum on unity in the charismatic movement.[38] In this forum, Copeland and Simpson engaged in mutual absolution of past abuses. They hailed Shepherding and Faith doctrine as valid and important parts of the multifaceted revelation given to the independent charismatic movement.

Copeland even called for a merger of the respective revelations given to the Faith and the Shepherding movements. Responding to the question, "Do the truths from the various streams work together?" Copeland responded: "Sure they do. While I was learning the principles of prosperity, Charles Simpson, Bob Mumford, Don Basham, and Ern Baxter got a hold of the importance of God's covenants." Copeland exhorted the two movements to stop criticizing one another and accept each other's revelation in order that the church might get deeper revelation.

> There is a place of revival and revelation in God that none of us can get to until we get together. We have a revelation of different truths that God has restored to the Body of Christ, but there is a deeper revelation to come because no one has ever seen Him in the fulness of His stature. We've come as far in what we're called to do as we're going to get until we come together and receive additional revelation from one another. I'm going to have to have your faith to help me get what else God has for me. You're going to have to have my faith to help you get what else God has for you.[39]

In response to Copeland's overtures, Simpson stated that

> I've always believed that those men [the Faith teachers] had something the church needed to hear, and I am moved by the openness I see among many of them. Ken [Copeland], for example, has taken some

daring and courageous steps to identify with us and other leaders. He has won my admiration for that.[40]

Regarding the unity of charismatics, Simpson stated that "the original problem is with the leaders" and that if the leaders would express their need of each others' revelations, then "that same attitude will follow in the people."[41] Simpson further proposed that leaders could unite the people by refraining from public criticism of each other's doctrine.

Although Simpson and Copeland were not acting as spokesmen for the Network, their statements were in perfect accord with its code of ethics. This code is the cornerstone of the Network and is binding upon all members. It strictly prohibits public criticism of another member's ministry and doctrine. Specifically, the code dictates that members: (1) "respect each person's differences in doctrine," (2) "maintain a teachable spirit towards the other leaders in the Network," (3) "speak only in an edifying manner regarding other ministers and ministries of the Body of Christ," and (4) "follow processes and procedures as commanded in Scripture when faced with a brother or sister in violation of these ethics."[42] The main scriptural procedure in the Network for correcting doctrinal and ethical violations requires that the offending party be confronted in private by his accusers. This policy is based largely on Matthew 18:15–18.

The ethical demand of the Network upon its members to cease public criticism of the ethics, morals, and doctrine of other ministers is nothing new in the independent charismatic movement. Historically, this tendency to suppress public debate about doctrine may be traced to a series of five charismatic leadership meetings on unity which began in Seattle in 1971 and ended in Oklahoma City in 1976. The purpose of these conferences was to reconcile the Shepherding controversy. At the Oklahoma City meeting, those present signed an agreement to "not voice publicly any criticism nor complaint against a fellow minister" in the areas of "ethics, morals and doctrine" unless they first approached the minister involved first privately, then with two other ministers, and finally, before a larger group of ministers.[43] This policy was also based on their interpretation of Matthew 18:15–18 and embodied a longstanding ethos of the charismatic renewal.[44]

A Critique of the New Charismatic Ecumenism

The goals of the Network are, on the surface, quite noble and embody the charity and ecumenism for which the charismatic renewal once stood.[45] Who could argue with an organization that brings Christians from different persuasions together to dialogue, love, and pray with one another? On another level, however, the Network embodies a spirit that has seduced more than one ecumenical movement, a spirit that in the name of love sacrifices biblical truth on the altar of church unity. Biblical unity involves both love and truth, and any attempt to achieve unity without sound doctrine is destined for heresy. In this respect, the Network differs little from the World Council of Churches, an organization whose concept of ecumenism some charismatics have long criticized, but are now unknowingly in the process of emulating.

The Network's interpretation of Matthew 18:15–18 may have legitimacy in the areas of ethics and morals of ministers, but the passage has nothing to do with doctrine, particularly false doctrine. The correction of false doctrine in the New Testament is always a public matter, and never a private one. For example, Paul "opposed" and publicly dressed down Peter "to his face" when the latter's hypocrisy threatened to undo the liberty of the gospel (Gal. 2:11–14). Paul did not take Peter aside and correct his doctrine privately. Concerning the fact Paul did not follow the prescriptions of Matthew 18:15–18, F. F. Bruce states that "since the offence was public, the rebuke had also to be public."[46] Paul was not at all shy about public correction of individuals (1 Tim. 1:20; 2 Tim. 4:14), nor was the Apostle John, who publicly named Diotrephes as a propagator of false doctrine and division in the church (3 Jn. 9, 10). False or heretical doctrine must always remain a matter of public evaluation in the church. To suppress this process is equivalent to what Dr. Howard Ervin called a "gag rule." This gag rule has been in effect since the Oklahoma City leadership conference in 1976 and apparently will remain the standard in the Network of Christian Ministries for what passes in the charismatic movement as "unity in the Body."

Biblical unity is not, as the Network seems to be saying, based just on love and acceptance; biblical unity is based on both love and truth (Eph. 4:13–15). A commitment to unity is not synonymous with the indiscriminate acceptance of "every wind of doctrine" blowing through the charismatic movement. Furthermore, the process towards unity is not helped by the suppression of doctrinal criticism through "craftiness in deceitful scheming" (or, for that matter, by any other method, even mutual agreement). On the contrary, "speaking the truth in love" is the Pauline formula for the unification and maturation of the body of Christ. Though it is an essential ingredient, love is not the only measure of Christian unity. A unity based solely on love is neither unity nor love. It is an affront to the concept of Christian unity to ignore or rationalize distortions of the truth that have destroyed numerous lives and deceived innumerable more and to call such profane sentimentality "love." A unity that cannot bear the truth has nothing to do with love.

Consequently, despite the noble intentions and sincere appeals of those who began the Network, to honor their unspoken "gag rule" on the public criticism of heretical and dangerous doctrine would be to compromise the Apostle Paul's identification of the church as the "guardian and pillar of the truth" (1 Tim. 3:15). It also spurns the Apostle Jude's commandment for the church to "contend earnestly for the faith which was once for all delivered to the saints" (Jude 2), and the Apostle John's admonition to "not believe every spirit, but test the spirits to see whether they are from God; because many false prophets have gone out into the world" (1 Jn. 4:1). The desire of the Network for unity in the charismatic movement cannot be honored at the expense of biblical doctrine. The church cannot abdicate its duty to examine the doctrine of those who claim to be in its ranks.

In the case of the Shepherding and the Faith movements, it is especially critical that the church do so for two reasons, one of which is doctrinal and the other pastoral. On the doctrinal level, the mutual absolution conferred by these two movements has not begun to answer the serious charges leveled against both by responsible leaders in the church. Neither the Shepherding nor the Faith movement has ever recanted the doctrines that incurred these charges in the first place. Until these charges are answered and these controversial doctrines recanted, there can be no real unity in the Network or the charismatic movement.

On the pastoral level, there is another reason why the Shepherding and Faith movements cannot be granted amnesty for their pasts. What the Network fails to mention are the thousands of believers whose faiths were destroyed by these two movements. Where are these believers now? Who cares for their souls? Who represents their interests in the Network? And most difficult of all to answer is who in the Network is going to ensure that even more believers in the future won't be hurt by the doctrine of the Shepherding and Faith movements? The pasts of these movements can be forgiven only if it is demonstrated their doctrine will not do similar damage in the future. The burden of proof lies with them to demonstrate that they have corrected their errors. Until they do so, to associate with them in the Network or in any other organized way is to condone their abuses. It is pastorally irresponsible.

The response of the main leaders of these movements is that they are not responsible for the misapplication of their teachings by their "imitators." The problem lies with their followers, not the teaching itself. For example, Kenneth Copeland recently stated that many of

> the problems have been caused not by the various leaders but by our imitators. A person takes something I've said and builds something that blows sky-high, and I get the glorious credit. The same thing has happened with other leaders.[47]

Likewise, Bob Mumford also blames the abuses associated with his teaching on his imitators. Although he has formally dissociated himself from Charles Simpson—who is now the sole head of the Shepherding denomination—Mumford still maintains that Shepherding doctrine is biblically sound: "Today I believe in the [Shepherding] principles as strongly as ever and am presently walking in the fruit of those principles."[48] He apologizes for his followers' misapplication of his teaching, but not for the teaching itself.

Such responses are grossly inadequate and misleading. If the Network is to have any credibility at all it cannot look the other way while some of its members commit doctrinal rape. Many whose lives have been devastated by the Faith movement, for example, were not "misapplying" the teaching at all. Their problem is that they applied the teaching all too well, and paid dearly for it. Unless the doctrines that inflicted these wounds are recanted, the tragedies will continue. When they do, how will the Network respond? Will its own code of ethics forbid corrective action? Or will the Network, like the Shepherding and Faith leaders themselves, blame the abuses on their followers? It is unconscionable that the Network would remain silent in such circumstances, but the truth is that it that it will be hard-pressed to do otherwise. The Network has no disciplinary response mechanism. And its code of ethics dictates acceptance of its members' doctrine, apparently even their bad doctrine. If the Network does speak out against doctrinal abuse, it will be in spite of its code of ethics, not because of it.

Some people are of the opinion that the Faith teachers have moderated their more extremist beliefs and practices and that the potential for future tragedies is minimal. I am not one of these people. The Faith teachers have toned down their rhetoric and made some superficial adjustments. But their basic theological system remains intact—the same system that produced the Faith controversy. There have been no retractions of major doctrines and no revisions of printed materials. The moderation of the Faith teachers is, therefore, more apparent than real. There can be no moderation without recantation and that simply has not occurred. Bruce Barron has recently implied that the Faith teachers are "moving toward the mainstream" of the independent charismatic movement.[49] If that is true, they are doing so on their own terms, for their theology is the same. Like the Shepherding controversy, the Faith controversy has never been resolved at the doctrinal level. Organizations such as the Network have healed some of the relationships damaged by the Faith controversy, but they have not reconciled the heart of the controversy: doctrine.

In my opinion, the Faith teachers are not moving toward the mainstream of the charismatic movement. Quite the opposite, the mainstream of the charismatic movement is moving toward the Faith teachers. As Pentecostal historian Vinson Synan has recently pointed out, Faith teachers are enjoying increasing acceptance and prestige outside of their own ranks—as witnessed by the selection of Kenneth Copeland as one of the main speakers at the 1987 North American Congress on the Holy Spirit and World Evangelization. The supposed moderation of the Faith teachers will only increase their acceptance in charismatic circles. If the "prophecies" of Copeland and Hagin are correct,[50] there will result from the efforts of organizations such as the Network a merging of Faith and Shepherding doctrine. If such a synthesis occurs, the errant and dangerous elements of both teachings will become (if they are not already) permanent fixtures in the independent charismatic movement.

Summary of the Historical Analysis of the Faith Movement

We began this book with the charge that the Faith movement believes and practices a "different gospel." So far, we have presented the historical evidence for this charge, which may be summarized as follows. (1) Kenneth Hagin did not author the teachings which bear his name and, thus, is not, as is claimed by both himself and his followers, the founding father of the Faith movement. (2) This title belongs to E. W. Kenyon, who authored most of the teachings on which the movement is based. (3) Kenyon freely admitted to close associates that he drew upon cultic, metaphysical sources in the formulation of his teaching. (4) During his time in Boston, and especially at Emerson College, Kenyon exposed himself both to Unitarianism and New Thought metaphysics. (5) Kenyon believed that the church of his day was based on "Sense Knowledge" rather than "Revelation Knowledge," and, as a result, it was impotent and ignorant in the areas of divine healing and supernatural manifestations. (6) Because of the rapid growth of the metaphysical cults, which both preached and practiced divine healing and supernatural manifestations, Kenyon attempted to formulate "a new type of Christianity," one that would include these practices, thereby enabling the church to compete with the New Thought cults. (7) As a result, Kenyon's Faith movement is a syncretism of New Thought metaphysics and radical fundamentalism; it is, in fact, a "different gospel." (8) Because of its cultic origins, the different gospel of the Faith movement has been responsible for much controversy, as its opponents have denounced its dangerous stance on healing and its materialistic obsession with prosperity.

Regarding its present status and relationship to the charismatic movement at large, our historical analysis reached the following conclusions. (9) The Faith movement is the second denomination produced by the independent charismatic movement, the first of which is the Shepherding-Discipleship movement. (10) Though repeatedly criticized for having destroyed the lives of people with their doctrines, both of these groups have claimed that their teachings are misunderstood and misapplied, and neither has ever publicly recanted and corrected these controversial teachings. (11) Although it is unlikely that they will ever merge in any organizational sense, the Faith and the Shepherding movements are currently involved in efforts to unite the independent charismatic movement. Unfortunately, these efforts are characterized by blind sentimentality and the repression of truth. Such "unity" refuses to confront doctrinal error, and naively disregards both the abuses of the past and the danger of continued abuse in the future.

Notes

1. According to David Edwin Harrell, Jr., Hagin has always emphasized that, unlike his competitors in the Healing Revival, his ministry was based on the Scriptures. For instance, at a healing conference in the 1950s, Hagin announced to a group of his colleagues: "When all these other things are gone, I'll be out there. Because the Word never fails. I built on the Word and they built on some kind of gift" (*All Things Are Possible: The Healing and*

Charismatic Revivals in Modern America [Bloomington, Ind.: Indiana University Press, 1975], p. 186).

2. Ibid. Although it would be difficult to prove, it is probably no coincidence that Hagin's ministry did not begin to take off until the Shepherding-Discipleship controversy of the mid-'70s. Hagin was only mildly involved in the controversy, but he was decidedly one of its biggest beneficiaries. After the rigid authoritarianism and austere discipline of the Shepherding movement, the laissez-faire prosperity orientation of the Faith movement was a welcome change to many charismatics. Hagin was definitely a man in the right place at the right time with the "right" teaching.

3. Andrews, p. 26; see also, Hagin, Jr. "Trend toward the Faith Movement," pp. 67–70.

4. Tom Carter, "Religion Without Hype: Kenneth Hagin's Ministry Doesn't Need the Spotlight," *Tulsa World: OK Magazine* (July 19, 1987), p. 5.

5. For example, 1979 Rhema grads Ray and Lynda McCauley returned to their native Johannesburg, South Africa to found "Rhema Ministries South Africa," which has a church of five thousand, a Training Center producing 300 graduates per year, and a distribution division which sells in excess of 10 thousand teaching tapes per month. The propagation of Hagin's doctrine in this manner is the purpose of Rhema. One Rhema student interviewed for this book stated that Rhema students are repeatedly told by their instructors that they are on the cutting edge of the charismatic renewal and are commissioned of God to spread "the Word of Faith" [i.e., Hagin's doctrine] throughout the world. The stated purpose of Rhema is "to prepare men and women for the full-time ministry" and "to produce graduates who will carry forth the great charismatic renewal that God has sent into our time" (*Rhema Bible Training Center Catalogue*, p. 3).

6. Many have already coronated Copeland as the new king of the Faith movement. In a recent article, even *Time* magazine refers to Copeland as the "chief exponent" of the Faith movement, and does not even mention the name of Kenneth Hagin, or his son, Kenneth Hagin, Jr. (see, Richard N. Ostling, "Religion: Power, Glory and Politics," *Time* 127 (Feb. 17, 1986, No. 7), 69.

7. For example, the dedication of Farah's book reads: "To encourage those for whom 'a faith-formula' has not worked and to liberate those who have come under unjust condemnation or, worse yet, lost their faith completely." Originally published by Logos, *From the Pinnacle of the Temple* is still available from Bridge Publications, South Plainfield, N.J.

8. Charles Capps, taped correspondence, Feb. 17, 1982.

9. Despite repeated attempts, Farah was unsuccessful in engaging Hagin or others in the Faith movement in any meaningful dialogue after his book was published.

10. Gordon Fee, "Some Reflections on a Current Disease," *Agora* 2 (Spring, 1979), pp. 12–16.

11. Ibid., p. 15.

12. Ibid., p. 16; for further critiques of the doctrine of prosperity, see Joe Magliato, *The Wall Street Gospel* (Harvest House, 1981); also, John White, *The Golden Cow: Materialism in the Twentieth-Century Church* (Downers Grove, Ill.: InterVarsity, 1979).

13. Fee, *Agora*, 3 (Summer/Fall, 1979), pp. 12–18.

14. Jim Quinn and Bill Zlatos, "Assembly's Message Ominous," *Fort Wayne* [Ind.] *News-Sentinel*, June 2, 1984, p. 1.

15. Besides Faith Assembly, Freeman ministered throughout the South in a network of sister churches based on his teaching. Although not to the same extent, these churches also experienced deaths due to non-treatment of sickness. The author is personally familiar with a tragic death as far south as Alabama in a church which practiced Freeman's teaching.

16. John Davis, "Freeman: Mystic, Monk, or Minister?" *Warsaw* [Ind.] *Times-Union*, Sept. 27, 1983, p. 1a.

17. Steven Lawson, "Faith Preacher Hobart Freeman Dies," *Charisma* (Feb., 1985), p. 110. A controversial point about Freeman's death is that the coroner was not summoned until 13 hours later, reportedly because of an all-night prayer vigil for his resurrection. Freeman was buried "in a pine box" with no public viewing and no graveside or memorial service (Kathy Muckle, "Faith Assembly Mourns Death of Leader," *Warsaw Times-Union*, Dec. 10, 1984, p. 1). The best information on Hobart Freeman is John Davis's four-part series in the *Warsaw Times-Union*, Sept. 27–30, 1984; Barron's chapter on Freeman in *The Health and Wealth Gospel* is also excellent.

18. See, "The Believer and Positive Confession," *Pentecostal Evangel* (Nov. 16, 1980), pp. 8–11, 18–20.

19. Phone interview with Joseph Flower, general secretary to the Assemblies of God, Springfield, Mo., Mar. 17, 1986.

20. The controversy at ORU reached a climax in a chapel service in which Fred Price was speaking on Sept. 19, 1980. Price was in the homiletical habit of interspersing within his sermon rhetorical questions to the audience, such as "Am I right?" or "Do you believe it?" Many of the ORU students wholeheartedly agreed with Price, but tension was growing within the seminary faculty during Price's week of messages in regard to his radical stance on healing. When in his chapel sermon, Price asked loudly, "It's not God who heals you, it's your faith! . . . Do you believe it?", one frustrated seminary professor couldn't remain silent any longer and shouted out equally loudly, "No!!!" Jumping up from his seat on the platform, President Oral Roberts immediately demanded and received an apology from the professor in question, but it was obvious from the subsequent reaction of the seminary faculty and many of the students, that the professor's "negative confession" had answered for many more than himself on that day.

21. Vinson Synan, "Faith-Formula Fuels Charismatic Controversy," *Christianity Today* 24 (Dec. 12, 1980), pp. 65–66. See also, Sherry Andrews, "The Controversy over Faith," *Charisma* 7 (Jan., 1982), pp. 44–49. Andrews wrote, "The controversy has become so intense that a group of theology professors at Oral Roberts University recently published a paper attacking the teachings of another charismatic school just eight miles away—Rhema Bible Training Institute headed by Kenneth Hagin. The group of professors were instrumental in having a faith teacher banned from the ORU campus. Although the faith controversy has not yet reached the proportions of the [Shepherding] discipleship controversy which nearly split the charismatic movement in two during the early '70's, it is causing consternation and

confusion among many. Many pastors and laypersons are taking a hard second look at the [Faith] movement" (p. 44).

22. Jimmy Swaggart, "The Balanced Faith Life," *The Evangelist* 12 (Dec., 1980), pp. 3–4.

23. "The Balanced Faith Life, Part II," *The Evangelist*, 13 (Jan., 1981), p. 11.

24. "Balanced Faith Life," pp. 4, 10.

25. Swaggart's claim that Faith teaching was "a new gnosticism" was based on an unpublished paper by Judith Matta, "The New Gnosticism: A Guide to the Faith Cult," La Miranda, Calif., 1981. A revised edition of Matta's work has since been published under the title of *The Born-Again Jesus of the Word-Faith Teaching* (Fullerton, Calif.: Spirit of Truth Ministries, 1984).

26. Jimmy Swaggart, *Hyper-Faith: A New Gnosticism?* (Baton Rouge, La.: Jimmy Swaggart Ministries, 1982), pp. 43–44.

27. Hunt and McMahon state, "Today's church is being swept by a revival of New Thought, now called Positive Thinking, Possibility Thinking, Positive Confession, Positive Mental Attitude, and Inner Healing. We are very concerned that this time New Thought, which represents inside the church what New Age is in the secular world, will not be forced out, but will remain within the evangelical church to contribute to the growing confusion and seduction" (*Seduction of Christianity*, p. 151).

28. See Demar and Leithe, *The Reduction of Christianity* (Dominion Press, 1988). Nevertheless, I do believe that *The Seduction of Christianity* has much of value to say to the charismatic movement and I strongly disagree with those who are advising charismatics not to read and evaluate it for themselves. The movement that does not listen to its critics is ripe for heresy.

29. Statement of History, Membership Solicitation Pamphlet, ICFCM, Tulsa, Okla.

30. John Jacobs, Executive Director of ICFCM, phone interview, July 1, 1982.

31. Kenneth Hagin Ministries, Inc. founded Rhema Ministerial Association International (RMAI) on Jan. 1, 1985 "for the purpose of becoming an assisting, equipping and governing organization to evangelize the world with the gospel of Jesus Christ through every possible medium." Although only Rhema Bible Training Center graduates may be licensed and ordained, the RMAI marks a significant step in the evolution of the Faith denomination. Ordination with RMAI demands (through signed affidavit) submission to "the Constitution, Ethics and Tenents [*sic*] of Faith proclaimed, practiced and set forth" by RMAI. One of the stated purposes of RMAI is "to supply a vehicle in which informative and encouraging counsel, and correction, and if necessary discipline, could be given to a member for the purpose of correcting error in doctrine, procedure, or ministerial ethics and conduct which could cause confusion and division in the Body of Christ" (*Statement of Purpose*). Furthermore, "any members of RMAI refusing to adhere to sound counsel, correction, or discipline will be removed from the membership of RMAI and their ministerial credentials will be revoked" (Article VI, *The Constitution of Rhema Ministerial Association International*). What this means for the future is uncertain, but the very least that can be said for now is that RMAI constitutes a national governing body, with full disciplinary powers of Rhema

ministers, not unlike the "trans-local authority" of the Shepherding denomination.

32. "A Voice of Victory: An Interview with Kenneth Copeland," *New Wine* 16 (Jan., 1984), pp. 6–11.

33. "Forum: Perspective on Unity," ibid., p. 10.

34. Reader reaction the month after Copeland appeared in *New Wine* was mixed. Many expressed appreciation to *New Wine* for helping them understand Copeland and his teachings. The emphasis on unity led one reader to claim that "the days of smiling at one another face-to-face and then backbiting one another are over." Others who wrote were less than impressed with both Copeland and the emphasis upon unity. "Kenneth Copeland," wrote one reader, "teaches blatant error" and informed *New Wine* that "If you are going to join together with the 'hyper-faith/prosperity' doctrine, I can no longer support your ministry in prayer or otherwise." See, "Letters to the Editor," *New Wine* 16 (Mar., 1984), p. 4.

35. In addition to these three men, the other members of the founding executive committee of the Network were: Mel Davis, K. R. Iverson, John Meares, Paul Paino, Thomas Reid, David Schoch, and Bob Weiner, (minutes, meeting of executive committee, Network, Nov. 26–27, 1984).

36. Emanuele Cannistraci, "What the Network Is," *The Network* (Jan.–Mar., 1986), p. 3.

37. "Network Statement of Purpose," *The Network* (Apr.–Aug., 1986), p. 4.

38. "The Year of Equipping the Saints," *New Wine* 18 (Jan., 1986), pp. 6–18.

39. Ibid., p. 16.

40. Ibid.

41. Ibid., pp. 14, 15.

42. "Code of Ethics," *The Network* (Feb.–Mar., 1987), p. 7.

43. *Report on the 1976 Charismatic Leaders' Conference*, p. 5.

44. Over the years, few have written more critically against the public criticism of doctrine than Jamie Buckingham, pastor, author, and editor-at-large for *Charisma* and *Ministries* magazines. As early as 1972, Buckingham wrote, "As members of this [church] 'family' we are commanded by our Father not to backbite, criticize, accuse or condemn. If we have a difference with a brother (doctrinal or personal) we are to go directly to him—or keep our mouth shut. There is no excuse for public condemnation of another in the Body" ("The First and Last Word," reprinted in *Logos Journal* 11 [Sept.–Oct., 1981], p. 40). In 1981, Buckingham stated that "pure doctrine is important. But who among us is qualified to define it?" His conclusion was that "since we can't decide, let's quit backbiting each other's ministries" ("Who Defines 'Correct Doctrine?' " *Charisma* [Mar., 1981], p. 11). In an interesting apologetic for doctrinal extremism among charismatics written in 1979, Buckingham admitted that "if the charismatic movement hasn't done anything else, it has at least re-instituted the office of the extremist in the kingdom." Claiming that "every genuine Christian movement in history has begun with extremism," Buckingham exhorted his readers to "thank God for extremists. Every movement needs just one" ("Thank God for Extremists!" reprinted in *Charisma* [Aug., 1985], p. 178). More recently, however, in

response to the question of how a pastor should respond to a guest speaker's doctrinal error, Buckingham stated, "By all means you correct it publicly. That's what pastors are for. . . . Then contact your guest speaker and let him know what you have done" ("Straight Answers to Specific Questions," *Solving the Ministry's Toughest Problems* [Altamonte Springs, Fla.: Strang Communications Co., 1984], 1:429–30).

45. For a summary of the history and goals of the Network of Christian Ministries, see "A Network for Unity," *New Wine* 17 (Dec., 1985), pp. 20–23.

46. F. F. Bruce, *Commentary on Galatians* (NIGTC; Grand Rapids: Eerdmans, 1982), p. 132.

47. Copeland, "The Year of Equipping the Saints," pp. 6, 15.

48. Mumford, "After Discipleship," p. 24.

49. Bruce Barron, "Faith Healers: Moving Toward the Mainstream?" *Christianity Today* 31 (July 10, 1987), pp. 50–52.

50. Although Hagin has been nowhere near as active in the unity movement as Copeland, he has prophetically predicted that such a movement would come in 1987. Speaking for God in 1984, Hagin had prophesied, "You wait till '87 comes. For that's the year that I'll join together streams of ministries that will flow mightily and great, and will cause the very earth to shake, will move heaven and stir hell, and bring you to the blessings that God intended on the earth to bestow, and many who stand here today will remember, saith the Lord, that I told you so. Amen" (tape entitled, "Prophecies for 1984–1987," spoken at Healing School, Rhema Bible Training Center, Tulsa, Okla., Dec. 12, 1984).

Part 2

A Biblical Analysis of the Modern Faith Movement

6 The Doctrine of Revelation Knowledge: Super Christians and the New Gnosticism

Now we are moving up into the big things. . . . I said softly as I walked into prayer meeting, We are coming into the spiritual redwoods. We are going to see spiritual giants, supermen. They have God dwelling in them. . . . They no longer walk as natural men. They belong to the love class, the miracle class. They are in the Jesus class. They have graduated from the lower class.

—E. W. Kenyon,
Identification, pp. 60, 61.

There is another similarity between the faith-formula teaching and Gnosticism. . . . Although its appeal is largely related to material benefits, there is a kind of dualism in which the material world is downgraded and set against the non-material world . . . it views the material world as misleading, inferior, and generally opposed to and disjunctive with the spiritual world.

—John Fickett,
Confess It, Possess It: Faith's Formula's? p. 12.

This chapter will examine how the cultic origins of the Faith movement have influenced its doctrine. If the biblical axiom is true that roots determine fruit, then we could expect that the fruits of the Faith movement (its doctrines, practices, and results) will show evidence of cultic influence as well. Since the Faith movement comes from the historical lineage of the metaphysical cults, they share many of the same doctrines and practices. Admittedly, much of the Faith theology is either evangelical or Pentecostal, but at key points its cultic origins are readily apparent.

The Cultic Nature of the Doctrine of Revelation Knowledge

Of all the major doctrines of Kenyon, the one that most dominates and permeates his writings is "Revelation Knowledge." Kenyon was the first to coin that term. He constantly distinguishes Revelation Knowledge from its opposite, "Sense Knowledge." Kenyon's book, *The Two Kinds of Knowledge*, is dedicated to this distinction, which came to be the guiding principle of his theology.

Sense Knowledge is the knowledge that comes through the five physical senses and is the source of all scientific and rational knowledge. As Kenyon put it, the physical senses are "the parents of all this knowledge."[1] Sense Knowledge is also responsible for modern technology and the tremendous advancement in the standard of living brought about by it.

But there are severe limitations to Sense Knowledge. Despite the material benefits derived from Sense Knowledge, it fails to answer the deepest and oldest questions of human existence. Because science is based on Sense Knowledge, it, too, is severely limited with regard to the ultimate issues of life.[2] The most serious limitation of Sense Knowledge is its inability to satisfy the "God hunger" that is in everyone.[3] Those who possess only Sense Knowledge are entirely unable to know God: "Sense Knowledge cannot find God and would not know God if it found Him."[4] Kenyon believed that to know God, one must transcend sensory and scientific knowledge in order to act upon the knowledge of the Bible.

Another type of knowledge is needed to answer the ultimate questions and that is "Revelation Knowledge." Only Revelation Knowledge can satisfy man's God hunger.[5] Revelation Knowledge is transcendent, supra-sensory knowledge "in the realm above Sense Knowledge."[6] It reveals the "reality" (a favorite Kenyon word) of the spiritual realm, as well as the illusory character of the physical realm. Although Kenyon nowhere offers a complete definition of Revelation Knowledge, a good working definition of the concept is: *Revelation Knowledge is that supernatural knowledge of God and the spiritual realm revealed in the Bible, particularly Paul's epistles, which enables man to transcend the limitations of Sense Knowledge and act in faith.*

The doctrine of Revelation Knowledge is especially crucial because it is the "epistemology" of the Faith theology. An "epistemology" is a theory about the nature of knowledge: how one gains knowledge, and how much can be known. Epistemology is important because it determines how one attempts to know God and the world. Kenyon's epistemology is determined by his radical distinction between Revelation Knowledge and Sense Knowledge. Epistemologically, this distinction produces two results. First, it produces *dualism.* Dualism is the belief that all of reality is reducible to just two opposite principles, with little or nothing in between: light versus darkness, spirit versus matter, good versus evil, etc. Second, it produces *fideism* (pronounced "fee-day-ism"). Fideism is the belief that religious truth is based solely on faith rather than reasoning or sensory evidence. Extreme forms of fideism reject science and common sense.[7] As we proceed, it will become apparent that both the dualistic and fideistic aspects of Revelation Knowledge come from the metaphysical cults.

There are five strong parallels between Kenyon's epistemology and that of the metaphysical cults. (1) Both epistemologies are radically dualistic. (2) Both teach that to possess one type of knowledge demands denial of the other type. (3) Both teach that perfect knowledge of God is attainable in this life. (4) Both claim to teach a way of knowing that will enable one to transcend physical limitations. (5) Both teach a way of knowing that creates classes of Christians: the haves and the have-nots. Let us examine more closely each of these parallels between the Faith theology and the metaphysical cults.

Dualism: Spirit Realm vs. Physical Realm

The doctrine of Revelation Knowledge exhibits the radical dualism of the metaphysical cults. For Kenyon, all knowledge is from two mutually exclusive sources: (1) Sense Knowledge from the physical realm below, or (2) Revelation Knowledge from the spiritual realm above. Knowledge from one realm is of no value to the other. The founding father of all the metaphysical cults, Phineas P. Quimby, also taught a radical dualism between physical and spiritual knowledge. "There are two ideas, one spirit and one matter," taught Quimby. "When you speak of man you speak of matter. When you speak of spirit you speak of the knowledge that will live after the matter is destroyed or dead. This [spiritual knowledge] is the Christian's wisdom."[8] Also like Kenyon, Quimby taught that the human spirit was "the real man" and that knowledge that comes through the spiritual senses "independently of the brain" is greater than that which comes through the physical senses.[9]

Quimby's chief disciple, Mary Baker Eddy, founder of Christian Science, taught an extreme form of spirit-matter dualism. She even denied the reality of physical matter, claiming that knowledge of matter through the physical senses was an "error" and "false belief" of the mind.[10] In her glossary of Christian Science terms, Eddy defines knowledge as "evidence obtained from the five corporeal [physical] senses," which "is not divine and is the origin of sin, sickness, and death." It is "the opposite of spiritual Truth and understanding."[11] Eddy's dualistic understanding of knowledge is almost exactly the same as Kenyon's.

Denial of Sensory Reality

Based on his dualistic epistemology, Kenyon taught that in order to walk in Revelation Knowledge, the believer must often deny Sense Knowledge. Just as knowledge of the physical realm must come to the brain through the senses, so also knowledge of the spiritual realm is revealed only in "the human spirit." In the Faith anthropology, man is compartmentalized into three radically distinct and mutually exclusive parts: spirit, soul, and body. The human spirit is man's fundamental identity and is his sole means of receiving and perceiving Revelation Knowledge. The human spirit has little or nothing to do with intellect, which can process only Sense Knowledge. Kenyon claims that "there will always be a conflict between our Senses and the Word."[12] Only as the human spirit "gains ascendency over your thinking faculties" do the "Senses take their proper place" and the "spirit becomes the master of your being."[13] The human spirit must subjugate the physical senses because "God cannot communicate with you through the Senses," but "He can communicate with your spirit."[14] Kenyon's strongly anti-intellectual bias is readily apparent in Hagin, who teaches that "one almost has to by-pass the brain and operate from the inner man (the heart or spirit) to really get into the things of God."[15]

The practice of sensory denial is essential to Kenyon's view of faith. Kenyon insists that "real faith is acting upon the Word independent of any sense evidence."[16] Faith often demands that the believer act solely upon Revelation Knowledge to the total exclusion of Sense Knowledge.[17]

One concrete example of the practice of sensory denial in the Faith movement is its doctrine of healing. "Confession [of faith] always goes ahead of healing," advises Kenyon. "Don't watch symptoms—watch the Word. . . . Don't listen to the senses. Give the Word its place."[18] People with Sense Knowledge faith "do not believe they are healed until the pain has left their body." Real faith would deny the "physical evidence" of pain and listen only to the Word.[19] This practice of the denial of physical symptoms has been the source of much controversy in the Faith movement. Many have practiced such denial to the point of death.

The practice of sensory denial also characterizes the metaphysical cults. Christian Science, for example, also teaches that knowledge from the senses lies and contradicts revelation. Mary Baker Eddy writes that

> the corporeal [physical] senses can take no cognizance of spiritual reality and immortality. . . . Corporeal sense defrauds and lies. . . . The corporeal senses are the only source of evil or error. Christian Science shows them to be false.[20]

Consequently, the knowledge of the senses must be denied in order to believe the teaching of Christian Science: "All the evidence of the physical sense and all the knowledge from physical sense must yield to [Christian] Science, to the immortal truth of all things."[21] All of the other New Thought cults also teach that in order to be healed, one must deny the knowledge of the senses.[22]

Perfect Knowledge of God

Another parallel between the cults and Kenyon's doctrine of Revelation Knowledge is that both teach that perfect knowledge of God is attainable in this life. "It goes without argument," proclaims Kenyon, "that God has the ability to give us exact knowledge in regard to spiritual things."[23] Unlike Sense Knowledge, which has limitations and imperfections, Revelation Knowledge is the "complete" and "full" and "perfect" knowledge of God.[24] This idea did not originate with Kenyon. One of Kenyon's classmates and a chief expositor of New Thought at the Emerson College of Oratory, Ralph Waldo Trine, spoke of "an inner spiritual sense through which man is opened to the direct revelation and knowledge of God."[25] As the human spirit opens itself to revelation, it becomes "unerring, *absolutely unerring*, in its guidance."[26]

Revelation Knowledge Transcends Physical Limitations

In both Kenyon's theology and that of Trine, as the believer attains "perfect knowledge" and learns to deny the physical senses, he transcends physical limitations and walks in continual revelation. Kenyon stated that "I am no longer hemmed in by limitations because I am united with the limitless One."[27] Trine taught likewise: "When the spiritual sense is opened, then it transcends all the limitations of the physical senses and the intellect."[28] Trine taught his followers that "it is not necessary that we live under the domination of any physical agent"[29] and that we are born to have "absolute control" over our own environment.[30] Trine's ideas could well have been the source of Kenyon's claim that through Revelation Knowledge, the believer can transcend and conquer any evil or deficiency in his life.

Knowledge Classifies Christians

One of the more disturbing aspects of Kenyon's doctrine of Revelation Knowledge is its tendency to create classes of Christians. The class lines are drawn between those who possess Revelation Knowledge and those who do not. In the quotation cited at the beginning of this chapter, Kenyon mentions the "supermen," the "miracle class," and those who have "graduated from the lower class." Some can even become "god men." These classifications are repeated with disturbing frequency in Kenyon's writings. The following is representative.

> We are not common folk. This [Revelation Knowledge] lifts us out of the common place into the super-realm. You are the real supermen and superwomen. You have gone outside of the realm of the senses, outside the realm of Sense Knowledge, and you have passed over into the realm of God, the spirit realm.[31]

In the same book from which this quotation is taken, there are chapters entitled "A New Class of Men" and "Some Characteristics of the Supermen." Such language cannot avoid creating categories or levels of Christians, some of which possess the knowledge to become "supermen," some of which do not.

Trine also could have been the source of Kenyon's belief that Revelation Knowledge create classes of Christians. He taught that those who received New Thought revelation would become the "saviors" of lesser men.[32] Through metaphysical revelation, a person receives "immediate inspiration from the Divine Omniscience, and the co-operative energy of the Divine Omnipotence, under which he becomes a seer and a master."[33] Thus, in Trine's theology, as in Kenyon's, those who possess metaphysical knowledge constitute a higher class of Christians than those who merely possess sensory knowledge.

They can even become gods through this knowledge. According to Trine, as a person cultivates his "inner spiritual sense," he "is opened to the direct revelation and knowledge of God, the secrets of nature and life . . . and made to realize his own deific nature and supremacy of being as the son of God."[34] Indeed, one of the original purposes of the International New Thought Alliance was "to teach . . . the Divinity of Man and his infinite possibilities through the creative power of constructive thinking and obedience to the In-dwelling Presence which is our source of Inspiration, Power, Health, Prosperity."[35] The ultimate goal of metaphysical revelation is the transformation of man into a god. In the next chapter we shall see that this is also the goal of Kenyon's Revelation Knowledge.

Biblical Analysis of the Doctrine of Revelation Knowledge

The major epistemological error of the metaphysical cults in-corporated into Kenyon's doctrine of Revelation Knowledge is that of gnosticism. The term "gnosticism" is derived from the Greek word *gnosis*, meaning "knowledge." It is the name given to a rather com-plicated religious heresy which in its Christian form came into prominence in the second century. *Gnosis* was "the supposedly re-vealed knowledge of God and of the origin and destiny of mankind, by means of which the spiritual element in man could receive re-demption."[36] In saying that Revelation Knowledge is gnostic, we are not implying that there is a direct historical connection between the Faith theology and ancient gnosticism. The gnostic concept of knowledge does, however, have strong parallels in thought with the metaphysical cults. Through Kenyon, these parallels found their way into the Faith theology.

Rudolf Bultmann pointed to three central aspects in the gnos-tic concept of knowledge. All three of these have already been dem-onstrated in both the metaphysical cults and the Faith theology. (1) *Dualism.* The gnostics taught that the knowledge of God is abso-lutely distinct from and mutually exclusive with all other kinds of knowledge. Only by turning away from sensory knowledge can one know God. (2) *Antirationalism.* The gnostics believed that the knowledge of God is "radically distinguished from rational thought." It is an esoteric illumination rather than an objective, historical revelation. (3) Classification. The gnostic concept of the knowledge classifies believers into classes or categories, the highest of which is divine.[37] Knowledge "invests the gnostic with the divine na-ture" through which "he is transformed from a man into God."[38] From these three points, we will further develop some analogies be-tween gnosticism and Kenyon's doctrine of Revelation Knowledge.

Gnostic Dualism vs. Biblical Revelation

The most obvious gnostic idea taught by the Faith theology is its dualistic definition of Revelation Knowledge as entirely spiritual in origin. Because it is spiritual, the physical senses are of no value in understanding it or using it. The Faith theology teaches the gnostic view that "man is a spirit being" who just happens to have a body. Only the "spirit man" has the capacity to receive revelation directly from the Holy Spirit. Because man's five bodily senses are physical, they are of no value in knowing God or his revelation. This view of revelation reflects the gnostic spirit-matter dualism that Kenyon learned from the metaphysical cults.

The Bible in no way justifies a dualistic view of revelation. Biblical revelation and salvation are physical as well as spiritual. The best proof of this is Jesus Christ himself, who is "the Word made flesh" (Jn. 1:14). In Jesus "all the fulness of Deity dwells in bodily form" (Col. 2:9). We are saved "through the blood of His cross" (Col. 1:20) and are reconciled to God "in His fleshly body through death" (Col. 1:22). In our treatment of the Faith theology's doctrine of redemption, known as "Identification," its gnostic spiritualization of the gospel will become further evident. Suffice it to say at this point, the Bible allows for no such spiritualization. The incarnation and death of Christ are the highest forms of revelation, and both are decidedly physical in nature.

Moreover, biblical revelation was not only physical in nature, it was perceived and understood through physical means. The apostles used their physical senses to understand the incarnation of the Word: "And we beheld His glory" (Jn. 1:14), wrote John. "We were eyewitnesses of His majesty" (2 Pet. 1:16), wrote Peter. "And we ourselves heard [God's] utterance . . . when we were with Him on the holy mountain" (2 Pet. 1:18). The apostles bore witness to what they had "seen and heard" and their "hands handled, concerning the Word of Life" (1 Jn. 1:1). The ultimate form of the Word of God—the incarnation and death of Jesus—was physical in nature and was perceived by physical means. This fact alone powerfully repudiates the gnostic spirit-matter dualism of Kenyon's Revelation Knowledge.

Gnostic Anti-Rationalism

We earlier described the Faith theology as fideism. The Faith theology rejects reason for the same reason as gnosticism: they both believe that revelation is spiritual and can only be perceived by spiritual means. One must, as Hagin puts it, "by-pass the brain to get into the things of God."

The Bible in no way justifies fideism. The human mind is just as much an instrument of revelation as the human spirit. In the *shema*, God commanded the Israelites "to love the Lord your God with all your heart and with all your *soul* and with all your might" (Deut. 6:5). Quoting the *shema*, Jesus commanded his disciples to love God "with all your *soul*, and with all your *mind*" (Mk. 12:30). Paul exhorted believers to "set your *mind* on the things above" (Col. 3:2) and Peter taught his followers to "gird your *minds* for action" (1 Pet. 1:13). If the mind is just as necessary in knowing God as the human spirit, then obviously this says something about the use of human reason. Reason is not the enemy of faith and God is not an irrational being. He is the source of all reason and he himself invites men to reason with him: " 'Come now, let us *reason* together,' says the Lord" (Isa. 1:18). Divine wisdom is *reasonable* (Jas. 3:17). It was Paul's custom to "reason" with the Jews "from the Scriptures" (Acts 17:2; cf., 17:17; 18:4, 19). The anti-rationalism of the Faith theology cannot be justified by an appeal to the Scriptures. Christianity may transcend reason, but it does not reject it.

Perfect Knowledge Not Available in This Life

The Faith teachers assert that it is possible to possess a "perfect" and "exact" knowledge of God. The belief in a perfect and mutual knowledge between God and man attainable in this life is a gnostic idea, not a biblical one. C. K. Barrett comments,

> Man's knowledge of God is imperfect; Paul remembers this when he uses gnostic language. . . . The gnostic found a saving relationship with God in the mutual knowledge that existed between the elect, gnostic, man, and God. According to Paul, this is not a possibility. Man's knowledge is not only dependent on God's gracious initiative, it is at best partial. It can therefore (even if gnostic premises are accepted) mean only a partial relationship and salvation.[39]

The Faith teachers would like to claim that they have discovered the way to a perfect knowledge of God. What they have, in fact, discovered is the gnostic epistemology of the metaphysical cults. As wonderful as perfect knowledge of God would be, it directly contradicts the only source of knowledge about God we do possess: the Bible. *The Bible itself denies that a perfect knowledge of God is attainable in this life.* The perfect knowledge of God—and of man, for that matter—

will not be attainable until "the perfect One" returns. This was clearly the teaching of Paul.

> For we know in part, and we prophesy in part; but when the perfect comes, the partial will be done away. . . . For now we see in a mirror dimly, but then face to face; now I know in part, but then I shall know fully just as I also have been fully known (1 Cor. 13:9, 10, 12; NASB).[40]

Paradoxically, God is both *Deus revelatus* ("the revealed God") and *Deus absconditus* ("the hidden God"). He is the God who "is revealed in hiddenness and hidden in his revelation."[41] Even to the greatest revelation of the hidden God—the Word made flesh—there remained much that was hidden. The Lord Jesus himself did not know the time of his return (Mt. 24:36). Clearly, if Jesus was content to remain ignorant of God's mysteries, then so must we.

Faith Measured By Love, Not Knowledge

The Faith theology exalts knowledge the same way that gnosticism does. Faith is preeminent for the Faith teachers, but they measure faith by the type and amount of knowledge one has. In the Bible, knowledge is not the measure of faith, not even Revelation Knowledge. Love is the measure of faith. Paul writes,

> We know that we all possess knowledge. Knowledge puffs up, but love builds up. The man who thinks he knows something does not yet know as he ought to know. But the man who loves God is known by God (1 Cor. 8:1, 2, 3; NIV).

Anyone who claims to have the knowledge of God must prove his knowledge by his love. As it is with knowledge, so also is it with faith. "The only thing that counts," proclaims Paul, "is faith expressing itself through love" (Gal. 5:6, NIV). In his famous "love chapter," Paul teaches that without love, both faith and knowledge amount to nothing: "And if I have the gift of prophecy, and know all mysteries and all knowledge; and if I have all faith, so as to remove mountains, but do not have love, I am nothing" (1 Cor. 13:3). Had the love ethic of Jesus prevailed in the Faith movement, many of the barbaric and tragic things done in his name—such as the fatal withholding of medication from young children—would never have happened.

Delusions of Grandeur

The exorbitant claims made for Revelation Knowledge have produced the same grandiose notions in the Faith movement that characterize gnosticism and the metaphysical cults. Through Revelation Knowledge, the Faith "supermen" become "kings in life" and "the bondage breakers for the rest of the human race."[42] Nowhere does the Bible teach that certain believers could attain to the status of a savior or redeemer. The "preacher-worship" that goes on in the Faith movement is analogous to the gnostic conception of an elite *pneumatikoi* who dispense saving knowledge as though it were resident in their own person. How this differs from the humility of the Apostle Paul! "Let a man regard us in this manner," wrote Paul, "as servants of Christ, and stewards of the mysteries of God" (1 Cor. 4:1). Paul stated that "we do not preach ourselves but Christ Jesus as Lord, and ourselves as your bond-servants for Jesus' sake" (2 Cor. 4:5). Even when their audiences attempted to worship them, the apostles steadfastly resisted the temptation to regard themselves as anything but mere men, humble servants of the Lord Jesus (Acts 10:26; 14:15). Certain charismatic preachers have not always done so.

The Faith theology's claim that Revelation Knowledge transforms men into the "masters" and "bondage breakers" of humanity is yet another example of the messiah-complex that permeates much of the charismatic movement. The history of the movement has seen an unbroken succession of personality cults promising far more than they can deliver and destroying people's faiths and lives in the process. One charismatic theologian writes,

> As time goes on, the [charismatic] renewal has been becoming not less but more dependent on strong leaders offering instant answers. There has been a sorry procession of panacea promises calling people successively to whatever was the fashion of the hour to solve their problems and cure their ills. . . . The oversimplification of the teaching offered and the response required bespeak the immaturity both of teachers and taught. And since each of these, although it helps some people, inevitably fails to live up to the universal claims made on its behalf, there is left behind a trail of disappointment and disillusionment that depresses the level of faith and expectation.[43]

The Faith theology is but the latest "panacea promise" to seduce the independent charismatic movement. It will probably not be the last.

Notes

1. Kenyon, *Two Kinds of Knowledge*, p. 11.
2. Ibid., p. 23.
3. Ibid., p. 25.
4. Ibid., p. 34.

5. Ibid., p. 19.

6. Ibid., p. 20.

7. Richard Popkin, "Fideism," *Encyclopedia of Philosophy*, ed. Paul Edwards (New York: Macmillan, 1967), 3:201.

8. Dresser, *Quimby Manuscripts*, p. 177.

9. Ibid., pp. 421–22.

10. Mary Baker Eddy, *Science and Health with Key to the Scriptures* (Boston: Trustees, 1934), p. 274.

11. Ibid., p. 590.

12. *Two Kinds of Knowledge*, p. 50.

13. Ibid., p. 39.

14. Ibid., p. 18.

15. Kenneth Hagin, *Right and Wrong Thinking* (Tulsa: Faith Library, 1966), p. 27.

16. *Two Kinds of Knowledge*, p. 34.

17. Ibid., p. 48.

18. E. W. Kenyon, *Jesus the Healer* (Seattle: Kenyon's Gospel Publishing Society, 1943), p. 26.

19. Kenyon, *Two Kinds of Faith*, p. 23.

20. Eddy, *Science and Health*, pp. 488–89.

21. Ibid., p. 493.

22. For example, one of the most important early New Thought authors, Warren Evans, writes, "That which we most need is to develop into our consciousness our inner and higher life and to give to it what rightfully belongs to it, an absolute sovereignty over all below it. It should be our aim to elevate the principle of thought above the plane of the senses and free it from their distorting influence" (Evans, *The Primitive Mind Cure* [n.p., 1885], p. 14).

23. Kenyon, *Hidden Man*, p. 167.

24. Kenyon, *Identification*, p. 52; Kenyon particularly emphasizes one of the Greek words for knowledge, *epignosis* (in contrast to plain *gnosis*) as the biblical justification of his claim to perfect knowledge. This distinction between *epignosis* and *gnosis* is common in the contemporary Faith movement as well.

25. Ralph Waldo Trine, *In Tune With the Infinite* (New York: Bobbs-Merrill Co., 1970), p. 35.

26. Ibid., pp. 35, 36.

27. Kenyon, *Two Kinds of Life*, p. 58.

28. Trine, *In Tune*, p. 93.

29. Ibid., p. 53.

30. Ibid., p. 54.

31. Kenyon, *The Hidden Man*, p. 158.

32. Trine, *In Tune*, p. 152.

33. Ibid., p. 36.

34. Ibid., p. 35.

35. *Constitution and By-Laws* (1916); quoted in Charles W. Ferguson, *The New Books of Revelation* (Garden City, N.Y.: Doubleday Doran, 1929), p. 168.

36. F. L. Cross and E. A. Livingstone, eds., *The Oxford Dictionary of the Christian Church*, 2nd ed. (Oxford: Oxford Univ. Press, 1983), p. 573.

37. Gnostic believers were classified according to what degree of knowledge they possessed. There were three classes of gnostics: (1) the *pneumatikoi*, the "spiritual ones" who possessed perfect knowledge; (2) the *psychikoi*, the "psychic ones" who possessed partial knowledge; and (3) the *sarkikoi*, the "fleshly ones," who possessed no spiritual knowledge, but instead were carnal.

38. Rudolf Bultmann, "*ginōskō*," *TDNT* (1964) 1:692–96.

39. C. K. Barrett, *The First Epistle to the Corinthians* (HNTC; New York: Harper & Row, 1968), p. 308.

40. According to Barrett, "the general drift of the verse is clear; it brings out the inadequacy of man's present knowledge of God in contrast with (a) God's knowledge of man now, and (b) the knowledge of God that man will have in the future. Then, not now (as in gnostic thought), there will be a complete mutuality of knowledge" (p. 307).

41. Richard A. Muller, *Dictionary of Latin and Greek Theological Terms* (Grand Rapids: Baker, 1985), p. 90.

42. Kenneth Hagin, "The Resurrection," *Word of Faith* (April, 1977), p. 6.

43. Thomas Smail, *The Forgotten Father* (London: Hodder and Stoughton, 1980), pp. 14–15.

7 The Doctrine of Identification: The Born-Again Jesus and the Atonement of the Devil

This book will blaze a new path in constructive interpretation of the Pauline revelation. It uncovers many new veins of primary truth long covered by sense knowledge interpretation of the Word. . . . They [the apostles] did not know what happened on the cross, or during the three days and nights before His resurrection, but we must know of these three days, for this is the thing that will build faith in us. The mystery is hidden in these three days.

—E. W. Kenyon,
What Happened from the Cross to the Throne, pp. 9, 12.

The Word-Faith teaching's mythological presentation of the fall of Jesus from Perfect Man to Satanic denies that the redemption of man took place on the Cross. It moves the redemption of Man to the time after the supposed double-death of Jesus on the Cross. . . . They assert that Jesus was the substitute for every man in Hell. . . . Sometimes the myth varies and includes Knowledge as the tool Jesus used in overcoming Satan in Hell. . . . Knowledge is the Way to being like God, and by knowing what happened to Jesus on the Cross, the believer is able to realize his equality with Jesus in all respects.

—Judith A. Matta,
The Born-Again Jesus of the Word-Faith Teaching, pp. 35, 37.

During the nineteenth century, the concept of "Identification" was popularized in a series of "deeper life" conventions, the first of which was held in Keswick, England, in 1875. "The Keswick movement," as it is now known, teaches that believers can, in part, overcome their inherent tendency toward sin through personal "Identification" with various aspects of Christ's redemptive act—specifically, his death, burial, resurrection, ascension, and exaltation. Identification forms something of an experiential bridge between anthropology and Christology. The Keswick movement teaches that to be identified through faith with Christ's redemptive work is to be "in Christ." His experience of the redemptive act then vicariously becomes man's experience. Identification is the way to appropriate in this life both the benefits and the demands of Christ's redemptive acts.

Whereas the Keswick movement began with biblically orthodox doctrines about Christ and man to form its doctrine of Identification, the Faith theology uses cultic, metaphysical concepts. This results in a heretical doctrine of Identification, which denies the physical nature of the atonement, asserts that Christ became a demoniac and was "born-again" in hell, and teaches that believers can be transformed into incarnations of God (=deification). In the remainder of this chapter, the term "Identification" will refer inclusively to Kenyon's and Hagin's bizarre doctrines of man, Christ, redemption, and deification.

The concept that Jesus died spiritually is so crucial to the Faith theology that some Faith teachers pronounce divine judgment on all who question it. For instance, in describing a minister who violently opposed Identification, Kenneth Copeland stated ominously, "That fellow is dead today. Now I said that to warn you. Don't criticize people for preaching [Identification]. If you don't understand it, keep your mouth shut and pray."[1] *Identification is so important because it is the basis of the Faith theology's claim that the believer is an incarnation of God.* Through his Identification with Jesus' "spiritual atonement," the believer is deified. Copeland's threats aside, it will now be demonstrated that the doctrine of Identification is based on cultic ideas.

The Cultic Nature of the Doctrine of Identification

According to Kenyon, the atonement is a truth that was unknown to Jesus' disciples, who comprehended neither the meaning of "spiritual death," nor the "mystery" of his three days of suffering in hell. Only Paul was given the "revelation" of the "mystery" of Christ's death.[2] Kenyon wrote two books on his version of Identification. The first was the pamphlet, *Identification: A Romance in Redemption*, and the second was the more expansive *What Happened from the Cross to the Throne*. Before turning to Identification itself, it is necessary to understand Kenyon's view of man.

Faith Anthropology: Man's Divine-Satanic Nature

Kenyon teaches that man as a species "is in God's class of being."[3] By this, he means that man and God possess a common nature: both are spirit beings. Kenneth Hagin goes so far as to say that "man is not a physical being. Man is a spirit."[4] The only difference in nature between man and God is of degree, not of kind. The common anthropological definition used throughout the Faith movement is that "man is a spirit, who possesses a soul, and who lives in a body."[5] According to Kenyon, "man's spirit is the real man."[6] Likewise, Hagin insists that "we live in a body, but we are spirit beings."[7]

Anyone vaguely familiar with metaphysics will recognize the cultic nature of the Faith view of man. All of the metaphysical cults teach the pantheistic idea that because God is in everything, everything is god (especially man). Thus Ralph Waldo Trine speaks for all of New Thought when he claims "*in essence the life of God and the life of man are identically the same, and so are one.* They differ not in essence, in quality; they differ in degree."[8] Like Kenyon, Trine also taught that by virtue of his oneness with God, man is a spiritual being, not physical.[9] All of the metaphysical cults insist that the "real" man is a spirit, not a body. Mary Baker Eddy, for instance, wrote that "spirit is real and eternal; matter is unreal and temporal. Spirit is God, man is His image and likeness. Therefore, man is not material; he is spiritual."[10] This spiritualized view of man is not the Judeo-Christian view revealed in the Bible.

Kenyon's susceptibility to cultic anthropology stemmed from his belief that man has no independent nature of his own (at least, not one that is uniquely and permanently human). Man is always "dependent upon a higher power than he is for his spiritual life. He must partake either of God's nature or of Satan's nature."[11] Man's nature was divine before the Fall, and demonic after the Fall.

Man was transformed from the divine to the demonic through "spiritual death." Spiritual death is more than just a spiritual counterpart to physical death.[12] In Kenyon's view, "spiritual death is in reality a nature."[13] It is the satanic nature imputed to man through sin, transforming him into a "new Satanic creation."[14] Similarly, Hagin teaches that "just as receiving eternal life means that we have the nature of God in us," so also, "spiritual death means having Satan's nature."[15]

Not only was each individual's nature corrupted by Satan, man's corporate dominion over the creation was also transferred to Satan through the Fall. Adam betrayed God by giving to Satan that which God had given to him, which is referred to in the Faith theology as "High Treason."[16] Thus, Satan is god and rules the creation by "legal right," not just by man's rebellion. In order to recapture the world, God must deal with Satan "justly" by paying him a ransom.[17]

Faith Christology: Spiritual Death and the Born-Again Jesus

According to Kenyon, Jesus died two deaths on the cross: the first spiritual, the second physical.[18] It was necessary that Christ die spiritually because sickness and sin are both *spiritual* in origin, not *physical*. Kenyon states that "sin and sickness come from the same Source. Satan is the author of both."[19] Likewise, "sickness is spiritual. It is manifested in our physical bodies as a disease."[20] The disease itself, however, is but a physical manifestation of a problem that is spiritual in origin.[21] Christ's physical death did fulfill perfect obedience, but it could never eradicate sin and sickness because both of these are spiritual.[22] The physical death of Christ was but the beginning of his redemptive work, not its end. Kenyon writes,

> All that Christ wrought in His Substitution was wrought in His Spirit. It was His Spirit that was made sin. It was His Spirit that suffered the torments of judgment on behalf of humanity. It was His Spirit that was declared righteous. . . . *It was His Spirit Resurrection that has given to humanity its Redemption.* Man is so tied up with Sense Knowledge that He has only seen the physical suffering of Christ on the Cross, and His physical Resurrection. *It was something infinitely beyond that.*[23]

Kenyon is herein claiming that the true redemptive work of Christ was not the agonies of his cross and the victory of his bodily resurrection, but instead, his "Spiritual Death" and "Spirit Resurrection" were his true redemptive acts.

In the Faith theology, Christ's physical sufferings and blood shed in death have no more power to atone and deliver than anyone else's. According to Kenyon, "if His [physical] death paid it, then every man could die for himself. Sin is in the spirit realm. His physical death was but a means to an end."[24] The "end" in view was his spiritual death and suffering in hell. The primacy of "spiritual death" is advocated by most of the major Faith teachers.[25] For example, Fred Price asks:

> Do you think that the punishment for our sin was to die on a cross? If that were the case, the two thieves could have paid your price. No the punishment was to go into hell itself and to serve time in hell separated from God . . . Satan and all the demons of hell thought that they had

him bound, and they threw a net over Jesus and they dragged Him
down to the very pit of hell itself to serve our sentence.[26]

Kenneth Copeland is even more direct in denying the atoning efficacy of Christ's blood: "Jesus went into hell to free mankind from the
penalty of Adam's high treason . . . *When His blood poured out it did
not atone* . . . Jesus spent three horrible days and nights in the bowels
of this earth getting back for you and me our rights with God."[27] It
was Jesus' suffering in hell that paid man's penalty and made him an
heir of eternal life. As Kenyon so succinctly put it, "He went to Hell
in order to take us to Heaven."[28]

It is not surprising that the metaphysical cults also deny that
Jesus' physical death atones for sin. Mary Baker Eddy states that "the
material blood of Jesus was no more efficacious to cleanse from sin,
when it was shed upon 'the accursed tree' than when it was flowing
in His veins."[29] She referred to the idea that God's wrath must be
propitiated by physical sacrifice as a "heathen conception."[30] Kenyon's commitment to such metaphysical concepts made it impossible for him to believe that Christ's physical sufferings on the cross
could be sufficient to win man's redemption without some supposedly more significant spiritual suffering in the spirit realm. This
spiritualization of Jesus' death, whether implicit (as in the Faith
theology), or explicit (as in metaphysics), destroys the very core of
the gospel. It is cultic and heretical.

So also is the Christology of the Faith movement. The "three
horrible days and nights" in hell inflicted much more than *external*
suffering upon Christ. Kenyon taught that when Jesus died spiritually, an *internal* transformation took place in his nature, just like
that which took place in Adam when he sinned. On the cross, when
man's sin and spiritual death were imputed to him, Jesus became a
"new Satanic creation." As a result, "Jesus became sin. His spirit was
separated from God."[31] This separation from God was more than
alienation because of man's sin. Spiritual death transformed Christ
from a God-man into a mortal (and satanic) man, thereby "sever-
ing" him from God.[32] In the Faith theology, Jesus was not a substitute for sin in any vicarious sense: he was transformed into a
demoniac.[33]

After Jesus suffered the penalty of man's sin and fulfilled all of
man's legal obligation towards Satan, God declared that justice had
been done. Because he had taken on spiritual death and become a
satanic creation, "Jesus was born again before He was raised from
the dead."[34] He went to hell a demon-possessed mortal man, and

emerged from hell a born-again, resurrected man.[35] This "born-again Jesus" then defeated Satan and his forces of darkness in hell. "It is important for us to realize," writes Kenneth Copeland, "that a born-again man defeated Satan."[36]

The Legal Side of Identification

For Kenyon, Identification refers to Christ's complete union with us in our fallen, demoniacal state, and "our complete union with Him in His Substitutionary Sacrifice."[37] Thus, Identification with Christ is two-sided: the "legal side" and the "vital side." The legal side of Identification "unveils to us what Christ did for us from the time He went to the Cross, until He sat down on the right hand of the Father."[38] It is considered "legal" because it fulfills the justice of God towards Satan, who owns the creation by virtue of Adam's High Treason. In order to redeem man from Satan's legal dominion, Jesus had to take upon himself spiritual death, the satanic nature, and "the curse of the Law," which is sin, sickness, and poverty.

The Vital Side of Identification

From the divine perspective, then, all that God must do to redeem man has already been done in the legal side of Identification.[39] From the human perspective, all that remains in redemption is for the believer to take his "place" in Christ, to exercise the "rights" Christ has given him, in short, to find his "identity" in Christ. The vital side is the faith actualization of the perfect redemption of Christ already credited to man in the legal side of Identification.

The ultimate end of the vital side of Identification is deification. "Deification" may be defined as the process whereby men are transformed into gods. In Kenyon's version of deification, man was created with the divine nature, sinned, and was filled with satanic nature; but through the new birth, he is again infused with the divine nature. "To be born again," claims Kenyon, is to receive "the nature and life of God in one's spirit."[40] Kenyon knew very well that deification was the teaching of the metaphysical cults. In one of his earliest newsletters, he wrote,

> Christian Science, Theosophy, New Thought and Modern Unitarianism teach, consciously or unconsciously, the Incarnation of the human family, that is, they teach that every man has a God in him. If a man has God in him then he and God are in union, and if united, Incarnated.[41]

Kenyon knew that the cults taught that man is an incarnation of God, and in this passage objected to it, but he taught virtually the same thing through his vital side of Identification.

Today, Kenneth Hagin continues to teach Kenyon's doctrine of human deification. Hagin says that "there is a real incarnation in the new birth!"[42] In the new birth, God imparts "His very nature, substance, and being to our human spirits."[43] Hence, Hagin maintains that "every born again man is an incarnation" and that "the believer is as much an incarnation as Jesus of Nazareth."[44] Lest the reader think that Hagin is only speaking metaphorically, consider the following quotations:

> That's who we are; we're Christ![45]

> In fact, in the Epistles, the Church is called Christ. The Church has not yet realized that we are Christ. When we do, we'll start doing the work we're supposed to do.[46]

> Christ is the Head—we are the Body—and the Body of Christ is Christ.[47]

On at least one occasion, Hagin seems to contradict the obvious intent of the above statements.[48] But for the most part, his meaning is clear: through Identification with Christ in the new birth, man becomes an incarnation of God.

As already mentioned, Kenyon's view of salvation as deification has strong cultic parallels. New Thought teaches that once a man recognizes that he is a spirit being in union with the Christ-Spirit, he is transformed into a god. According to Trine, "in the degree that we open ourselves to this divine inflow are we changed from mere men into God men."[49] Like the Faith teachers, Trine taught that believers needed to realize their true "identity" as God men.[50] Both Trine and Kenyon teach that believers who are in union with God are themselves incarnations of God. They also both teach that believers in union with God can transcend all physical limitations. Kenyon maintained that if all believers were vitally identified with Christ's rebirth in hell, then the church would be elevated above every sickness, pain, circumstance, and imperfection.[51] Where these things exist in the church, it is only because believers have failed to realize their Identification with Christ.[52]

Although his emphasis is slightly different, Trine also claimed that through union with God, the believer could transcend every sickness and circumstance of the physical body. The believer who recognizes that he is a spirit-being, no longer makes the mistake of regarding himself as body, subject to ills and disease, but he realizes the fact that he is spirit, spirit now as much as he ever will or can be, and that he is the builder and so the master of the body, the house in which he lives; and the moment he thus recognizes his power as master he ceases in anyway to allow it the mastery over him.[53]

Thus, both Trine and Kenyon insist that like God himself, believers should be the absolute masters of all sin, sickness, and circumstances.

Biblical Analysis of the Doctrine of Identification

Anthropology: Is Man a Spirit Residing in a Body?

The basic underlying error of Kenyon's doctrine of Identification is its faulty understanding of man and the Fall. Man is *not* a spirit being who possesses a soul and just happens to live in a body, as the Faith teachers claim; rather, man is an integrated being of spirit, soul, and body (1 Thess. 5:23). The Hebrew understanding of man is wholistic; it depicts man as an organic whole, rather than merely as the sum of his parts. In Hebrew anthropology, the body is every bit as important to one's personal identity as the spirit.[54] When God created man, he formed him from the dust of the ground, breathed into his nostrils the breath of life, and, as a result, man became a *nephesh haya*, "a living soul" (Gen. 2:7)—a phrase which "does not refer to the soul merely, but to the whole man as an animated being."[55] Man is not just "dust in the wind," but neither is he just "God's breath." The "real you" is all of you: dust and breath, body and spirit. Contrary to Faith anthropology, the "spirit man" is not the "real you." The extreme trichotomism of the Faith anthropology, which identifies man's "true inner self" as fundamentally divine, residing exclusively in his spirit, in radical contradistinction to his body and soul, transmuted by demonic powers, is far more characteristic of gnostic mythology than of the Judeo-Christian view of man.[56]

Did the Fall Make Man's Nature Satanic?

The Faith theology's doctrine of the fall of man is hopelessly distorted by its view of man himself. Kenyon and Hagin's teaching that fallen humanity was filled with the "satanic nature" and became a "new satanic creation" is utterly indefensible. In the first place, it attributes far too much power to Satan, who has no creative powers of his own and who is himself a created being. Satan can, indeed, possess men on an individual basis, but there is no reason to believe that he has the power to alter the nature of man on a universal level. Only God has the power to create and recreate.

Moreover, God created man with a nature all his own. Man does *not* draw his nature from whatever deity owns the "rights" to him at any given moment. Man's nature is in "the image of God," (*imago Dei),* but it is a distinctly *human* nature. To be created in the "image" and "likeness" of God is to reflect God's glory and, in a limited sense, his capacities, but it is *not* to be a god. The concept of the *imago Dei* has, admittedly, born a wide range of interpretation, and there should be a liberality of opinion on the matter.[57] For the purposes of our treatment, the *imago Dei* may be defined as the spiritual, psychological, and, yes, even physical endowments created in man whereby he alone of all creatures might live in relationship with God and others, and exercise dominion and stewardship over creation in the name of God. This definition differs from that of the Faith theology in that it preserves a clear and permanent distinction between the divine nature and human nature. The *imago Dei* makes man *like* God, but it does not make him a god.

Nor did the fall of Adam transform man into a creation of Satan. Even after the Genesis account of the Fall, man is still described as a creature in the image of God. On the basis of his permanent possession of that image, murder is prohibited (Gen. 9:6). The *imago Dei* was damaged by Adam's sin, but not eradicated. To use John Calvin's example, after the Fall, the image of God was shattered within man, but like reflections of one's face in a broken mirror, distorted images of God's glory can still be seen within fallen man. If the image of God were completely destroyed or possessed by Satan, then there would be no difference between man and the animals. Man would cease to be man and could no longer be held morally accountable to God or respond to him for salvation. In Christ Jesus, the shattered mirror of God's image is restored, and man is once again "the image and glory of God" (1 Cor. 11:7). "The restoration of the *imago Dei,* the new creation of the original image of God in man, is identical with the gift of God in Jesus Christ received by faith"[58] (cf. Rom. 8:29; 2 Cor. 3:18; Eph. 4:24; Col. 3:10).

Deification: Is the Believer an Incarnation of God?

Contrary to the Faith theology and metaphysical cults, salvation is not deification. In the biblical view of salvation, fallen man is not a demoniac, and restored man is not a god. *In the Bible, salvation is the process whereby through faith in Christ Jesus man is restored to all that Adam was created to be.* Christ is Adam-in-reverse, the restorer of the image of God. Man is, indeed, "a new creature in Christ" (2 Cor. 5:17), but the emphasis in this verse is upon Christ: the creature remains a creature.[59] The "new man" who has "been created in Christ Jesus" (Eph. 2:10) is still a man. Paul's exhortations to "put off the old man" (Eph. 4:22) and "put on the new man" (Eph. 4:24) both refer to distinctly human natures: the former fallen and the latter redeemed.[60] What we "put off" is not a satanic nature, and what we "put on" is not a god nature. The Faith doctrine of deification can be justified only by an appeal to the metaphysical cults, not by an appeal to the Bible.

Atonement: Was Christ Sacrificed to Satan?

Because of all its emphasis upon Satan as "the god of this world," Kenyon's doctrine of Identification particularly damages what some theologians refer to as "the God-ward" aspect of the atonement, which is its primary meaning. The underlying assumption of Identification is that Satan owns man by "legal right" and that a ransom must be paid to him if man is to be redeemed. Kenyon's concept is thus a "Satan-ward" view of the atonement. Christ's spiritual death is interpreted as Satan's price of redemption. This is not a new idea and is known in theology as a "ransom theory" of the atonement.

The central focus of any doctrine of atonement should be on the fact that Christ's death is a *sacrifice to God.* The righteous and holy God is the party that must be satisfied by atonement, not Satan. Paul tells the Ephesians that "Christ loved you and gave himself up for us, an offering and sacrifice to God as a fragrant aroma" (Eph. 5:2). Elsewhere, Paul writes, "For there is one God, and one mediator also between God and men, the man Christ Jesus, who gave himself as a ransom for all" (1 Tim. 2:5, 6). As the mediator, Christ's "ransom" was to God, not to Satan.

This God-ward interpretation of the atonement does not deny that Satan exercises a real dominion in the world; neither does it deny that a major part of Christ's mission was to destroy Satan's dominion. Satan is called the "god of this world" (2 Cor. 4:4) and "the ruler of this world" (Jn. 14:30). "The whole world lies in the power of the evil one" (1 Jn. 5:19). Christ did come to destroy his power (1 Jn. 3:8). Where Kenyon errs is not in asserting the reality of Satan's dominion, but in claiming that he possesses it by "legal right." If that were true, Satan would be entitled to atonement. Satan's dominion is, however, a usurped dominion. He stole it. He maintains it by accusation (Rev. 12:10), by deception (2 Cor. 4:4; Rev. 12:9), by enslavement to sin (2 Tim. 2:26), by the fear of death (Heb. 2:15), and by the power of death (Heb. 2:14; Rom. 5:17). In exercising his stolen dominion, Satan does use God's law for his own evil purposes, but he has no legal right of ownership of the world. God doesn't owe Satan a ransom. *God owes Satan nothing!* (Nothing, that is, except eternal punishment in hell.)

Christ destroyed Satan's dominion not by paying a ransom to him, but by fulfilling the law of God, which Satan used to condemn man before God. He broke the power of the devil, when he freed us from "the law of sin and death" (Rom. 8:2; cf., Col. 2:14, 15). The two primary agents of Satan's rule, sin and death, are based on the law. "The sting of death is sin, and the power of sin is the law" (1 Cor. 15:56). Millard Erickson writes,

> It was not the payment of a ransom to Satan that ensured his defeat and the triumph of God, but Christ's taking our place to free us from the curse of the law. By bearing the penalty of our sin and thus satisfying once and for all the just requirements of the law, Christ nullified Satan's control over us at its root—the power to bring us under the curse and condemnation of the law. Christ's death, then, was indeed God's triumph over the forces of evil, but only because it was a substitutionary sacrifice.[61]

Thus, the doctrine of Identification rests upon the false premise that Christ's ransom was paid to Satan. And if its premise is false, so are its conclusions.

Christology: Did Jesus Become Sinful/Satanic?

One false conclusion of the Faith theology is its belief that Christ ransomed man from sin by becoming sinful. To support this view, the Faith teachers repeatedly cite (and misinterpret) 2 Cor. 5:21: "He made Him who knew no sin to be sin on our behalf, that we might become the righteousness of God in Him." This scripture is interpreted to mean that Jesus ransomed man's sin not by dying on the cross, but by taking on human nature, which, according to Faith anthropology, is satanic. But this interpretation ignores the fact that the context of 2 Cor. 5:21 is clearly God's redeeming activity in the bodily crucifixion of Christ (2 Cor. 5:14–19), not some alleged spiritual transmutation of his nature into sin. God was the primary player in the atonement, not the devil. Moreover, God made Christ sin in "the forensic [i.e., legal] sense of the word" only; as payment for our sin, God "treats the sinless Christ as though he were a sinner" by delivering him up to death on the cross.[62] According to Leon Morris, "all the verbal juggling in the world cannot make 'made sin' mean 'took upon himself human nature.' "[63] To be "made sin" refers to the legal nature of Christ's substitutionary death on the cross, not his transformation into a demoniac.

This Faith teachers' belief that Jesus became sinful indicates a gross misunderstanding of the Old Testament concept of substitutionary sacrifice. The Levitical concept of substitution, which is the background of Christ's atonement, was based on the perfection and holiness of the sacrificial victim. The sacrificial animals chosen for the sin offering were to be a bull "without defect" (Lev. 4:3), a goat "without defect" (Lev. 4:23), and a lamb "without defect" (Lev. 4:32). The person presenting these holy offerings would lay his hand on the animals to symbolize the transfer of his sin and guilt (Lev. 4:4, 24, 33). This transfer of sin was symbolic, not literal. Kenyon's doctrine of Identification would claim that at the moment of transference of sin, these animals *became* unholy, that they *became* sin. Just the opposite was true. At the moment of transference, the offering became holy to Lord; anybody who touched or ate the sin offering also became holy (Lev. 6:25–27, 29). The sacrificial animal did not *become* sin; sin was symbolically *imputed* to it. It was a substitute for sin: a holy offering that atoned for sin by virtue of its perfection and consecration to the Lord.

These Levitical concepts of substitution and imputation are the background of 2 Cor. 5:21. Jesus did not literally *become* sin; sin was symbolically *imputed* to him. The Scriptures clearly teach that Jesus' sacrifice was a fit substitutionary offering because it was a sinless offering. Peter draws upon Levitical images when he writes that we are redeemed "with precious blood, *as of a lamb unblemished and spotless*, the blood of Christ" (1 Pet. 1:19).[64] The writer to the Hebrews does likewise when he states that Christ "offered himself *without blemish to God*" (Heb. 9:14). Here again, as in 1 Pet. 1:19, "without blemish" (*amōmos*) is a reference to the Levitical requirement of an externally perfect sacrifice (cf. Ex. 29:1, LXX). The writer to the Hebrews is here indicating that "that which was required outwardly in the Levitical victims was satisfied absolutely by

Christ."[65] The doctrine of Identification contradicts the fact that Christ "offered himself without blemish to God" and that as a sin offering, he was "most holy to the Lord." If he was not, then his offering for sin was not accepted by God.

Atonement: Did Jesus Have to Die Spiritually?

Another major problem with Kenyon's view of the atonement is the notion that Jesus had to die spiritually in order to atone for sin. The Scriptures in no way justify the claim that Jesus died twice on the cross: first, spiritually, and then physically. The Faith teachers base their case for the "double-death" of Jesus exclusively on Isa. 53:9, "His grave was assigned with wicked men, yet He was with a rich man in His death." Interpreting the passage messianically, Kenyon notes that the Hebrew word for "death" in this verse is in the plural, from which it is deduced that Jesus died twice.

The problems with the double-death theory are both numerous and massive. Its greatest deficiency is that it is based on a single word of a single text of Scripture. As one scholar has noted, any doctrine that can claim only *one* proof-text probably can claim *none*! This axiom certainly holds true for the double-death theory, which depends upon a mistranslation of its sole proof-text. It is no accident that there is not a major English version of the Bible which translates the Hebrew plural "deaths" in Isa. 53:9 with the English plural. To do so would defy one of the most basic rules of Hebrew grammar. Plural nouns are extremely common in the Hebrew Scriptures. They are not just used to denote numerical plurality, but also to emphasize a particular meaning of the noun. In Hebrew, plural nouns express majesty, rank, excellence, magnitude, and intensity.[66] In Isa. 53:9, "deaths" is a *plural of intensity* used by the writer to indicate that the death mentioned was a particularly violent one.[67] It no more means that the king of Tyre died two deaths than that the Messiah died two deaths.

Even if Isa. 53:9 is a messianic reference to Jesus, the double-death theory simply does not fit the facts of his death as they are recorded in the gospels. Immediately before his death, Jesus committed his spirit into the hands of the Father (Lk. 23:46). At the moment of death, he cried out loudly, bowed his head, and "yielded up His spirit" to God (Mt. 27:50; Jn. 19:30). The moment of yielding up his spirit coincided with the death of his physical body; thus, Jesus did not "die spiritually before he died physically." Moreover, if as the Faith teachers say, Jesus was immediately taken to hell after his death, why then did he tell the thief on the cross "today you shall be with me in Paradise"? Although we do not know definitively "what happened from the cross to the throne," the above passages would indicate one thing that did *not* happen. Jesus was *not* taken to hell by the devil after his death. Thus, the house of cards constructed on the double-death of Jesus by the Faith teachers comes crashing to the ground.

And with it crashes the most overtly heretical aspect of Identification: the denial of atonement by physical death. Although the importance of the blood of Jesus may seem so fundamental to the gospel as to be beyond question, *the Faith doctrine of atonement subtly, but clearly, teaches that Christ's physical death alone cannot atone*. The Scriptures, however, clearly teach the contrary. Jesus defeated Satan on the cross through physical death, not in hell through "spiritual death" (which does not even exist apart from physical death anyway). For Paul, Christ's triumph over and humiliation of the demonic powers took place on the cross when he liberated man from the law: "And having disarmed the powers and authorities, he made a public spectacle of them, *triumphing over them by the cross*" (Col. 2:13–15, NIV; italics added). Jesus did not liberate man from the law one way and from the "powers and authorities" of the devil another. Man was liberated from both on the cross.

Furthermore, it was not Jesus' "spiritual sufferings," "spiritual death," and "spiritual resurrection" that defeated Satan. The atonement is grounded in the fact that Jesus suffered in the *flesh* and died in the *flesh*. Peter states that "Christ has suffered in the flesh" (1 Pet. 4:1) and that "He Himself bore our sins in His *body* on the cross" (1 Pet. 2:24). The writer to the Hebrews teaches that "since the children share in flesh and blood, He Himself likewise also partook of the same, *that through death He might render powerless him who had the power of death, that is, the devil*" (Heb. 2:14). The nature of Satan's defeat described in this passage seems abundantly clear. In the incarnation, Christ partook of the "flesh and blood" of God's children. In his death on the cross, Christ shed his blood and suffered in his flesh, thereby defeating death and "him who had the power of death, that is, the devil."

All of the biblical writers assert that it is Jesus' physical death that atones for sin and redeems man from death. It is evident from the usage of "blood" in the Bible that it is a symbol of physical life given in death, particularly sacrificial and violent death.[68] The atonement of Christ was a physical act involving the shedding of his blood in bodily crucifixion. The writer to the Hebrews, for example, teaches that the whole Levitical system is expressed in the statement that "all things are cleansed with blood, and without the shedding of blood there is no forgiveness" (Heb. 9:22). With the Levitical sacrifices in mind, Peter tells his readers they are redeemed "with precious blood, as of a lamb unblemished and spotless, the blood of Christ" (1 Pet. 1:19). Likewise, Luke refers to believers as "the Church . . . which He purchased with His own blood" (Acts 20:28). Paul states that "we have redemption through His blood, the forgiveness of our trespasses" (Eph. 1:7). John tells us that Christ "released us from our sins by His blood" (Rev. 1:5). In referring to the blood, all of these biblical witnesses point to the fact that the atonement of Christ was an overtly physical act.

Notes

1. Kenneth Copeland, tape entitled, "How to Receive Revealed Knowledge," (n.d.).

2. Kenyon, *Identification*, p. 18; here again, one sees Kenyon's selective use of Scripture. Kenyon taught that the Gospels were written by men who understood Jesus only by Sense Knowledge. Through Revelation Knowledge, Paul alone of all the biblical writers understood the true nature of the atonement.

3. Kenyon, *Hidden Man*, p. 7; cf., Kenneth Hagin, *The Human Spirit*, vol. 2 (Tulsa: Faith Library, 1980), p. 12.

4. Kenneth Hagin, *Redeemed* (Tulsa: Faith Library, 1981), p. 27.

5. Ibid.

6. Kenyon, *Two Kinds of Knowledge*, p. 22; cf., *Hidden Man*, p. 74: "Your spirit is your real self."

7. Kenneth Hagin, *Having Faith in Your Faith* (Tulsa: Faith Library, 1980), p. 3.

8. Trine, *In Tune*, p. 16.

9. Ibid., p. 46.

10. Eddy, *Science and Health*, p. 468.

11. Kenyon, *The Bible in the Light of Our Redemption*, 2nd ed. (Lynnwood: Kenyon's Gospel Publishing Society, 1969), p. 28.

12. Ibid.; cf. Hagin, *Redeemed*, p. 28.

13. Kenyon, *The Bible*, p. 28.

14. Ibid.; cf., Hagin, *Redeemed*, p. 29.

15. Hagin, *Redeemed*, p. 29.

16. Kenneth Hagin, *Authority of the Believer* (Tulsa: Faith Library, 1967), p. 15.

17. Kenyon, *The Bible*, p. 43.

18. Kenyon, *Identification*, p. 16.

19. Kenyon, *Jesus the Healer*, p. 17; cf., Kenneth Hagin, *Seven Things You Should Know About Divine Healing* (Tulsa: Faith Library, 1981), pp. 13–15.

20. Kenyon, *Identification*, p. 15.

21. Kenyon, *What Happened*, p. 50; cf., Hagin, "Looking at the Unseen," *Word of Faith* (June, 1974), p. 2.

22. According to Kenyon, Jesus' cry of "It is finished" and subsequent physical death did not at all mean that redemption from sin was accomplished. All that the physical death accomplished was perfect obedience to the Father's will and fulfillment of the Abrahamic and Mosaic covenants (*What Happened*, p. 50).

23. Kenyon, *Hidden Man*, p. 47; italics added for emphasis.

24. Kenyon, *What Happened*, p. 47; cf., Hagin, "Christ Our Substitute," *Word of Faith* (March, 1975), pp. 1, 4. In his pamphlet entitled *The Precious Blood of Jesus* (Tulsa: Faith Library, 1984), Hagin appears to have an orthodox understanding of the blood atonement. It is interesting to note, however, that "spiritual death" and the "satanic nature" of man are not mentioned in this pamphlet. Moreover, his position in this one writing contradicts his numerous other statements denying the efficacy of Christ's death. In a letter dated April 23, 1986, Hagin wrote that "because Jesus was made sin with our sins He had to pay the penalty for sin. . . . This, as we know, cannot be referring to natural, physical death or else any sinner following his death could say he had paid the penalty for his sins."

25. Not all of the Faith teachers, however, hold to Kenyon's view of the spiritual death of Jesus. The most notable of these dissenters is the late Hobart E. Freeman, whose opposition to the doctrine is expressed in his book, *Did Jesus Die Spiritually?: Exposing the JDS Heresy* (Warsaw, Ind.: Faith Ministries & Publications [n.d.]).

26. Frederick K. C. Price, *Ever Increasing Faith Messenger* (June, 1980), 7.

27. Personal letter from Kenneth Copeland, Ft. Worth, Tex., March 12, 1979; italics added for emphasis.

28. Kenyon, *Identification*, p. 8.

29. Eddy, *Science and Health*, p. 330.

30. Mary Baker Eddy, *No and Yes* (Boston: Christian Science Publishing Society, [n.d.]), pp. 44–45.

31. Hagin, *The Name of Jesus*, p. 32.

32. Copeland, "What Happened from the Cross to the Throne" (tape).

33. Kenyon specifically rejects a vicarious interpretation of substitution: "He was our sin Substitute. Sin was not reckoned to Him. Sin was not set to His account. He became sin" (*What Happened*, p. 12).

34. Kenyon, *What Happened*, p. 64; cf., Hagin, "Made Alive," *Word of Faith* (April, 1982), p. 2.

35. "See you have to realize that He [Jesus] died; you have to realize that He went into the pit of hell as a mortal man made sin. But He didn't stay there, thank God. He was reborn in the pit of hell and resurrected" (Copeland, "What Happened").

36. Kenneth Copeland, "Jesus: Our Lord of Glory," *Believers' Voice of Victory* (April, 1982), p. 3.

37. Kenyon, *Identification*, pp. 6, 7; cf., Hagin, "The Resurrection: What It Gives Us," *Word of Faith* (April, 1977), p. 5.

38. Kenyon, *Identification*, p. 7.

39. Ibid., p. 52.

40. Kenyon, *Hidden Man*, 26.

41. Kenyon, "Incarnation," *Reality* (Dec., 1911), p. 49.

42. Kenneth Hagin, *Zoe: The God-Kind of Life* (Tulsa: Faith Library, 1982), p. 42.

43. Hagin, "Walking in the Light of Life," *Word of Faith* (Jan., 1978), 3.

44. Hagin, "The Virgin Birth," *Word of Faith* (Dec., 1977), p. 0.

45. Hagin, *Zoe*, p. 41.

46. Hagin, *The Name of Jesus*, p. 105.

47. Ibid., p. 66.

48. Kenneth Hagin, *The Key to Scriptural Healing* (Tulsa: Faith Library, 1977), p. 25.

49. Trine, *In Tune*, p. 21.

50. Ibid., p. 20.

51. Kenyon, *Two Kinds of Righteousness*, p. 41.

52. Kenyon, *Jesus the Healer*, p. 54.

53. Trine, *In Tune*, p. 46.

54. One prominent OT scholar states that "it is precisely the distinctive characteristic of Hebrew thought that it constantly sees the whole in the individual part. . . . For the body is not an object which we possess, but which stands outside our real being; it is not simply the natural basis and instrument to which we are assigned, but which does not belong to our essential self. It is the living form of that self, the necessary expression of our individual existence, in which the meaning of our life must find its realization" (Walter Eichrodt, *Theology of the Old Testament* [Philadelphia: Westminster, 1967], 2:148–49).

55. C. F. Keil and F. Delitzsch, *The Pentateuch*, vol. 1, *Commentary on the Old Testament* (Grand Rapids: Eerdmans, 1985), p. 79.

56. "The gnostic myth recounts . . . the fate of the soul. . . . The soul—or, more accurately in the language of gnosticism itself, man's true inner self, is a part, splinter, or spark of a heavenly figure of light, the original man. Before all time this figure was conquered by the demonic powers of darkness. . . . [who] tore the figure of light into shreds and divided it up. . . Man's true Self is differentiated not only from the body and its senses, but also from his soul. The anthropology of gnosticism is therefore trichotomous. It distinguishes body, soul, and self" (Rudolf Bultmann, *Primitive Christianity in its Historical Setting* [New York: World Pub., 1972], p. 163).

57. For a general discussion of the major views of the *imago Dei*, see Millard Erickson, *Christian Theology* (Grand Rapids: Baker, 1984), 2:498–517.

58. Emil Brunner, *The Christian Doctrine of Creation and Redemption*, vol. 2, *Dogmatics* (Philadelphia: Westminster, 1952), p. 58.

59. 2 Cor. 5:17 speaks of man's new relationship to God through Christ, not his ontological transformation into a divine being. "Man's existence is new in virtue of a new relation to God. . . . This new relation is bound up with Christ, through whom it has entered into and become history" (W. Foerster, "*ktizō*," *TDNT*, 3:1034).

60. The act of "putting off" and "putting on" refers to human participation in the process of Christ's renewal of human nature. Eph. 4:22–24 "sug-

gests neither a magical transformation, nor a mystic loss of personality, nor a cheap escape from captivity" (Markus Barth, *Ephesians* [2 vols.; Garden City, N.Y.: Doubleday, 1979], 2:472).

61. Erickson, *Christian Theology*, 2:822.

62. Herman Ridderbos, *Paul: An Outline of His Theology* (Grand Rapids: Eerdmans, 1975), p. 165.

63. Leon Morris, *The Cross in the New Testament* (Grand Rapids: Eerdmans, 1965), p. 221.

64. "Without blemish" (*amōmos*) "recalls the Jewish requirement that such an offering must be faultless" and "spotless" (*aspilos*) emphasizes "that in Christ's case the faultlessness must be understood in terms of sinlessness and holy consecration" (J. N. D. Kelly, *A Commentary on the Epistles of Peter and Jude* [Grand Rapids: Baker, 1981], pp. 74–75.

65. B. F. Westcott, *The Epistle to the Hebrews* (Grand Rapids: Eerdmans, 1980), p. 262.

66. For a summary of these usages of the Hebrew plural form, see *Gesenius' Hebrew Grammar*, E. Kautzsch, ed., A. E. Cowley, trans. (Oxford: Clarendon Press, 1910), pp. 396–401.

67. Another example of this usage is Ezk. 28:8–10, which describes the violence and certainty of the death of the king of Tyre: "you will die the *death* of those who are slain." Keil and Delitzsch state that the plural form for death used in both Isa. 53:9 and Ezk. 28:10 is an example of *pluralis exaggerativus*: "it is applied to a violent death, the very pain of which makes it like dying again and again" (*Commentary on the Old Testament*, vol. 7, *Isaiah*, p. 329).

68. Of the 362 uses of the Hebrew word for blood (*dam*) in the OT, 103 refer to sacrificial blood and 203 refer to violent physical death of some kind. Likewise, of the 98 uses of the Greek word for blood (*haima*) in the NT, 25 refer to violent physical death, 12 refer to animal sacrifice, and 37 refer to the physical death of Christ (Leon Morris, *The Apostolic Preaching of the Cross* [Grand Rapids: Eerdmans, 1980], pp. 112–23).

8 The Doctrine of Faith: Faith in God versus Faith in Faith

Did you ever stop to think about having faith in your own faith? Evidently God had faith in His faith, because He spoke words of faith and they came to pass. . . . In other words, *having faith in your words is having faith in your faith.* That's what you've got to learn to do to get things from God: *Have faith in your faith.*

—Kenneth Hagin,
Having Faith in Your Faith, pp. 4–5.

What you believe about faith tells me the kind of God in whom you believe. . . . You cannot escape it: The kind of God on whom you have risked everything comes shining through when you tell me what you believe about faith. If you believe in a God who answers prayer only according to the *amount* of faith a person has, you have to deal with my question: How much faith does it take? Does it take a pound? A gallon? An ounce? . . . Once more: What you believe about faith reveals the kind of God in whom you believe.

—Arnold Prater,
How Much Faith Does It Take?
(Nashville: Thomas Nelson, 1982), pp. 15–17.

If Arnold Prater's above thesis is correct, what a movement teaches about faith reveals the kind of God which that movement is attempting to serve (or have serve it). And since faith is the proud banner under which the Faith movement marches, we would have to agree with Kenneth Hagin that the god of the Faith movement must, indeed, "have faith in his own faith." But Hagin's statement begs the question. Why does Hagin's god need faith? How much and what kind of faith pleases him? And, ultimately, what kind of God is it that needs faith in his faith?

The Cultic Nature of the Doctrine of Faith

The Faith theology provides clear but unacceptable answers to these questions. The answers are objectionable because of the type of god that they reveal. Any god who has to "have faith in his own faith" is not the God and Father of our Lord Jesus Christ. He is really no god at all. He (it?) is the impersonal "force" of the metaphysical cults. This force is the slavish puppet of anybody who knows the "formulas" and "spiritual laws" of how to control him. These formulas and laws are called "faith" in the Faith movement, but in reality, they are nothing more than recycled New Thought metaphysics.

Faith as a Formula

Several of its critics have characterized the conception of faith in the Faith movement as a "formula." Words such as "formula," "law," "steps," and "principles" do appear quite often in Faith literature, which lends credence to this characterization. For example, Hagin claims that Jesus appeared to him in a vision and said, "If anybody, anywhere, will take these four steps or put these four principles into operation, he will always receive whatever he wants from Me or God the Father." With these "steps," Jesus said to Hagin, "You can write your own ticket with God." The four steps that Jesus gave to Hagin were: "(1) Say it, (2) Do it, (3) Receive it, and (4) Tell it."[1]

The formulaic nature of Faith theology is based upon its world view. The world was created by God speaking the Word and calling into being everything that is. The Faith theology claims that "God is a faith God" because he had faith that his words would bring forth creation *ex nihilo* ("out of nothing"). As a result, the Word is woven into the very fabric of creation. Indeed, the Word is what holds the creation together and maintains its operation. Kenyon teaches that "faith-filled words brought the universe into being, and faith-filled words are ruling that universe today."[2] Following Kenyon's lead, Hagin claims that through the discovery of the "spiritual laws" established by God to run the universe, the believer can put these laws to "work" for his own use.

> In the spiritual realm God has set into motion certain laws, just as He set laws in the natural realm. Those laws in the natural realm work, don't they? Just as you get into contact with those natural laws or put them into practice they work for you. Over in the spiritual realm the same thing is true. I have come to the conclusion that the law of faith is spiritual law, that God has put this law into motion, and that as surely as you come into contact with it it will work for you.[3]

The "law of faith" is to the spiritual realm what the law of gravity is to the physical realm. Whenever the law is set into motion, it works.

Thus, anybody, Christian or non-Christian, can plug into this universal law of faith and get "results." "It used to bother me," explains Hagin, "when I'd see unsaved people getting results. Then it dawned on me what the sinners were doing: they were cooperating with the law of God—the law of faith."[4] Since the law of faith is impersonal, just like the law of gravity, it works regardless of who the person is or where he or she stands with Christ. To get these "results," the Faith teachers often recommend "little formulas" to follow for whatever a person needs from God. Fred Price, for instance, teaches that Rom. 10:10 is a "formula" and that anybody "could put anything in there [the formula] you want—healing, your needs met, new job, car, home, whatever you need."[5] Formulas such as these will, for anybody who uses them, place the resources of the world, heaven, and the universe at one's disposal.

The Faith theology's view of spiritual laws and formulas can only be understood in the light of the doctrine of God in the metaphysical cults. The god in which the metaphysical cults believe is not a *personal* god who *sovereignly* governs the universe. Their god is an *impersonal* force: "the Infinite Power," "the Spirit of Infinite Life," and "the Infinite Intelligence." This infinite, but impersonal, force rules the universe indirectly through "immutable laws" rather than directly through his presence and wisdom. Historically, this concept of God could be categorized as a spiritualized form of "deism" so prevalent in the late nineteenth century.[6] Concerning the existence of spiritual laws governing the universe, New Thought advocate Trine writes:

> This Infinite Power is creating, working, ruling through the agency of great immutable laws and forces that run through all the universe, that surround us on every side. Every act of our every day lives is governed by these same great laws and forces. . . . In a sense there is nothing in all the great universe but law.[7]

Another New Thought cult, the Unity School of Christianity, also teaches a deistic view of the universe. One of its early founders and prophetesses, H. Emile Cady, states:

> The mental and spiritual world or realms are governed by laws that are just as real and unfailing as the laws that govern the natural world. Certain conditions of mind that are so connected with certain results that the two are inseparable. If we have the one, we must have the other, as surely as night follows the day.[8]

Cady claims that there is a cause-and-effect relationship between these spiritual laws and the human mind. Every thought of the human mind causes an effect in the universe through the operation of spiritual laws. Man does not, therefore, have to deal with a *personal* God, but rather, with *impersonal* laws that can be manipulated by anyone, regardless of their relational standing with God through Christ.

When Kenyon refers to "the great spiritual laws that govern the unseen forces of life,"[9] he is espousing the metaphysical version of deism: a universe governed by spiritual laws, instead of by God. The Faith theology in principle teaches a personal God. But in practice the Faith god differs little from the god of the metaphysical cults. Both must do the bidding of the spiritual laws that govern the universe. Neither is free to disregard these laws. It is precisely because of this universal system of spiritual laws that the numerous formulas of the Faith theology (supposedly) work. Just like the formulas of the metaphysical cults, the Faith-formulas operate the spiritual laws, and the spiritual laws control the Faith god. That this god is controlled by the spiritual laws of Faith theology is evident from the fact that even unbelievers unknowingly obtain his blessings by using them. Neither the Faith god nor "the Infinite Power" of metaphysics are at liberty to refuse the bidding of these formulas and laws.

Faith as Positive Confession

Positive confession is, undoubtedly, the most distinctive doctrine of the Faith movement, and it originated with Kenyon, not Hagin. The most popular saying about the nature of faith, though attributed to Hagin, actually was coined by Kenyon: "What I confess, I possess."[10] Confession is commonly defined in Faith theology as "affirming something we believe . . . testifying to something we know . . . witnessing for a truth that we have embraced."[11] The secret to confession is to know the nature and extent of the perfect redemption in Christ, to know one's "identity" and "rights" in Christ, and to confess verbally the provision of Christ in every need and problem of life. The working presupposition of positive confession is that one's mental attitude determines what one believes and confesses, and what one believes and confesses determines what one gets from God. As Hagin puts it, "What we believe is a result of our thinking. If we think wrong we will believe wrong. . . . If we believe wrong, our confession will be wrong. In other words, what we say will be wrong and it will all hinge on our thinking."[12] Positive mental attitude (PMA) is the fount from which all positive confession flows.

The concept of positive confession fits well into the world view of Faith theology. Positive confession is the spiritual shove that sets into motion the "spiritual laws" that govern the universe. "A spiritual law that few of us realize," states Kenyon, "is that our confession rules us."[13] A "right" or "wrong" confession is the determining factor in one's harmony with these universal spiritual laws. Confession is the catalyst that evokes their blessings, or their curses. A person will possess only to the extent he has faith to confess these spiritual laws: "Sooner or later we become what we confess."[14] A believer will only grow in faith to the degree which he practices positive confession.[15]

Kenyon's emphasis upon positive mental attitude (PMA) and positive confession as the basis of "faith" also finds its roots in the metaphysical cults. Since all of these cults teach that reality is the sum total of whatever man thinks it to be, man possesses the innate ability to shape and reshape reality through the powers of his mind and his words. As the founder of the Unity School of Christianity, Charles Fillmore, puts it, "What we think, we usually express in words; and our words bring about in our life and affairs whatever we put into them."[16] Like Kenyon and Hagin, Ralph Waldo Trine teaches that a man's state of mind—what he believes and con-fesses—will eventually produce a corresponding reality, whether good or bad.

> There is in connection with thought a law that we are now beginning to understand that may be termed "the drawing power of the mind." We are continually attracting to us, from both the seen and the unseen sides of life, influences and conditions corresponding with the type of thought we most habitually allow to take form in our minds, and that we consequently most habitually live with.[17]

Trine similarly defines faith as "the drawing power of the mind," which confesses into physical existence the resources of the spiri-tual realm.

> Faith is nothing more nor less than the operation of the *thought forces* in the form of an earnest desire, coupled with expectation as to its fulfillment. And in the degree that faith, the earnest desire thus sent out, is continually held to and watered by firm expectation, in just that degree does it either draw to itself, or does it change from the unseen into the visible, from the spiritual into the material, that for which it is sent.[18]

Like Kenyon, Trine teaches his followers to expect God's fulfillment of the confession *before* there is any visible evidence in the material realm. Indeed, the highest form of faith in the metaphysical cults is to believe against all contradictory "Sense Knowledge." Such belief changes the unseen into the seen. The power to transform the unseen into the seen characterizes both the metaphysical cults and the Faith movement.

The Faith teachers, of course, would deny that they teach "the drawing power of the mind." They would say that faith comes from the "recreated human spirit," not the human mind. They would also say that their confession is based on the Word of God. Both of these objections do not alleviate the charge of cultism. In the first place, the cults refer to the spirit as often as they do the mind; they are basically synonyms in metaphysical literature. Second, like the Faith movement, these cults also use the Word of God as the basis of their PMA and positive confession. Third, both the cults and the Faith theology base their confession on a deistic system of spiritual laws that work for anybody, independently of the specific will of God.

In a universe ruled by spiritual law, neutrality is impossible. A negative confession can effect as much evil as a positive confession can effect good. In the Faith theology, "what you say is what you get," whether good or bad. Kenyon writes,

> It is what we confess with our lips that really dominates our inner being. . . . [People] confess their fear and they become more fearful. They confess their fear of disease and the disease grows under the confession. They confess their lack and they build up a sense of lack which gains the supremacy in their lives.[19]

Unbelief is not the mere absence of belief. Unbelief is a destructive belief that inevitably expresses itself in a negative confession. This negative confession then produces the particular form of destruction in which one believes.

This, too, is a cultic belief. The association between the metaphysical cults and the Faith movement regarding PMA and positive confession becomes evident from the fact that both groups affirm the power of a *negative* as well as a *positive* mindset. The Faith theology teaches that *fear* as well as *faith* creates reality. So do the metaphysical cults. Like Kenyon, Trine believed that "the moment we fear anything we open the door for the entrance of the actualization of the very thing we fear."[20] The issue, then, is not, as the Faith teachers claim, the power of the Word of God. If that were the case, *fear* would not be exalted as the flipside of the same coin with *faith*. The issue is the power of thought, naked thought, whether good or bad, to draw unseen, *impersonal* forces into play. In Faith theology, a *personal* loving God does not determine what comes into the believer's life. PMA and positive confession do. The Faith god can neither withhold the good, nor inhibit the bad from happening to those whose confessions invoke his spiritual laws. This is not the sovereign, personal God of the New Testament. This is the god of metaphysics.

Faith as Creative Power

Based on his view that the universe is "ruled by words," Kenyon advocates "creative faith" by which the believer can use God's formula for creation—"Let there be"—to create his own reality.[21] Charles Capps expands Kenyon's concept of "creative faith" to the point that man, not God, is the only creator left in the universe. Capps claims to have received this revelation of man's role as creator from God himself:

> In August of 1973, the Word of the Lord came unto me saying, "If men would believe me, long prayers are not necessary. Just speaking the Word will bring what you desire. My Creative power is given to man in Word form. I have ceased for a time from my creative work and have given man the book of MY CREATIVE POWER. That power is STILL IN MY WORD."[22]

Through "creative faith," man becomes not only a god. He becomes a creator.

As with the Faith theology, the metaphysical cults also teach that through the power of spoken words, man has "creative power" just like God. Trine writes, "The 'power of the word' is a literal, scientific fact. Through the operation of our thought forces we have creative power."[23] Unity leader H. Emile Cady taught a concept much like the Faith teachers' "creative faith":

> God creates. Because man was created or brought into the visible universe in the same image and likeness of God, he spiritually has like powers like with God: he has the power of creating, of bringing into visible form that which before did not exist.[24]

Other Unity leaders claim that "if God created by the power of his word it is fair to assume that He gave like powers to man, who has in miniature all the abilities of his Father."[25] Thus, the metaphysical cults teach man is a "miniature" god whose words possess the power to create his own little world. This notion is alive and well in the Faith movement.

The Force of Faith

As the result of his book *The Force of Faith*, Kenneth Copeland has made popular the term "faith-force." Copeland teaches that "in the reborn human spirit there are four major forces": the force of faith, the force of righteousness, the force of wisdom, and the force of love.[26] Although the basic formula that confession brings possession is the same, the unique aspect of faith-force is its definition that

> Faith is a power force. It is a conductive force. It will move things. Faith will change things. Faith will change the human body. It will change the human heart. Faith will change circumstances. . . . The force of faith is released by words. Faith-filled words put the law of the Spirit of life into operation.[27]

Copeland teaches that since "God is a faith being" and since man is "a faith being," man has the faith "to operate in the same way" that God operates.[28] As a believer grows in his faith-force, he possesses more power and can move bigger obstacles in the spirit realm.[29] With faith and patience, "the power twins," a believer can receive whatever his faith-force is powerful enough and patient enough to believe for.

The God Kind of Faith

Another popular Kenyonism in the Faith movement is "the God Kind of Faith." Rather than the customary translation of Mk. 11:22, "Have faith *in* God," Kenyon proposes the translation "Have the faith *of* God." From this translation, Kenyon deduces that "We have God's faith produced in us by His living word, by His nature that is imparted to us."[30] Hagin develops Kenyon's interpretation into the concept of "the God Kind of Faith." According to Hagin, "the kind of faith that spoke the universe into existence is dealt to our hearts."[31] The God Kind of Faith is, in reality, a combination of the principles of positive confession and creative faith. It is to be distinguished from the "man kind of faith," which is dependent upon the physical senses. The God Kind of Faith is the faith that prays once, speaks the word into existence, and then holds to the confession of the word despite all contradictory evidence of the physical senses. To pray more than once is to destroy one's confession.

Faith in the Name

In his book *The Wonderful Name of Jesus*, Kenyon states that God has given the church his "power of attorney" in the name of

Jesus: "it is legally ours."[32] Before he ascended, Jesus left his name
to the church. When the believer uses Jesus' name, God *must* respond favorably, because all authority is in that name. Kenyon
teaches that "when we pray in Jesus' Name we are taking the place
of the absent Christ; we are using his name, his authority, to carry
out his will on earth."[33] Through its use of the name of Jesus, the
church takes his place on the earth. Whatever the church prays in
faith using the name, God has to answer. In his book *The Name of
Jesus*, Hagin claims that "I have not prayed one prayer in 45 years . . .
without getting an answer. I always got an answer—and the answer
was always yes."[34] The name of Jesus is the believer's carte blanche
with God. It confers unconditional authority upon the believer.

Faith and the Authority of the Believer

Because all authority is in the name of the Jesus and that name
is now the "legal" possession of the church, believers have all the
authority of Jesus. According to the Faith theology, "when Christ
ascended, he transferred his authority to the church."[35] Christ can
no longer work on earth apart from the church.[36] If the church fails
to exercise its authority in a particular situation, God's hands are tied
and nothing more can be done.

Biblical Analysis of the Doctrine of Faith

Although there is much that is praiseworthy about its emphasis
on faith, the Faith theology ultimately advocates faith in a god other
than the God of the Bible. That the Faith god is the god of metaphysics becomes evident from its view that spiritual laws rule the universe, not God. This Faith cosmology (view of the universe) is a
spiritualized form of deism. It destroys either the *sovereignty* of God
or the *personality* of God.

Is God a Sovereign or a Subject?

If, for instance, the Faith cosmology teaches that God *must*
obey these spiritual laws and cannot do otherwise, it has destroyed
his *sovereignty*, his right of self-determination and self-rule in the
universe. The Bible clearly teaches the absolute sovereignty of God's
will. "Our God is in the heavens; He does whatever he pleases" (Ps.
115:3). No man can force God's hand with formulas, and there are no
spiritual laws apart from his will (e.g., Dan. 4:34–35). In the universe,

God "works all things after the counsel of His will" (Eph. 1:11), not according to the formulas of man's will. God's reign in the universe is a classic example of autocracy: a government by a single person having unlimited power. God is a benevolent despot, it is true, but he is a despot nonetheless. None can force his hand.

Is God a Person or a Principle?

If, on the other hand, the Faith teachers accept God's *sovereignty*, but believe that his mind and will are indistinguishable from his spiritual laws, they have destroyed his *personality*: his self-consciousness, his self-existence, and self-will, all of the attributes that make God a person. The Faith conception of God's personality fails to acknowledge that God could have a will apart from the so-called spiritual laws that govern his universe. In describing faith as a "force" with which the believer can "move things," the Faith theology depersonalizes God. It renders him an impersonal force that must do man's bidding because it is capable of doing nothing else. The "Force of Faith" is, in reality, "Faith in the Force." Just as Luke Skywalker in the *Star Wars* trilogy learns how to manipulate "the good side of the Force" with his mind-control, so also the Faith theology teaches how to manipulate the Faith god with positive confession. When it comes to manipulating deities, however, one must remember that there is a "dark side of the Force" as well. "Faith in the Force" made for an entertaining movie, but its view of god was sub-biblical and sub-Christian.

Taking Jesus' Name in Vain?

The Faith theology's teaching on Jesus' name violates one of God's primary commandments. In the Decalogue, Yahweh told the people of Israel, "You shall not take the name of the Lord your God in vain, for the Lord will not leave him unpunished who takes his name in vain" (Ex. 20:7; cf., Lev. 19:12; Deut. 5:11). The intent of the third commandment is far broader than a mere prohibition of cursing or profanity; it also prohibits and threatens to punish any attempt to use the divine name to manipulate or control Yahweh. In Canaanite and Egyptian mythology, to discover a god's secret name is to control the god. The magical arts of the diviners and sorcerers consisted of constant muttering of the divine names of their gods.[37] The diviner-magician usually had selfish goals in mind and had little regard for the will of the deity.[38] After the return from captivity, so great in Israel was the fear of profaning the name of Yahweh that the Jews ceased to use it in conversation. According to Jewish scholar Ephraim Urbach, "the discontinuance of the enunciation of the Name was intended to prevent the blurring of the distance between God and man and the use of the Name for magical purposes."[39]

How this Jewish reverence differs from the way Faith teachers use the divine name! They imply that God will answer any egocentric prayer a believer prays if it is accompanied by Jesus' name. The Faith theology's teaching on Jesus' name is dangerously close to the beliefs and practices of the diviner-magicians. Jesus did, indeed, promise his disciples that "if you ask Me anything in My name, I will do it" (Jn. 14:14). But his promise was not unqualified. It requires believers to abide in him and allow his words to abide in them (Jn. 15:7). It requires them to keep his commandments (1 Jn. 3:22). It requires them to pray according to his will (1 Jn. 5:14, 15). The motives and objects for which one prays are vitally important: "You ask and do not receive, because you ask with wrong motives, so that you may spend it on your pleasures" (Jas. 4:3). Believers who use the name of Jesus for their lusts should expect nothing from God. Those who use his name to manipulate God should heed the warning of the third commandment. When someone is able to get results from his "faith" for selfish (or even immoral) purposes, it is evidence that something other than God is answering his prayers. The Bible teaches that God wants his power to control us; he wants our wills to be subject to his will. Any attempt to reverse this arrangement, to attempt to control or manipulate supernatural power, thereby subjecting God's will to ours, is magic or witchcraft.

Is Man a Creature or a Creator?

There is a saying in theology that goes something like this: "The denigration of God leads to the exaltation of man." Nowhere is there a better example of the denigration of God than in the idea that man has "creative powers" by speaking the word of faith. Besides being cultic in origin, the concept of creative faith denigrates the entire Trinity: the Father's exclusive role as the *source* of creation (Gen. 1:1; Neh. 9:5, 6; Ps. 90:2; Isa. 44:24; Jer. 32:17); the Son's exclusive role as the *agent* of Creation (Jn. 1:3; Col. 1:16; Heb. 1:2); and the Spirit's exclusive role as *executor* of creation (Gen. 1:2; Job

26:13; 33:4; Ps. 104:30; Isa. 40:12–13). The creation is *from* the Father, *through* the Son, and *by* the Holy Spirit. Man is a creature and no creature in the Bible is ever accorded creative powers: no man, no angel, no devil, no animal. The closest that the Bible comes to investing man with creative powers is God's command to be fruitful and multiply. But if procreation constitutes creative powers then animals are creators, too. Besides, the issue is creation *ex nihilo* ("out of nothing"), not procreation. Creation *ex nihilo* is entirely the prerogative of God.

God's Word and God's Will

The Faith theology badly distorts the relationship between God and his Word. The universe is held together by God himself, not by spiritual laws. The Bible clearly teaches that Christ "upholds all things by the word of His power" (Heb. 1:3) and "in Him [in His very person] all things hold together" (Col. 1:17). God did not need faith to create the world, and he does not need faith to hold the world together. God's Word has no power apart from God himself: his will, his sovereignty, his holiness, and his love. His Word has all power because God has all power. Man can, indeed, appropriate God's power by believing his Word, but the power is from God, not from positive confession. Man's confession of the Word has power if, and only if, the sovereign God wills to empower the confession. The Word of God is subject to the will of God: it is not an independent force to which God must dance. God is faithful to his Word, but he is not enslaved to it.

Man-Centered Faith

The Faith teacher's concept of the "God-kind of faith" illustrates well the man-centered nature of the Faith theology. This concept is based on their erroneous translation of Mk. 11:22 as a subjective genitive: "Have the faith *of* God." One prominent NT scholar has written that such a translation "is surely a monstrosity of exegesis."[40] In the NT, *pistis* (faith) is frequently followed by a genitive construction, and is always translated as an objective genitive: "Have faith *in* God."[41] Jesus was not conferring godhood upon men who have faith. He was exhorting men to have faith *in* God, that is, in his person, his character, and his saving deeds. This is yet another example of the disturbing tendency of Faith theology to

144 A DIFFERENT GOSPEL

reduce faith to an abstract human concept, such as PMA or positive confession, thereby divorcing it from God. God is both the subject and object of faith, both its source and its goal.

Charismatic Humanism

This anthropocentric focus is the basis of Charles Farah's charge that the Faith theology constitutes "charismatic humanism." The humanistic nature of the Faith god is revealed in Hagin's phrase, "having faith in your faith." A man whose faith is in his own faith is a man whose faith is in himself: it is faith in self, not in God. Biblical faith is always *theocentric* (God-centered) rather than *anthropocentric* (man-centered). Although this phrase "charismatic humanism" may appear to be a contradiction in terms, its truth-value lies in its expression of the man-centered supernaturalism of PMA and positive confession. PMA and positive confession are humanistic in the sense that they confer upon man the unrestrained power to meet his own self-defined "needs." A man's faith is placed in his own faith: the optimism of his thinking and the positiveness of his confession. The man who is positive enough can manipulate the spiritual laws that control God. Thus, just as in humanism, man, not God, is in the driver's seat.

Notes

1. Hagin, *How to Write Your Own Ticket with God*, pp. 5, 20, 21, 32.
2. Kenyon, *Two Kinds of Faith*, p. 20.
3. Hagin, "The Law of Faith," *Word of Faith* (Nov., 1974), p. 2; cf., "The Secret of Faith," *Word of Faith* (March, 1968), p. 2.
4. Hagin, *Having Faith in Your Faith*, pp. 3–4.
5. Frederick K. C. Price, *How Faith Works* (Tulsa: Harrison, 1976), pp. 110, 111; cf., Hagin, *Four Steps to Answered Prayer* (Tulsa: Faith Library, 1980), p. 7.
6. "Deism" is a system of natural theology first developed in England in the seventeenth and eighteenth centuries. There were many varieties of deism, but the later use of the term "restricts the meaning to belief in a God or first cause, who created the world and instituted immutable, universal laws that preclude any alteration" (M. H. McDonald, "Deism," *Evangelical Dictionary of Theology*, p. 304). Thus, deism teaches that the universe is ruled by natural law rather than divine providence. Whereas deism proper refers only to the *physical* laws governing the universe, the metaphysical cults (and Kenyon) maintain that there are *spiritual* laws as well.
7. Trine, *In Tune*, pp. 15, 16.

8. H. E. Cady, *Lessons in Truth* (Lee's Summit, Mo.: Unity, 1955), pp. 64, 65.

9. Kenyon, *Hidden Man*, p. 35.

10. Kenyon, *Hidden Man*, p. 98; Cf., Kenneth Hagin, *Bible Faith Study Course* (Tulsa: Faith Library, 1980), p. 92; Charles Capps, *Releasing the Ability of God through Prayer* (Tulsa: Harrison, 1973), p. 67.

11. Kenneth Hagin, *New Thresholds of Faith* (Tulsa: Faith Library, 1980), p. 40.

12. Hagin, *Right and Wrong Thinking*, p. 3.

13. Kenyon, *Two Kinds of Faith*, p. 67. This same exact statement appears undocumented in Kenneth Hagin's *In Him* (Tulsa: Faith Library, 1975), p. 1.

14. Kenyon, Ibid., pp. 65, 66.

15. Kenyon teaches that "you rise or fall to the level of your confession." *Hidden Man*, p. 147. Cf., Hagin, "Words," *Word of Faith* (April, 1979), pp. 4, 5; "You never realize beyond your words. . . . You will never realize beyond that which you say. . . . Faith never grows beyond our words."

16. Charles Fillmore, *Christian Healing* (Unity Village, Mo.: Unity, [n.d.]), p. 16.

17. R. W. Trine, *The Winning of the Best* (Indianapolis: Bobbs-Merrill Co., 1917), p. 64.

18. Trine, *In Tune*, pp. 32, 33.

19. Kenyon, *Two Kinds of Faith*, p. 72; cf., Hagin, *Right and Wrong Thinking*, p. 24.

20. Trine, *In Tune*, p. 93.

21. Kenyon, *Two Kinds of Faith*, p. 20.

22. Capps, *God's Creative Power Will Work for You* (Tulsa: Harrison, 1976), pp. 5, 6; cf., Capps, *The Tongue: A Creative Force* (Tulsa: Harrison, 1976), pp. 8–14.

23. Trine, *In Tune*, pp. 25, 26.

24. H. E. Cady, *How I Used Truth* (Lee's Summit, Mo.: Unity, 1957), p. 64.

25. Charles and Cora Fillmore, *Teach Us to Pray* (Kansas City, Mo.: Unity, 1944), p. 73.

26. Kenneth Copeland, *The Force of Faith* (Ft. Worth: Kenneth Copeland Pub., 1983), p. 6.

27. Ibid., p. 10, 16.

28. Ibid., p. 14.

29. Fred Price, *Faith, Foolishness, or Presumption?* (Tulsa: Harrison, 1979), pp. 46–47.

30. Kenyon, *Two Kinds of Faith*, p. 103; here Kenyon accepts both translations of Mk. 11:22. This is not so in the modern Faith movement (see Price, *How Faith Works*, p. 95).

31. Hagin, *New Thresholds*, p. 74.

32. Kenyon, *The Wonderful Name of Jesus*, p. 26.

33. Ibid., 20.

34. Hagin, *The Name of Jesus*, p. 16.

35. Hagin, *Authority*, p. 11.

36. Ibid., pp. 27, 47.

37. Ephraim E. Urbach, *The Sages* (Cambridge, Mass.: Harvard Univ. Press, 1987), p. 124.

38. G. Herbert Livingston, *The Pentateuch in its Cultural Environment* (Grand Rapids: Baker, 1974), p. 170.

39. Urbach, *The Sages*, p. 134.

40. C. E. B. Cranfield, *The Gospel According to St. Mark* (Cambridge: Cambridge Univ. Press, 1983), p. 361.

41. Cf., Acts 3:16; Rom. 3:22, 26; Gal. 2:16 (twice); 3:22; Eph. 3:12; Phil. 1:29; 3:9; Col. 2:12; 2 Thess. 2:13; Rev. 14:12.

9 The Doctrine of Healing: Sickness, Symptoms, and Satan

I know that I am healed because He said that I am healed and it makes no difference what the symptoms may be in the body. I laugh at them, and in the Name of Jesus I command the author of the disease [Satan] to leave my body.

—E. W. Kenyon,
The Hidden Man, p. 99.

For the most part we need encouragement to believe that God *does* heal people. But after we do summon up the courage to launch out and start praying we may get discouraged when we realize that people are not always healed through our prayers. This is especially puzzling to those who have been exposed to a very simplistic approach to healing: "All you have to do is claim your healing."

—Francis MacNutt,
Healing
(Notre Dame: Ave Maria Press, 1974), p. 248.

Healing is a way of life for those in the Faith movement. Though difficult to document because of the countless thousands who claim healing "by faith" (Revelation Knowledge) rather than fact (Sense Knowledge), it must be admitted that there are probably more *claimed* healings in the Faith movement than any period of the church since the apostles. Whether or not all these healings really happen is irrelevant to members of the movement. The point is that those claiming these healings believe that they have been healed, and nothing, not even pain and continued symptoms of illness, will convince them otherwise.

What is the source of this dogmatic insistence that *all* can be healed *any* and *every* time they exercise faith? Those in the Faith movement would answer that the Bible is the source of their beliefs about healing. The Bible is *a* source of these beliefs, but it is not *the* source. Another possible source is the post–World War II Healing Revival, which unquestionably influenced Kenneth Hagin and the other Faith teachers. The Pentecostal Healing Revival produced more than its share of radical doctrines of faith-healing, many of which required believers to reject medical science. Nevertheless, there are elements of the Faith doctrine of healing that have no precedent in the Healing Revival. These elements do, however, have strong precedent in the metaphysical cults.

Do miracles prove truth? Before turning to this contention, we need to restate two very important points about healing and miracles. The first point is this: *Healing and miracles do not prove the truth of one's interpretation of the Bible.* American pragmatism dictates that whatever produces results is true. But surely pragmatic results cannot be the sole measure of truth. If healing and miracles are the standard by which a doctrine of healing is established as truth, then one would have to say that the doctrine and practices of the metaphysical cults are also truth.[1] An impressive number of healings occur in Christian Science, New Thought, Unity, Religious Science, etc. The second point is this: *Healing and miracles come from more than one source.* Not all healings are divine healings, and not all miracles are from God. The metaphysical cults, for example, use positive mental attitude and positive confession to heal disease. The occult openly invokes satanic power in its practice of healing. Even though the cults and the occult can claim many healings, most Christians would accept neither the doctrine nor the practices of such groups. Thus, if it can be shown the doctrine of healing practiced by the Faith movement is cultic in origin, then it might give charismatics occasion to question the source of their apparent "success" in the area of healing.

The Cultic Nature of the Doctrine of Healing

The doctrine of healing in the Faith theology is based on its understanding of the atonement of Christ. In the Faith theology, the purpose of the atonement is as much to provide healing of disease as it is the forgiveness of sin.[2] On the basis of passages such as Isa. 53:5, Mt. 8:17, and 1 Pet. 2:24—the typical texts appealed to by those Pentecostals who believe healing is in the atonement—Kenyon and Hagin insist that Christ has provided complete physical healing from all sickness. But unlike classical Pentecostals, the Faith teachers believe that diseases are healed by Christ's *spiritual* atonement in hell, not his physical death on the cross.

Disease Is Spiritual, Not Physical

Christ had to suffer spiritually in hell to provide healing because all diseases are but a physical effect of a spiritual cause. Kenyon taught that "sickness is a spiritual condition manifested in the physical body."[3] Ultimately, all disease comes from the spiritual realm of Satan.[4] Following his mentor's lead, Hagin states that because all disease is spiritual in origin, God's method of healing must be purely spiritual as well.[5] Hence, the Faith teachers conclude that the atonement had to be a spiritual act, not physical.

The idea that all disease is a physical manifestation of something spiritual in origin comes directly from the metaphysical cults. The founding father of New Thought, P. P. Quimby, also defines sickness completely in terms of spiritual causes.[6] The spiritual causality of disease, indeed, of all life, is a central dogma of metaphysics. Kenyon's New Thought classmate at Emerson, Ralph Waldo Trine, writes that "everything in the visible, material world has its origins in the unseen, the spiritual, the thought world."[7] Trine explains further:

> Everything exists in the unseen before it is manifested or realized in the seen, and in this sense it is true that the unseen things are the real, while the things that are seen are the unreal. The unseen things are the *cause*; the seen things are the *effect*.[8]

Several startling parallels can be drawn between the Faith theology and metaphysics. Both systems of thought deny that disease has any physical or organic causes, teaching instead that disease is entirely the physical effect of a spiritual cause. Both systems teach that since disease is spiritual, the highest form of healing must be spiritual as well. This exclusively spiritual understanding of disease, on which Kenyon's doctrine of healing rests, is probably derived from his background in metaphysics.

A Sick Believer Is Abnormal

In the Faith theology, a true believer should never be sick. By confessing his faith in the healing redemption of Christ, the Christian can and should know perfect health. Thus, Kenyon concludes that "it is wrong for us to have sickness and disease in our bodies when God laid those diseases on Jesus."[9] Since it is always God's will to heal, the believer who is not healed is obviously out of the will of

God. "Sickness does not belong to the body of Christ," says Kenyon. "It is not normal or natural."[10]

The metaphysical cults also teach that sickness is an abnormal condition for which the believer is directly responsible through his violation of spiritual law. Trine comments,

> Full, rich and abounding health is the normal and the natural condition of life. Anything else is an abnormal condition, and abnormal conditions as a rule come through perversions. God never created sickness, suffering and disease; they are man's own creations. They come through his violating the laws under which he lives.[11]

The Faith teachers assert the metaphysical dogma that sickness is always caused by unbelief and sin. They claim that God has done all that he is going to do to provide healing and it is up to the believer to appropriate the perfect healing that is in the atonement. The believer who fails to do so has only himself to blame. He has failed not only himself, but also God.

Negative Confession Produces Sickness

One sure way a believer can become sick is by uttering a negative confession. A "negative confession" is any mental or verbal acknowledgment of the presence of disease in one's body. The verbal acknowledgment of a disease gives Satan the "right" to inflict it.[12] To talk about illness is tantamount to devil worship and is expressly forbidden by Kenyon.[13] When a believer worries or complains about an illness, he has forfeited his "right" to the perfect healing redemption of Christ. In the Faith movement, the truly mature rarely even admit they are ill, much less talk about it.

Such paranoia about the verbal acknowledgment of disease also characterizes the metaphysical cults. The admission of disease in public is simply not tolerated in these cults, for reasons that should be obvious. Among those who believe that negative attitudes and confessions have the power to inflict disease, conversation about one's illness must be severely restricted. Negative confessions, Trine warns, have the power to "infect" others with disease.[14] The Faith teachers frequently issue similar warnings to their audiences. In more radical Faith churches, a Christian is not even allowed to speak of sickness in order to request prayer. Those who do are often rebuked and told that they need to "confess the Word" and "give thanks for their healing."

Believers Should Deny Symptoms

In the Faith movement, the believer is instructed that healing is an accomplished "faith fact," but that it is not instantaneously manifested as a physical fact in the believer's body. During the interlude between the confession of healing and its manifestation, the believer might encounter "symptoms" of a disease. These symptoms are not the disease itself. The disease itself was laid on Jesus when he died spiritually. Any symptoms of illness are spiritual decoys with which Satan is attempting to trick the believer into making a negative confession, thereby forfeiting his healing.[15] Hence, Kenyon advises believers to hold to their confession of healing no matter what they, or anybody else, perceive their symptoms to be. He writes,

> Confession always goes ahead of healing. *Don't watch symptoms—* watch the Word; and be sure that your confession is bold and vigorous. *Don't listen to people.* Act on the Word. Be a doer of the Word. It is God speaking. You are healed. The Word says you are. *Don't listen to the senses.* Give the Word its place. God cannot lie.[16]

Hagin also teaches that "real faith in God—heart faith—believes the Word of God regardless of what the physical evidences may be" and that "a person seeking healing should look to God's Word, not to his symptoms."[17] The symptoms should be denied because they are not real.

Believers Should Endure Pain

The pain produced by these delusive symptoms can, however, be frighteningly real. According to Kenyon, "Faith declares that you are healed while the pain is wracking your body."[18] Hagin states that it's easy to believe God for healing when there is no pain; the real test of faith comes when one must deny pain to make a positive confession.[19] One of Hagin's disciples, Fred Price, describes an instance in which following his mentor's teaching incurred him a considerable amount of pain.

> I have been attacked to such a degree, and been in such pain that I almost wished that I had never heard about faith and healing. Sometimes I would hurt so badly until I wanted to go to the doctors and let them give me a shot, and knock me out for six weeks, and that would have been easy. But I knew better. . . . I refused to give into it.[20]

From this story, one may deduce that the real issue of healing is one's ability to endure physical pain. Price states that he "knew better" than to take the "easy" solution of seeking medical help. In Price's mind, to have done so would have been a sign of hypocrisy and a repudiation of his own teaching.

The notion that a believer should never acknowledge or talk about symptoms of illness is also cultic. Because Christian Science rejects the reality of the physical body altogether, Mary Baker Eddy likewise denied physical symptoms. She considered them an "illusion" and "error" that can be overcome by the power of thought. Eddy advises,

> When the illusion of sickness or sin tempts you, cling steadfastly to God and His idea. Allow nothing but His likeness to abide in your thought. Let neither fear nor doubt overshadow your clear sense and calm trust. . . . [21]

Eddy contends that "the way to cure the patient is to make the disease unreal to him."[22] In other words, the person who is ill must be shown that he cannot trust what his physical senses are telling him about his symptoms. "To prevent disease or to cure it," claims Eddy, "the power of Truth, of divine Spirit, must break the dream of the material senses."[23] The sick person must be taught to "turn his gaze from the false evidence of the senses" to the truths of Christian Science.[24] Eddy advises, "When the first symptoms of disease appear, dispute the testimony of the material senses with divine Science."[25] Thus, symptoms of illness only have reality to the degree that the sick person acknowledges and speaks of their existence.

The New Thought understanding of symptoms is slightly different from Christian Science and is the more likely source of the Faith theology. For the most part, New Thought writers do not deny the reality of physical matter as does Christian Science. Instead, they assert that the higher reality of spiritual truth can overcome any reality perceived by the physical senses. But in practice, New Thought writers recommend the same denial of physical symptoms practiced by Christian Science. Ralph Waldo Trine quotes with approval the following statement from a New Thought writer.

> Never affirm or repeat about your health what you do not wish to be true. Do not dwell upon your ailments, nor study your symptoms. Never allow yourself to be convinced that you are not completely master of yourself. Stoutly affirm your superiority over bodily ills, and do not acknowledge yourself the slave of any inferior power.[26]

Like New Thought, the Faith theology *in theory* does not deny the reality of physical matter. *In practice*, however, the Faith theology engages in the same sort of denial of physical symptoms advocated by both New Thought and Christian Science. The Faith teachers may have a more sophisticated set of biblical proof-texts to justify the practice of denial, but the source of the practice itself is decidedly cultic.

Outgrowing the Need for Medical Science

The attitude of the Faith teachers toward the medical profession also has strong parallels in the metaphysical cults. On the one hand, the Faith teachers warn their followers not to get off medication until their faith is strong enough to handle it. On the other hand, by precept and example, they implicitly challenge their followers to abstain from medication whenever possible. Kenyon, for instance, believed that taking medication contradicts a confession of faith.[27] Hagin seldom comments directly upon medicine and doctors, other than his constant boast of needing neither since 1933. Once, however, when asked what medication he took when he felt ill, Hagin responded, "I take what I preach. If it doesn't work for me, I don't know how in the world it will work for anybody else."[28] The other Faith teachers are somewhat more cynical about doctors. Kenneth Copeland states flatly, "The world has a system of healing which is a miserable failure."[29] "Doctors are fighting the same enemies that we are," says Fred Price, "the only difference is they're using *toothpicks* and we are using *atomic bombs*."[30] Price often depicts medicine as a "crutch" upon which the immature believer relies: "If you need a crutch or something to help you get along, then praise God, hobble along until you get your faith moving to the point that you don't need a crutch."[31]

Price's statement on medicine is typical of the ambiguity that exists in the Faith movement. His book *Faith, Foolishness, or Presumption?* is one of the few that deals directly with the subject of doctors and medicine. It, too, is inconsistent on the subject of medical science. Price goes to great length to establish that "it is not a sin to use medication" and that medicine "is not in opposition to divine healing" (pp. 92–93). He instructs his followers not to "let medicine be the thing that decides whether you are operating in faith or not" (p. 93). A much subtler, yet just as clear, attitude is communicated in Price's book, one which subverts medicine and forces a choice upon those who want to be like the Faith teachers. First, Price himself notes several times that "I don't use pills myself" because "I have

my faith operating to such an extent that I don't need them" (p. 65).
Second, Price often depicts medicine as a "lower level" response to
illness that the true believer will eventually outgrow: "Medicine is
not God's highest or best. There is a better way when you know how
to use your faith. When you have developed your faith to such an
extent that you can stand on the promises of God, then you won't
need medicine" (p. 88). Third, Price places medication in the "gray"
area in which "each person ought to be persuaded in his own mind
whether or not he wants to take medication" (p. 66). Fourth, Price
repeatedly encourages, on the basis of his own example, abstinence
from medication in the "little issues" of illness, such as colds and
headaches, in preparation for terminal illnesses. "If you can't believe
God for a headache," says Price, "there is no way in the world that
you are going to believe God for the healing of terminal cancer"
(p. 91). Fifth, medication only helps relieve the pain and symptoms
of illness. It does not heal the illness itself (p. 87). Finally, any physical pain experienced by the believer in abstaining from medication
is described in such noble phrases as "making a stand," "believing
God," "moving in faith," "using faith," and "a commitment of the
heart." In a movement in which faith is exalted above all other
Christian virtues, the message of Price is clear. Those who really walk
in faith can, like the Faith teachers themselves, learn to do without
the benefits of medical science.

The Faith theology's position on medical science is based on its
metaphysical understanding of physical symptoms. Medicine is a
physical science. The whole science of medicine is based on the
ability to detect, diagnose, and prescribe treatment of disease and
its symptoms. Because the Faith teachers believe that disease is
spiritual (metaphysical) in origin, they must, by definition, also
consider the *physical* science of medicine an inferior means of healing. The Faith theology of healing is based, not on the ability to *detect*
physical symptoms, but to *deny* them. The physical symptoms are
not real. They will become real, however, if the believer acknowledges their existence and fails to apply the principles of spiritual
healing. Only people who do not know how to believe God for *spiritual* healing resort to medical science.

The Faith view of medical science is cultic. It is metaphysical in
origin, not biblical, and is the same view preached by the founder of
nineteenth-century metaphysics, P. P. Quimby. Quimby blames doctors for convincing people to "believe" in the symptoms of their
disease, thereby making the disease real. Quimby articulates well

the innate hostility of the metaphysical cults towards the medical profession:

> A physician may tell you what is not true about yourself. If you believe it and he deceives you that is no disgrace to you, for it shows an honest heart and confidence in the physician. Then follows the creation and appearance of the thing he has told you. As far as you are concerned you are blameless, but the physician is a liar and a hypocrite and has used your creative powers to deceive you for his own selfish ends. . . . Now when people are educated to understand that *what they believe they will create*, they will cease believing what the medical men say, and try to account for their feelings in some more rational way.[32]

Because he teaches that disease is a *spiritual* belief, Quimby claims that "there is no curative virtue in medicine" and any apparent cures effected by medicine are "all owing to the patient's belief," not to the work of the doctors.[33] According to Quimby, doctors are "slavedrivers" whose only motivation is to make money from illnesses which they themselves help to create in their patients.[34] Predictably, the official position on medicine of Eddy's Christian Science is that "Material medicine has no place in the life of a Christian Scientist."[35]

Unlike Christian Science, New Thought metaphysics allows for the combined use of medical and spiritual healing. Nevertheless, just as in the Faith theology, New Thought prophets see the day when people can outgrow the need of doctors, and when spiritual "principles" will do away with medicine. "The true physician . . . of the future," predicts Trine, "will not medicate the body with drugs so much as the mind with principles."[36] Like the Faith teachers, Trine regards medicine and drugs as stop-gap measures at best. "*The real healing process must be performed by the operation of life forces within.*"[37] Trine prophesies that many will learn how to heal themselves and, thus, no longer need physicians and drugs.

> The time will come when the work of the physician will not be to treat and attempt to heal the body, but to heal the mind, which in turn will heal the body. . . . *and still beyond this there will come a time when each will be his own physician.*[38]

Trine claims that he knows of numerous cases of people who were given up on by medical science, but who were later healed by New Thought. While not as hostile as Christian Science towards medicine, Trine exhorts his followers to transcend the need for doctors and drugs. The similarities of Trine's views on medicine with the Faith theology cannot pass unnoticed.

Believers Should Never Die of Disease

The promise of a disease-free existence is, to say the least, one of the more attractive appeals of the Faith theology. This promise begs the question, however, of just *how* a true believer is "supposed" to die. Kenyon answers this question with typical abandon: "I believe that it is the plan of the Father that no believer should ever be sick, that he should live his full length of time and actually wear out and fall asleep."[39] Elsewhere, he states, "We should simply wear out and fall asleep without pain, without these hideous diseases that dishonor the Lord."[40] Following Kenyon's lead, Hagin states,

> I believe that it is the plan of God our Father that no believer should ever be sick. That every believer should live his full length of time and actually wear out, if Jesus tarries, and fall asleep in Jesus. It is not—I state boldly— it is not the will of God my Father that we should suffer with cancer and other dread diseases which bring pain and anguish. No! It is God's will that we be healed.[41]

Disease should have no place in the life of a Christian. The Faith theology has never gone as far as the "Manifest Sons of God" doctrine that argues that believers can learn to overcome death altogether. Nevertheless, *how* a believer dies is an indicator of the power of his faith. Believers die, but according to Kenyon and Hagin, they should not die of disease.

Believers Should Never Die Before Age 70

Not only *how* a believer dies is determined by his faith, the question of *when* he is supposed to die is also answered by the Faith theology. Kenyon proclaims that a believer should live out his "full-length of time" and should not die before that time is expired. Just how long a person's "full-length of time" is intended by God to be is never stated by Kenyon,[42] but a popular doctrine circulating in the contemporary Faith movement is that the Bible unconditionally guarantees that Christians will live long and healthy lives. For example, Price comments,

> Your minimum days should be 70 years, that's just the bare minimum. You ought to live to be at least 120 years of age. That's the Bible. God out of his own mouth—in the Old Testament—said the number of your days shall be 120 years. I didn't write it! God said it. The minimum ought to be 70 years, and you shouldn't go out with sickness and disease then.[43]

The Faith theology teaches that after 70 years of life, a Christian then "chooses" his time to die. The believer who dies before his 70 to 120 years could have lived longer had he exercised faith in the promises of the Bible. "The only reason people die before their time," claims Price, "is because they do not understand how to exercise their faith according to the Word to prevent death, or they choose to die before their time."[44] In response to the question of why children sometimes die or are born dead, Price states: "Children that are born dead had no control over their life, but their parents had that control. However, if the parents do not know the Word of God and to claim their rights in Christ, the child suffers the loss."[45] Thus, the responsibility for any premature death lies squarely with the believer.

The belief that people choose their time to die and should live for over a century has antecedents in New Thought. Trine's views on the longevity of life achieved through metaphysical healing are very similar to those of the Faith theology. Although he does not claim to base his belief on the Bible, Trine does assert that "our natural age should be nearer a hundred and twenty years than we commonly find it today."[46] People fail to live to the age of 120 because when they see others aging, they believe that they, too, must age. "By taking this attitude of mind," explains Trine, these people "many times bring upon themselves these very conditions long before it is necessary."[47] An unfortunate footnote to Trine's thesis is that he himself lived only to the age of ninety-two, a long life, to say the least, but somewhat short of his own standards. It will be interesting to see how many of today's Faith teachers fulfill their standards of a "full life."

Biblical Analysis of the Doctrine of Healing

Because of its metaphysical background, the Faith theology has transformed healing, a biblical practice of long standing in the church, into a cultic obsession. Healing is, indeed, a gift of the Holy Spirit (1 Cor. 12:9). The church has been commissioned to pray for the sick (Jas. 5:14, 15). Signs, healings, and exorcisms do often follow those who preach the gospel (Mk. 16:15–20).[48] These supernatural experiences and ministries are the heritage of the people of God. This heritage is not, however, the gospel itself. Christianity is not a healing cult and the gospel is not a metaphysical formula for divine health and wealth. The Faith theology's inordinate emphasis on healing is a gross exaggeration of the biblical doctrine and distorts the centrality of Christ and the gospel.

Must God Always Heal?

Healing is an iron-clad doctrine of the Faith theology, and therein lies the problem. Like the metaphysical cults, the Faith teachers dogmatize what is primarily an experience. In doing so, they claim a cause-and-effect power for their healing formulas, and since it is impossible that God would fail to comply with these Scripture formulas, the believer has only himself to blame for sickness. Thus, healing is not a sovereign miracle bestowed by a merciful God. Healing is a cause-and-effect formula that works every time the Christian applies it in "faith."

In critiquing the Faith doctrine of healing, it is difficult to resist the extremes either of denying healing altogether or of formulating yet another doctrine of healing in response. Neither is appropriate here. Healing is a divine gift and ministry of the church. This cannot be denied. My conviction, however, is that the gift of healing was never intended to be reduced to a doctrinal formula. We must neither deny healing, nor simplify it into "steps" or "principles" or "formulas" to which God *must* respond. Again, to quote Gordon Fee, "God *must* do *nothing!*" God does, indeed, respond to faith, but he does not always respond with healing. Just as in all areas of prayer, we must pray and exercise faith under the lordship of Christ. His lordship demands that we abandon ourselves to his will. Any doctrine of healing that teaches, as does the Faith theology, that "we don't have to wait until the Spirit wills" is not true faith. Call it metaphysics. Call it positive mental attitude. Call it magic. But don't call it faith.

Those who use healing formulas to claim that God heals *all* of our diseases *every* time are denying reality. They are ignoring the obvious fact that Christians get sick all the time. Some recover from their illnesses; others do not. Every day, somewhere in the world, Christians die of the same diseases that everybody else dies of. This is not a pleasant fact, but it is an undeniable one. If we deny it, then we deny not only reality, but also what the Bible itself has said of life in this physical body.

Do Believers Suffer in Their Bodies?

The Bible teaches that believers will not be entirely free from bodily suffering until the return of Christ and the general resurrection. Kenyon's and Hagin's thesis that believers can be fully redeemed from bodily suffering in this life directly contradicts Pauline teaching on bodily redemption. In Romans, Paul teaches that all of creation "groans" under the curse of suffering (Rom. 8:19–21), and that believers "groan" right along with it. Just as fallen creation awaits eagerly its recreation at Christ's return (Rom. 8:19; Rev. 21:1–5), so also believers await the completion of redemption: "the redemption of our bodies." Although through the Holy Spirit we have the "first fruits" of redemption, even believers "groan" in hope of bodily redemption. Along with the rest of creation, we, too, must "with perseverance wait eagerly for it" (Rom. 8:24, 25).

This theme of "groaning" while we wait for the redemption of our bodies through resurrection is also seen in 2 Corinthians. Paul admits that our "our outer man is decaying," but exhorts believers not to "lose heart" because "our inner man is being renewed day by day" (2 Cor. 4:16). The basis of his confidence, even in the face of physical decay, is the certainty of bodily redemption (2 Cor. 5:1–4). Though we "groan" in this earthly body, we have the Spirit as "the pledge" that God will give us a new body, a body in which suffering and sickness will be "swallowed up by life" (2 Cor. 5:4, 5).

Paul teaches that believers will not be fully redeemed until Christ returns and transforms "the body of our humble state into conformity with the body of His glory, by the exertion of the power that He has even to subject all things to himself" (Phil 3:21). The human body, in all its weakness and frailty, will be marvelously transformed into a body in which disease and death will have no place. Referring to "the resurrection of the dead," Paul writes,

> It is sown a perishable body, it is raised an imperishable body; it is sown in dishonor, it is raised in glory; it is sown in weakness, it is raised in power; it is sown a natural body, it is raised a spiritual body (1 Cor. 15:42–44).

Contrary to the Faith anthropology, the believer's body is not made impervious to disease through faith, the new birth, positive confession, or anything else. It remains a "perishable" body of "weakness" and "dishonor." But at the return of Christ, the believer's decaying and mortal body will undergo an incredible change (1 Cor. 15:51–55). *Disease* will be defeated only when *death* is finally defeated: at the return of Christ and the general resurrection. *The error of the Faith theology is that it ascribes a power to faith healing that will be manifest only at the end of the age.* This is but one of many examples of its overrealized eschatology. As wonderful as it is, healing power is only a stopgap provision. At best, it can only ward off disease and death.

Were Believers Always Healed in the Bible?

Not only does the Faith doctrine of healing contradict Pauline teaching, it also contradicts Paul's life and ministry. One would expect that had Paul known and taught Faith theology, both his life and the lives of those who followed him would have been free of illness and suffering.[49] Such was not the case. God frequently performed "extraordinary miracles by the hands of Paul" (Acts 19:11), yet Paul frequently was unable to heal his closest and dearest associates. For example, he admits that "Trophimus I left sick at Miletus" (2 Tim. 4:20). In the case of Epaphroditus, Paul describes his relief that by God's mercy his friend's deathly illness had run its course, sparing his life (Phil. 3:25–27).

Elsewhere, Paul advises Timothy to "use a little wine for . . . your stomach and your frequent ailments" (1 Tim. 5:23). Perhaps in his advice to Timothy, Paul was merely passing on the prescription of another of his traveling companions, "Luke the beloved physician" (Col. 4:14). In standing with Paul in his imprisonments, sometimes all by himself (2 Tim. 4:11), did Luke ever administer medicine to Paul's body? We are not told for certain, but it is not inconceivable that Luke acted not only as a companion and historian of Paul, but as his personal physician as well.

The Sickness and Suffering of Paul

Paul certainly had need of a personal physician, for he himself was also subject to illness. He reminds the Galatians that their response to his illness provided the occasion for his ministry among them.

> But you know that it was because of a bodily illness that I preached the gospel to you the first time; and that which was a trial to you in my bodily condition you did not despise or loathe, but you received me as an angel of God, as Christ Jesus Himself. Where then is that sense of blessing you had? For I bear you witness, that if possible, you would have plucked out your eyes and given them to me (Gal. 4:13–15).[50]

Paul also mentions a cryptic "thorn in the flesh" which he unsuccessfully entreated the Lord to remove on three occasions (2 Cor. 12:7–9).[51] Scholars speculate much as to the exact nature of Paul's illness. A commonly held opinion is that Paul experienced occasional epileptic seizures.[52] A stronger possibility is periodic malaria fever, which frequently plagues many modern missionaries.[53] Numerous other suggestions have been made.[54] For our purposes, it is not necessary to know the exact nature of Paul's illness, but its facticity is hardly in question, and is enough to cast serious doubt upon the Faith teachers' claim that a believer can and should always manifest perfect health.

Moreover, one cannot help but wonder how Paul's bodily illness would have been received today among charismatics. Would charismatics "despise" and "loathe" his illness as an indication of his immature faith? Or, like the Galatians, would we respond to his ministry with "a sense of blessing," receiving him as "an angel of God," as "Christ Jesus himself"? Would there be those among us who would be willing to "pluck out" our own eyes that Paul might see? What a tremendous blessing would be missed if through our distorted and cultic view of healing we rejected Paul's ministry because he struggled with bodily illness.

The Sickness and Suffering of Job

The interpretation of Job's sufferings is another example in which the Faith theology directly contradicts biblical teaching. The Faith teachers contend that Job brought all of his problems on himself through negative confession and unbelief. God did not afflict Job, argue the Faith teachers, Satan did. And the reason that Satan was able to do so was Job's fear. God had built a "hedge" (Job 1:10) around Job, but Job had pulled it down through his negative confession of fear: "For what I fear comes upon me, and what I dread befalls me" (Job 3:25).[55] When Job eventually repented of his fear and prayed for his friends, God restored his health and fortunes (Job 42:1–10). This is the "true" story of Job, say the Faith teachers.

Although their interpretation is certainly novel, the Faith teachers twist the meaning of the above passages and omit other important texts altogether. Their desire to exonerate God of any involvement in Job's afflictions may seem noble, but it contradicts the direct testimony of the Bible, Job, and, ultimately, God himself. The Bible plainly teaches that although Satan was the *agent* of Job's trials, God was the ultimate *source*. God was the one who removed the "hedge" and who placed Job under Satan's power (Job 1:12, 2:6). Satan could not have touched Job without God's permission. God gave his permission in order to test Job's faith and to answer Satan's accusing question, "Does Job fear God for nothing?" (Job 1:9). In the first trial, God allowed Satan to wipe out Job's children and servants through the sword of the Sabeans (1:15), through "the fire of God"

(1:16), through the sword of the Chaldeans (1:17), and through a strong wind (1:19). If Satan were acting unilaterally in his afflictions of Job, why is it said that "the fire of God" destroyed Job's sheep and shepherds? This is consistent with Job 42:11, in which his family comforts him "for all the evil the Lord had brought upon him."

Job clearly ascribes his suffering to the hand of God. His response to these tragedies was that of a pious and grieving Jew:

> Then Job arose and tore his robe and shaved his head, and he fell to the ground and worshipped. And he said, "Naked I came from my mother's womb, and naked I shall I return there. The Lord gave and the Lord has taken away. Blessed be the name of the Lord" (Job 1:20–21).

Notice that though Satan was the direct agent of the affliction, Job perceived correctly that ultimately it was the Lord who had *given* him his children and estate, and it was the Lord who had *taken* them away. Amazingly, some Faith teachers have the audacity to claim that Job's statements in this regard were neither "true" nor "inspired."[56] They claim that Job was in error in ascribing his trial to God. What they fail to see is precisely what Job saw so clearly: both good and adversity come from the will of God, either his direct will, or his permissive will. For instance, after his second trial, in which God allowed Satan to afflict Job's own body, Job rebuked his wife when she pressured him to surrender his integrity and to "curse God and die!" (Job 2:9). "You speak as one of the foolish women speaks," replied Job. "Shall we accept good from God and not . . . adversity?" (Job 2:10). Job recognized that though the Lord is not the author of evil, he does frequently permit it in the lives of even the godliest of people.

The Faith teachers deny what God himself readily admits. Though Satan was the instigator and executor of Job's afflictions, it was God who accepted the responsibility for the experiment to test Job's integrity. After the first set of trials, Satan again appears before God.

> And the Lord said to Satan, "Have you considered My servant Job? For there is no one like him on the earth, a blameless and upright man fearing God and turning away from evil. And he still holds fast his integrity, *although you incited Me against him, to ruin him without cause*" (Job 2:3).

Satan acted as the "inciter" of God. He is "the accuser of our brethren . . . who accuses them before our God day and night" (Rev. 12:10). Satan was, indeed, both the inciter of God and accuser of Job. Nevertheless, God admits that indirectly, but ultimately, *he* was the one who tested Job and allowed his ruin.

Job 2:3 also contradicts another central claim of the Faith teachers regarding Job. It is claimed that Job's fear tore down the hedge that allowed Satan's attacks. Nothing could be further from the truth. In Job 2:3, God states that he ruined Job *"without cause."* There is nothing in the first two chapters of Job to indicate that he caused his own problems through fear or unbelief. Quite the contrary, the very first verse of the book states that Job "was blameless, upright, fearing God, and turning away from evil" (Job 1:1). Twice the Lord asks Satan, "Have you considered My servant Job?"—his uprightness, blamelessness, and integrity (Job 1:8, 2:3). Fear neither was the *cause* of Job's afflictions, nor was it their *result*. For twice also is it affirmed that Job did not sin as a result of God's trials. After his first trial, it is written that "through all this Job did not sin nor did he blame God" (Job 1:22). Likewise, after his second trial, it is written that "in all this Job did not sin with his lips" (Job 2:10). His hope in God was strong throughout his trial: "Though He slay me, I will hope in him" (Job 13:15). Job's faith was steadfast, even when facing death: "And as for me, I know that my Redeemer lives, and at the last He will take His stand on the earth. Even after my skin is destroyed, yet from my flesh I shall see God" (Job 19:25, 26). Job asked many questions of God in the midst of his suffering, some for which he later repented (Job 42:6). But in the end, "the Lord accepted Job" (Job 42:9) and rebuked his "comforters," informing them that they had "not spoken of Me what is right as My servant Job has" (Job 42:7).

It appears that in the Faith teachers, Job still has his "comforters," those who would accuse him with simplistic and trite answers. In blaming Job, the Faith teachers have slandered a man whom the Lord not once, but twice said was "blameless and upright." Admittedly, the sufferings of Job caused him to question God. But his questions were not sin, and they were not the cause of his sufferings. The Faith teachers have committed the error of Eliphaz, Bildad, Zophar, and Elihu. In trying to exonerate God, they have unjustly condemned an innocent man. They have "not spoken what is right," either of Job or of God.

A Concluding, Non-Theological Postscript

Although there are serious *theological* errors in the Faith doctrine of healing, its most critical errors are in the area of *practice*. The theological errors of the Faith teachers lead them inevitably into many dangerous practices. Though we are citing these errors in a postscript, this is no indication of their importance. In many cases, these errors are a matter of life and death.

One of the most dangerous practices encouraged by the Faith teachers, by both precept and example, is denial. Because of its background in the metaphysical healing cults, the Faith theology instructs believers to deny any physical symptom of illness. Christian Science denies symptoms because it denies the reality of physical matter and the reliability of the physical senses to perceive reality. Unlike Christian Science (but like New Thought and Unity), the Faith theology does not deny the reality of physical matter or the reliability of the physical senses. All three of these systems (New Thought, Unity, and Faith), however, do teach that believers should deny physical reality and their physical senses in order to confess a higher *spiritual* reality: divine healing. The Faith teachers claim that Satan has the power to rob them of this higher reality by presenting lying symptoms to a believer. For this reason, symptoms of illness, including pain, should be denied.

Such denial is a most dangerous game to play. In diseases such as cancer, where early detection is directly proportional to cure rates, it is not only dangerous: it can be deadly. As Kübler-Ross has pointed out in *On Death and Dying*, people with serious illnesses have a strong tendency to engage in various forms of denial anyway. The Faith theology gives such people a multitude of religious rationalizations to practice denial, particularly the denial of symptoms of illness. In illnesses such as headaches and colds, the denial of symptoms is usually not too serious, and by enduring a little pain, the believer can claim that God healed him.[57] In more serious diseases, however, in which symptoms persist and worsen, the practice of denial can result in a progression of the disease beyond the point which medical science can help.[58] In some cases, the symptoms are denied to such an extent that a *serious* illness becomes a *terminal* one.

Another practice common in the Faith movement is the refusal to seek medical care for illnesses. This practice could easily be the result of Hagin's participation in the radical healing revivalism common among the Pentecostal evangelists of the 1950s and 1960s. Even if, however, we are willing to concede that the rejection of medical care is a Pentecostal phenomenon rather than a cultic one, we still must point out two facts. First, the more moderate faith healers of the Healing Revival, such as Oral Roberts and Kathryn Kuhlman, consistently warned their followers not to reject medicine. Indeed, whenever possible, Roberts and Kuhlman always made it a practice to verify claimed healings with doctors.[59]

Second, even if the practice of rejecting medical care is not *directly* cultic, it is *indirectly*; that is, it has strong parallels in cultic thought and practice. The bottom line is that those in the Faith movement and the metaphysical cults have three general similarities. (1) They rarely seek medical care and when they do, they wait as long as possible. (2) They feel a strong sense of guilt and failure when their faith "fails" and they are forced to go to the doctor. (3) When they finally do go to the doctor, they are often reluctant and uncooperative patients. In summary, their "faith" inhibits medical healing rather than promotes it.

Finally, the most consistent reports of abuse caused by the Faith doctrine of healing involve the treatment of those in the movement with chronic and/or terminal illnesses. Because of the belief that listening to a "negative confession" can infect one's faith, not many in the Faith movement are willing even to be around, much less listen to, those who are seriously ill in their own churches. Basically, the Faith churches have little or no concept of pastoral care for the chronically and terminally ill believer. Such a believer is shunned, isolated, and ostracized as though he was an unbeliever— which, by definition, is precisely what he is, or else he would not be ill in the first place. Those who are willing to risk exposing themselves to a negative confession frequently minister to the terminally ill person the brand of "comfort" given to Job by his "friends." The time when a dying believer needs a word of encouragement is when he receives a sermonette on the failure of his faith. The time when a dying believer needs his faith the most is when he is told that he has it the least. The time when he needs the support of a sensitive, supportive body of believers is when he is ostracized and isolated as though he was himself infectious. Perhaps the most inhumane fact revealed about the Faith movement is this: when its members die, they die alone.

Notes

1. An example of the fallacy that signs and miracles validate one's teaching is William Branham, one of the original and greatest evangelists of the post–World War II Healing Revival. Branham worked astounding miracles of healing in his crusades. To this day his gifts of supernatural knowledge of those to whom he ministered remain unparalleled, even among modern healing evangelists. Despite all of his gifts, however, Branham's doctrine was always marginal at best, and towards the end of his ministry, it became

outright heretical. He denied the doctrine of the Trinity, teaching instead the "Jesus only" doctrine. He taught that he was the prophet Elijah, whose ministry would result in the return of Jesus. There were pockets of his followers who believed that he was not just a prophet, but also the incarnation of Jesus himself. Although Branham's is an extreme example, it illustrates that a ministry of miracles and healing in no way proves soundness of doctrine.

2. Kenneth Hagin, *Healing Belongs to Us* (Tulsa: Faith Library, 1977), pp. 16, 17. The title of Hagin's book is also the title of a key chapter in Kenyon's book, *Jesus the Healer*.

3. Kenyon, *Identification*, p. 15.

4. Kenyon, *Jesus the Healer*, p. 81.

5. K. Hagin, "Looking at the Unseen," *Word of Faith* (June, 1974), p. 2.

6. "What is disease?" asks Quimby. "It is what follows the effect of a false direction given to the mind or spiritual matter" (*Quimby Manuscripts*, p. 186).

7. Trine, *In Tune*, p. 112.

8. Ibid., p. 25.

9. Kenyon, *Jesus the Healer*, p. 44.

10. Ibid., p. 67.

11. Trine, *In Tune*, p. 65; cf., pp. 45, 50.

12. Kenyon, *Power of Positive Confession*, p. 119; Hagin, *Right and Wrong Thinking*, p. 27; Price, *How Faith Works*, p. 23.

13. Kenyon, *Power of Positive Confession*, p. 80.

14. Trine, *In Tune*, p. 66.

15. Kenyon, *What Happened*, p. 109.

16. Kenyon, *Jesus the Healer*, p. 26; italics added for emphasis.

17. Kenneth Hagin, *The Real Faith* (Tulsa: Faith Library, 1980), p. 13.

18. Kenyon, *Hidden Man*, p. 107.

19. Hagin, *Real Faith*, pp. 19–20; cf., *The Key to Scriptural Healing*, p. 28.

20. Price, *Faith, Foolishness, or Presumption?* pp. 76–77.

21. Eddy, *Science and Health*, p. 495.

22. Ibid., p. 417.

23. Ibid., p. 412.

24. Ibid., p. 420.

25. Ibid., p. 390.

26. Trine, *In Tune*, p. 67.

27. Kenyon, *Two Kinds of Faith*, p. 42; cf., *Jesus the Healer*, pp. 80–81.

28. Kenneth Hagin, *God's Medicine* (Tulsa: Faith Library, 1977), pp. 17, 18. In this same book, Hagin teaches that "God's Medicine is His Word" (p. 5). He claims that when he feels the symptoms of illness, he simply "doubles up" on his Bible reading and "it works wonders."

29. Kenneth Copeland, *The Laws of Prosperity* (Ft. Worth: Kenneth Copeland Publications, 1974), p. 22.

30. Frederick K. C. Price, *Is Healing for All?* (Tulsa: Harrison, 1976), p. 113.

31. Price, *How Faith Works*, pp. 92–93.

32. Dresser, *Quimby Manuscripts*, pp. 262–63.

33. Ibid., p. 290.

34. Ibid., pp. 318–19.

35. Quoted in Charles Braden's *Christian Science* (Dallas: S.M.U. Press, 1958), p. 256.

36. Trine, *In Tune*, p. 67.

37. Ibid., p. 43.

38. Ibid., pp. 65–66; italics added for emphasis.

39. Kenyon, *Jesus the Healer*, p. 65.

40. Kenyon, *Two Kinds of Faith*, p. 109.

41. K. Hagin, "Healing: The Father's Provision," *Word of Faith* (Aug., 1977), p. 9.

42. There are rumors in the Faith movement that Kenyon himself chose his time to die and when the moment of death came, he supposedly "dismissed his spirit" just like Jesus on the cross. His daughter, Ruth Houseworth, denies these rumors, stating, "The Faith teachers are trying to make a legend out of my father" (personal interview).

43. Price, *Is Healing for All?* p. 104.

44. Fred Price, *Ever Increasing Faith Messenger* (Fall, 1980), p. 3.

45. Ibid.

46. Trine, *In Tune*, p. 60.

47. Ibid.

48. Although it is all but certain that Mk. 16:9–20 is a later addition to the text of Mark—and thus is noncanonical—the passage does give us some insight into the experience of the primitive church community. As C. S. Mann points out, with the exception of the drinking of poison, all of the miraculous signs mentioned in this passage are elsewhere in the NT associated with the preaching of the gospel (*Mark* [AB 27; Garden City, N.Y.: Doubleday, 1986], pp. 675–76).

49. Some of the more radical Faith teachers maintain that if Paul knew what the Faith movement knows today, he never would have allowed his coworkers to be sick, or been sick himself. Gratefully this is not a widely held belief in the movement.

50. Not all scholars are agreed that Gal. 4:13, 14 refers to a bodily illness. Herman Ridderbos believes that Paul's "bodily condition" was the physical wounds and exhaustion suffered in the intense persecution of his missionary work in Galatia (*The Epistle of Paul to the Churches of Galatia* [Grand Rapids: Eerdmans, 1984], pp. 30, 166–67). The majority of scholars believe that it was a disease of some kind, but refuse to diagnose it (Bruce, *Galatians*, pp. 208, 209; cf., Hans Dieter Betz, *Galatians* [Hermeneia; Philadelphia: Fortress, 1979], p. 225).

51. There is no consensus on the nature of Paul's "thorn in the flesh." The three major positions are: (1) psycho-spiritual torment and temptation; (2) persecution; (3) bodily illness. The trend in recent scholarship is towards bodily illness (Victor Paul Furnish, *II Corinthians* [AB 32A; Garden City, N.Y.: Doubleday, 1984], pp. 548–49). One fact in strong favor of interpreting Paul's thorn as a disease is that he describes it as "a messenger of Satan." In the first century, disease was often attributed to Satan (K. L. Schmidt, "*kolaphizo*," *TDNT*, 3:819).

52. Krister Stendahl, *Paul Among Jews and Gentiles* (Philadelphia: Fortress, 1980), p. 42; cf., Martin Dibelius, *Paul* (Philadelphia: Westminster, 1953), pp. 42–43.

53. Sir William Ramsay, *St. Paul: The Traveller and the Roman Citizen* (Grand Rapids: Baker, 1962), pp. 95–97.

54. Besides malaria and epilepsy, F. F. Bruce provides the most comprehensive list of opinions on Paul's illness: pain in the ear or head (Tertullian), ophthalmia (J. T. Brown), sufferings caused by persecution (J. Munich), concern for his unsaved Jewish brethren, painful memories of his own persecution of the church (Menoud), and attacks of depression caused by the exaltation of the divine revelation that was manifested through him (*The Epistle of II Corinthians* [Grand Rapids: Eerdmans, 1980], p. 248).

55. Price, *Is Healing for All?* p. 11; cf., Don Hughes, *What About Job?: The Truth* (Broken Arrow, Okla.: Don Hughes Evang. Assoc., 1984), pp. 13–15.

56. Price, ibid., p. 10; Hughes, ibid., p. 16. This is a fairly common tactic. Although the Faith teachers claim to believe in an inerrant Bible, they do not hesitate to deny the truth and inspiration of passages that contradict their position. Apparently the integrity of their theology means more to them than the integrity of the Bible.

57. Occasionally, however, tragic consequences result. For example, one woman described to the author the results of following the teaching to deny the reality of a sore throat. Although her sore throat persisted and worsened to the point that she grew seriously ill, she still did not seek medical attention. When she finally did see her doctor, her sore throat turned out to be advanced rheumatic fever. Her health and mental clarity have been permanently affected by her practice of denial of what she thought to be only a common cold.

58. Several physicians in Tulsa have described to the author the frustration of attempting to treat serious illnesses that could have been prevented had they been diagnosed sooner. In many cases, by the time these people go to the doctor, it is too late. One cancer specialist formerly at a local religious hospital commented that on a weekly basis he encountered believers who were denying symptoms of cancer. In "numerous" cases, this denial made a significant difference in their chances of recovery.

59. Today, the name of Oral Roberts is synonymous with the merging of prayer and medicine. Roberts has always taught his followers the co-equality of prayer and medicine as "delivery systems" of God's healing power.

10 The Doctrine of Prosperity: Success and the Upwardly Mobile Christian

God has certain benefits attached to walking by faith. Most employers at least have enough common decency about them that they don't ask somebody to work for them *for free*. . . . If a man has enough nicety about him to do that, can't you at least believe that the Father God is not asking you to serve Him *for free* either?

—Fred Price,
Faith, Foolishness or Presumption, p. 7.

American Christianity is rapidly being infected by an insidious disease, the so-called "wealth and health" Gospel—although it has very little of the character of the Gospel in it. In its more brazen forms . . . it simply says, "Serve God and get rich" . . . in its more respectable—but pernicious—forms it builds fifteen million dollar crystal cathedrals to the glory of affluent suburban Christianity.

—Gordon Fee,
"The Cult of Prosperity," p. 13.

In his book *All Things Are Possible,* David Harrell states that the doctrine of prosperity has come to be "the most important new idea of the charismatic revival," an idea which has "almost supplanted the earlier emphasis on healing."[1] The Faith movement has definitely proven Harrell's thesis true. Whereas in its infancy, the Faith movement was known for its radical emphasis upon healing, today the Faith movement is one of the major sources of prosperity teaching among modern charismatics. Although they did not originate the teaching and are by no means the only ones propagating it, the Faith teachers have with typical abandon made the most outrageous claims for the doctrine. Their promises of material prosperity and financial success are undoubtedly a major source of motivation for many to join their movement.

The Cultic Nature of the Doctrine of Prosperity

Teachings on prosperity have always characterized the ministry of faith-healing evangelists. For the most part, these teachings fall into one of two types. First, there is the *egocentric* teaching on prosperity. This type of teaching promises success and prosperity from God to those who give to the evangelist's ministry. It is egocentric because it centers on the personality of the evangelist and the welfare of his ministry. Second, there is the *cosmic* teaching on prosperity. This type of teaching promises success and prosperity from God to those who know the spiritual laws of the universe that govern financial prosperity. It is *cosmic* because it centers on the universal principles of prosperity that God has set up in the cosmos. Although there were cosmic teachings on prosperity in the post–World War II Healing Revival, the vast majority were of the egocentric variety and promised success and finances to those who bankrolled the evangelist's ministry.

At times Faith teachers become slightly egocentric in their appeals for money, but generally they teach prosperity on a cosmic scale. Their purpose is to impart the knowledge of the spiritual laws that govern prosperity in the universe. The following quotation from Kenneth Copeland is typical of this cosmic view of prosperity taught in the Faith movement.

> We must understand that there are laws governing every single thing in existence. Nothing is by accident. There are laws of the world of the spirit and there are laws of the world of the natural. . . . We need to realize that the spiritual world and its laws are more powerful than the physical world and its laws. Spiritual laws gave birth to physical laws. The world and the physical forces governing it were created by the power of faith—a spiritual force. . . . It is this force of faith which makes the laws of the spirit world function. . . . This same rule is true in prosperity. There are certain laws governing prosperity in God's Word. Faith causes them to function. . . . The success formulas in the Word of God produce results when used as directed.[2]

Unlike the egocentric variety of prosperity teaching, Copeland does not usually claim that those who give to his ministry will prosper. His intent is to explain "the success formulas" of the Bible which release "the force of faith." This faith causes the spiritual laws governing prosperity in the universe to function.

One example of a "success formula" is the Copelands' principle of giving based on Mk. 10:30 known as "the hundredfold return." Gloria Copeland explains this spiritual law.

> You give $1 for the Gospel's sake and $100 belongs to you; give $10 and receive $1000; give $1000 and receive $100,000. I know that you can multiply, but I want you to see it in black and white and see how tremendous the hundredfold return is. . . . Give one house and receive one hundred houses or one house worth one hundred times as much. Give one airplane and receive one hundred times the value of the airplane. Give one car and the return would furnish you a lifetime of cars. In short, Mark 10:30 is a very good deal.[3]

This "very good deal" is claimed to be a universal spiritual law. It is claimed to work for anybody and everybody who knows it, as do all of the other laws of prosperity. Regarding a non-believer who applied a law of prosperity, Hagin writes,

> God didn't bless him because he was a sinner. He received God's blessing because he honored God. God has a certain law of prosperity and when you get into contact with that law and those rules, it just works for you—*whoever you are.* When you come into contact with God's laws, they work.[4]

Thus, even a "sinner" who "comes into contact" with the laws of prosperity will reap their rewards. The believer who lives in poverty, though he knows Christ, dishonors God.

The cosmic type of teaching about prosperity is another example of the influence of the metaphysical cults on the Faith movement. These cults teach prosperity almost exactly like Copeland. One of the major attractions of the Unity School of Christianity has always been its teaching on prosperity. In his book *Prosperity*, Charles Fillmore, the founder of Unity, insists that Unity's "law of prosperity has been proved time and time again. All men who have prospered have used the law, for there is no other way."[5] Long before Copeland claims to have "discovered" the laws of prosperity, Fillmore wrote that "everything is governed by law" and that "there is a law that governs the manifestation of supply."[6] Just like Copeland, Fillmore claims that to operate the law of prosperity, first one must *understand* it; second, one must have *faith* in it; and third, one must *apply* it to one's need.[7] Thus, the prosperity of both the metaphysical cults and the Faith theology is based on impersonal knowledge of how to manipulate spiritual laws rather than personal trust in the provision of a sovereign God.

Kenyon's New Thought classmate, Ralph Waldo Trine, also describes a cosmic view of prosperity that sounds very much like Copeland's. In a chapter of *In Tune with the Infinite* entitled, "Plenty of All Things—The Law of Prosperity," Trine writes,

> If one holds himself in the thought of poverty, he will be poor, and the chances are that he will remain in poverty. If he holds himself, whatever present conditions may be, continually in the thought of prosperity, he sets into operation forces that will sooner or later bring him into prosperous conditions. The law of attraction works unceasingly in the universe.[8]

Like the Faith teachers, Trine teaches that there are "laws" in the universe that govern prosperity and that faith is the key to operating these laws.[9] Both Trine and Copeland teach that faith is the "law of success," which imparts the power to create prosperous circumstances.

They also both teach that these laws are set into motion by positive mental attitude and positive confession. Copeland definitely links prosperity to one's attitude and confession.

> *You can have what you say!* In fact, what you are saying is exactly what you are getting now. If you are living in poverty and lack and want, change what you are saying. It will change what you have. . . . Discipline your vocabulary. Discipline everything you do, everything you say, and everything you think to agree with what God does, what God says, and what God thinks. God will be obligated to meet your needs because of His Word. . . . If you stand firmly on this, your needs will be met.[10]

This relationship between prosperity and positive thinking is nothing new. Many years prior to Copeland's claims of receiving the revelation, New Thought leader Trine wrote,

> This is the law of prosperity: When apparent adversity comes, be not cast down by it, but make the best of it, and always look forward for better things, for conditions more prosperous. To hold yourself in this attitude of mind is to set into operation subtle, silent and irresistible forces that sooner or later will actualize in material form that which is today merely an idea. But ideas have occult power, and ideas, when rightly planted and rightly tended, are the seeds that actualize material conditions.[11]

It is significant to note that Trine attributes the confession of prosperity to "occult power." Trine believed that "thought is a force, and it has occult power of unknown proportions when rightly used and wisely directed."[12] This usage of occult powers is, of course, a practice that the Faith teachers would publicly reject. *Nevertheless, the Faith teachers must come to grips with the fact that those who began the practices of positive mental attitude and positive confession attributed their ability to acquire riches to psychic and occultic power.*

For example, Trine advocated the occultic practice of visualization as a means to become prosperous. He instructs his followers in the art of visualizing prosperity through mental suggestion and verbal affirmation.

> Suggest prosperity to yourself. See yourself in a prosperous condition. Affirm that you will before long be in a prosperous condition. Affirm it calmly and quietly but strongly and confidently. Believe it, believe it absolutely. Expect it—keep it continually watered with expectation. You thus make yourself a magnet to attract the things that you desire.[13]

In *The Seduction of Christianity*, Dave Hunt warns against the practice of visualization on the basis of its origins in the occult and Eastern religions. While there may well be some harmless uses of visualization, Hunt is quite correct in pointing out that its origins are decidedly non-Christian. To the degree that the Faith teachers recommend faith-visualization and mind discipline to obtain prosperity, they are introducing an alien and, perhaps, occultic practice as a substitute for biblical faith.

As with its doctrine of healing, the Faith theology teaches that if a man is poor, he has only himself to blame. Since Christ died to redeem man from poverty, Kenyon insists that "it is abnormal for believers to be in bondage to poverty so that they have to go to the world for help."[14] A man is poor, whether Christian or non-Christian, for one reason: he dishonors God. Hagin comments,

> You know friends, most of us are not so poor because we have honored God—but because we have dishonored Him. You might as well say Amen because it's so. I've given you scriptures to prove it.[15]

The believer who is poor dishonors God because he has failed to appropriate the deliverance from poverty provided for in the atonement.

Kenyon preached prosperity, but he did not condone materialism or greed. To his credit, Kenyon defines prosperity as not just "the ability to make your life a success," but rather "the ability to use the ability of God to help humanity."[16] Biblical prosperity "is not the prosperity of the senses, which thinks gold and political favor is [*sic*] prosperity." Biblical prosperity is ultimately the presence of God himself.[17] Although all of the seminal concepts on prosperity are present in his writings, Kenyon defined prosperity in terms of deliverance from poverty, and the power to deliver others.

The modern Faith movement has gone far beyond Kenyon's doctrine of prosperity. Whereas Kenyon interpreted prosperity in terms of the believer's fundamental *needs*, many modern Faith teachers claim that God wants to grant every *desire* as well. Hagin teaches that God not only wants to deliver believers from poverty, "He wants His children to eat the best, He wants them to wear the best clothing, He wants them to drive the best cars, and He wants them to have the best of everything."[18] Nothing is too good for the "king's kids." As children of royalty, believers are to live in a manner befitting their exalted station in Christ. Fred Price, for example, teaches that God not only wants to provide the believer's need of transportation; he wants to provide any (and every) *luxury* automobile the believer so desires. After all, asks Price, "if the Mafia can ride around in Lincoln Continental town cars, why can't King's Kids?"[19] On the contrary, "King's Kids ought to ride in Rolls Royces."[20] Price warns, however, that a young "Word" Christian might not have sufficient faith to believe God for a luxury car and, perhaps, should begin believing God for loan payments on a Volkswagen.[21] A believer can keep buying and selling cars until "finally you will be believing for a Rolls Royce, if that's what you want." Personally, says Price, "I would rather have a Lincoln Continental. So whatever it is, different strokes for different folks."[22] Price teaches that "it doesn't make [God] any difference" if believers have a different car for every day of the week (except Sunday).[23] This is but one of many examples in the doctrine of prosperity in which there is a noticeable absence of any distinction between a believer's *needs* and his *desires*.

Biblical Analysis of the Doctrine of Prosperity

The Faith teachers are quite correct in directing believers to God and the promises of his word in order to get their needs met. The Bible does promise that, under normal circumstances, God both is aware of and will meet every legitimate need of the believer. In his Sermon on the Mount, the Lord Jesus taught that "your Father knows what you *need* before you ask Him" (Mt. 6:8). He taught us to not be anxious about the necessities of life, such as food, drink, and clothing (Mt. 6:25–31). These necessities were what the Gentiles so anxiously and eagerly spent all their time seeking (Mt. 6:32a). Jesus did not at all deny that these were legitimate needs. He assured his followers that "your heavenly Father knows that you *need* all of these things" (Mt. 6:32b). If they would "but seek first His kingdom and His righteousness," promised Jesus, "all these things [food, drink, and clothing] shall be added to you" (Mt. 6:33). As the believer is faithful to seek as his first priority the kingdom of God, God promises his faithfulness to meet the basic needs of the believer.

How Much Do We Really Need?

The distorted view of prosperity in the Faith theology centers on its definition of "need." The word for "need" used by Jesus in the Sermon on the Mount is the noun *chreia* (Mt. 6:8), and its verb form *chrēzō* (Mt. 6:32), the basic meaning of which is "necessary."[24] According to Jesus, we have "need" (*chreia*) of very few things in life. The Sermon on the Mount mentions only three: food, drink, and clothing. Paul limits "need" to two: "And if we have food and covering, with these we shall be content" (1 Tim. 6:8). Elsewhere, Jesus said that "only a few things are necessary, (*chreia*) really only one" (Lk. 10:42). In the context of Lk. 10:42, the one thing which is necessary (*chreia*) is to seek to spend time with Jesus and his word. This does not, of course, mean that Jesus was denying work as the means whereby men acquire food, drink, clothing. What Jesus says in Lk. 10:42 is perfectly consistent with his teaching in Mt. 6:33. Only those who purpose to "seek first the kingdom of God" can expect God to supply their needs.

In defining "need," the Faith teachers have gone far beyond Jesus and Paul, who limited need to food, drink, and clothing. If we accept the dictionary definition that a need is something without which we will die or no longer be able to function, then we would have to say that the Faith teachers have gone far beyond the confines of even the English language. New houses, fancy cars, and fine clothing hardly qualify as "needs," as items without which we will surely perish. The doctrine of prosperity fails to make any distinction between a *need* and a *want*, and a *want* and a *lust*. Under normal circumstances, God has promised to meet every legitimate *need*. He has also stated his desire to fulfill many of our *wants*. But nowhere has God given any indication that he would ever cater to our *lusts*. The only "promise" that God has made with regards to our lusts is his promise to crucify them (Rom. 6:1–14; 8:12, 13; Gal. 5:16–24).

Was Paul Prosperous?

Just as with their views of healing, the Faith teachers' doctrine of prosperity is a direct contradiction of Paul's teaching and lifestyle, which did not always reflect "perfect health," "prosperity," and "abundance." He often "suffered need" and knew lack. To those Corinthians who fancied themselves "filled" and "rich," who had become "kings," Paul wrote,

> For, I think, God has exhibited us apostles last of all, as men con-
> demned to death; because we have become a spectacle to the world,
> both to angels and to men. We are fools for Christ's sake, but you are
> prudent in Christ; we are weak, but you are strong; you are distin-
> guished, but we are without honor. To this present hour we are both
> hungry and thirsty, and are poorly clothed, and are roughly treated,
> and are homeless; and we toil, working with our own hands; when we
> are reviled, we bless; when we are persecuted, we endure; when we are
> slandered, we try to conciliate; we have become as the scum of the
> world, the dregs of all things, even until now (1 Cor. 4:9–13).

As the original "charismatics," the Corinthians manifested the same doctrinal error as many modern day charismatics. They fancied themselves "king's kids" who had already begun their royal reign in this life. These Corinthian charismatics were embarrassed by the sacrificial life and suffering of the apostle Paul. Little wonder is it that in the Corinthian epistles, more than any of his other writings, Paul finds it necessary to defend repeatedly his apostolic ministry (see 2 Cor. 10:7–18; 11:5–33; 12:1–6). Like many modern charismatics, the Corinthians were impressed only by preachers who possessed the three "P's": power, prestige, and prosperity. One wonders whether Paul would fare any better defending his ministry in the present charismatic milieu. For example, many faith teachers have claimed—usually, off the record— that if Paul knew what the Faith movement knows today, his poverty and sufferings would not have been necessary.

Prosperity and the Cross

The Corinthians misunderstood Paul for the same reason that many modern Faith teachers do today. They did not understand that the cross of Christ was the foundation of both Paul's theology and his life. In other words, because the Corinthians misunderstood Paul's gospel, they could not possibly appreciate his life, *for his life was but an expression of his gospel.* Paul's gospel was "the word of the cross" (1 Cor. 1:18). This word of the cross was nothing less than a crucified Messiah: "We preach Christ crucified" (1 Cor. 1:23). Unlike many modern pulpiteers, Paul did not preach "in cleverness of speech, that the cross of Christ should not be made void" (1 Cor. 1:17). On the contrary, he determined to know nothing among the

Corinthians "except Jesus Christ, and Him crucified" (1 Cor. 2:2). Paradoxically, the shameful execution of Jesus of Nazareth, and his subsequent resurrection, was the central event of Paul's gospel. Paul would speak no further of God until this event was established as "the first truth" in the minds of his audience.

The Faith teachers do not, of course, deny the necessity of the death of Jesus. On the contrary, they incessantly proclaim the *benefits* of the cross of Christ for the believer, such as prosperity and healing. But rarely, if ever, do they speak of the *claims* of the cross on the life of the believer. *Their basic attitude is that Jesus went to the cross so the believer would not have to.* How far this is from the word of the cross preached by Paul! The Faith teachers criticize Paul for his poverty and his acceptance of suffering, even sickness, as the will of God. What they fail to recognize is what Paul knew so well: *to believe in the crucified Messiah is to submit to the claim of his cross.* One cannot exploit the benefits of the cross without submitting to its claims. To reject the cross of Jesus is to reject his lordship.

The Believer and the Cross

For Paul, the cross of Christ crucified the totality of the believer's existence. This includes both the believer's life and his lusts for the things of this world. The crucifixion of the believer even extends to his relation to God's law. This last theme is especially strong in his letter to the Galatians. The death and resurrection of Jesus is not just an event to be believed. Jesus' cross became Paul's cross. Jesus' resurrection became Paul's resurrection. To believe in the cross meant the death of the believer's claims on his own life. To believe in the cross meant the death of the believer's claims on God through the law. To believe in the cross is to deliver the totality of one's existence unto him who delivered himself up for us. Anything less "nullifies" the grace of God and renders meaningless the death of Jesus (Gal. 2:20–21).

The Demands of the Cross

It is also evident from Galatians that Paul did not conceive of Jesus' cross in terms of its worldly benefits. He realized that identification with the cross of Jesus entailed the crucifixion of the believer's relation to the world and its lusts. Paul's "boast" was that the cross of Jesus had crucified both his desire for the world, and the desire of the world for him: "But may it never be that I should boast, except in the cross of our Lord Jesus Christ, through which the world has been crucified to me, and I to the world" (Gal. 6:14). The hall-mark of the believer should be his willingness to have crucified his fleshly lusts and worldly desires: "Now those who belong to Christ Jesus have crucified the flesh with its passions and desires" (Gal. 5:24). Paul both lived and taught the crucified life.

In teaching his followers the crucified life, Paul was inventing no new doctrine. The other apostles also clearly taught that to be-lieve in Jesus demanded renunciation of this world's lusts. James admonishes his worldly readers with the following question: "You adulteresses, do you not know that friendship with the world is hostility toward God? Therefore whoever wishes to be a friend of the world makes himself an enemy of God" (Jas. 4:4). The believer can-not be friend of the world without being an enemy and adulterer towards God. John likewise teaches that the love of God and love of the world's lusts are mutually exclusive (1 Jn. 2:15–17). What was the origin of this unanimity of opinion among the apostles? Undoubt-edly, it was the Lord Jesus himself, who had taught them, "No one can serve two masters; for either he will hate the one and love the other, or he will hold to one and despise the other. You cannot serve God and mammon" (Mt. 6:24). Jesus did not endure the cross so that his followers could indulge in the lusts of this world. Quite the contrary, only those who make Jesus' cross their cross can even claim to be his followers. Those who would teach that the purpose of the cross was to bestow worldly prosperity on believers should heed again the words of the crucified Messiah: "If anyone wishes to come after Me, let him deny himself, and take up His cross, and follow Me" (Mk. 8:34). . . . "And he who does not take his cross and follow after Me is not worthy of Me" (Mt. 10:38).

The primary error of the Faith doctrine of prosperity, then, is not just in its claim that God wants to make believers rich. The problem is much more fundamental than that. At stake is nothing less than the meaning of the central event of Christianity: the cross and resurrection of Jesus. The Faith teachers interpret the cross of Jesus exclusively in terms of the benefits it confers upon the believer, such as prosperity. In so doing, they create a mind-set in their fol-lowers which is entirely antithetical to the true meaning of the cross.

The Problem with Prosperity

This prosperity mind-set contradicts the cross in at least three ways. First, it subverts the demand of the cross for self-denial. The will of God is assumed to be synonymous with the self-indulgent will of man. The believer can rest assured that it is God's will to grant him "whatever his li'l ol' heart desires." Second, the doctrine of prosperity reduces God to a means to an end. Many who practice it become seekers of status (and all its external symbols) rather than seekers of God. A fundamental shift occurs in their conception of God. God becomes the *means* whereby the *end* of prosperity is attained. He becomes the *source* from which prosperity flows, rather than the *sovereign* to whom prosperity in this life is sacrificed. Third, the mind-set of prosperity is focused on the things of this world as the sign of God's approval and the means of God's blessing. The demand of Jesus to leave the world behind and to take up the cross to follow him is blunted, if not silenced, by the doctrine of prosperity. The Jesus of the prosperity doctrine is not the crucified Messiah.

But what, then, is the correct biblical attitude towards money and prosperity? The question of the believer's relation to monetary riches is, admittedly, a difficult one, a full answer to which is beyond the scope of this present volume. Gordon Fee, the Pentecostal scholar who has written the most on the prosperity doctrine, cites two extreme viewpoints that one should avoid in relation to wealth. The first is *rejection.* In this viewpoint, the believer rejects all prosperity in the belief that money is inherently evil. The second extreme is that of accommodation. In this viewpoint, the believer accommodates himself to worldly cultural values with little or no thought about the demands of Jesus and his cross, or the tremendous economic disparity which exists in the world today.[25]

The Bible and the Poor

We see such cultural accommodation in the Faith theology's doctrine of prosperity. The doctrine of prosperity is, in fact, a carnal accommodation to the crass materialism of American culture. It ignores and/or compromises the demands of the New Testament upon the affluent and constructs a theology that not only rationalizes the disparity between rich and poor. It actually degrades the poor, claiming that their poverty is the result of "dishonoring" God. Poverty is, indeed, a curse, as the Faith teachers say, but it is not a curse that God inflicts upon people. It is a curse that people inflict upon one another by means of oppression.

Even a cursory reading of the Bible reveals that the doctrine of prosperity cannot stand up to an examination of the biblical evidence. Prosperity is based on a very selective set of biblical texts, the majority of which are from the Old Testament. It can be held only to the exclusion of countless passages of the Bible which address the subject of wealth and poverty. These passage are so numerous that it is possible to cite only the major ones from the New Testament. The following passages were chosen because they reflect both God's concern for the poor and his warning to the rich.

God's Concern for the Poor

Blessed are you who are poor, for yours is the kingdom of God (Lk. 6:20).

The Spirit of the Lord is upon Me, for He has anointed Me to preach the gospel to the poor (Lk. 4:18).

One thing you [the rich young ruler] lack: go and sell all you possess, and give to the poor, and you shall have treasure in heaven; and come, follow Me (Mk. 10:21).

For the poor you always have with you, and whenever you wish, you can do them good (Mk. 14:7).

This poor widow put in more than all the contributors to the treasury; for they all put in out of their surplus, but she, out of her poverty, put in all she owned, all she had to live on (Mk. 12:43–44).

They [the apostles] only asked us to remember the poor—the very thing I [Paul] also was eager to do (Gal. 2:10).

Or do you despise the church of God, and shame those who have nothing? What shall I say to you? Shall I praise you? In this I will not praise you (1 Cor. 11:22).

God's Warning to the Rich

But woe to you who are rich, for you are receiving your comfort in full (Lk. 6:24).

It is easier for a camel to go through the eye of a needle than for a rich man to enter the kingdom of God (Mk. 10:25).

Do not lay up for yourselves treasures upon earth . . . But lay up for yourselves treasures in heaven . . . for where your treasure is, there will your heart be also (Mt. 6:19–21).

No one can serve two masters; for either he will hate the one and love the other or he will hold to one and despise the other. You cannot serve God and mammon (Mt. 6:24).

And the worries of the world, and the deceitfulness of riches, and the desires for other things enter in and choke the word, and it becomes unfruitful (Mk. 4:19).

Instruct those who are rich in this present world not to be conceited or to fix their hope on the uncertainty of riches, but on God, who richly supplies with all things to enjoy (1 Tim. 6:17).

Instruct them [the rich] to do good, to be rich in good works, to be generous and ready to share, storing up for themselves the treasure of a good foundation for the future (1 Tim. 6:18, 19).

Listen, my beloved brethren: did not God choose the poor of this world to be rich in faith and heirs of the kingdom which He promised to those who love Him (Jas. 2:5).

Come now, you rich, weep and howl for your miseries which are coming upon you. Your riches have rotted and your garments have become moth-eaten. Your gold and your silver have rusted; and their rust will be a witness against you and will consume your flesh like fire. It is in the last days that you have stored up your treasure (Jas. 5:1–3).

In conclusion, the doctrine of prosperity is the result of two influences, one cultic, the other cultural. First, it is the result of metaphysical influences upon the founding father of the Faith theology, E. W. Kenyon. The metaphysical cults, particularly New Thought and the Unity School of Christianity, were the first to propagate the idea that God will make rich all those who know "the laws of prosperity" which govern the universe. Through Kenyon, this cultic belief entered the Faith movement and was expanded by Hagin and the other Faith teachers to a degree which even he himself would never have approved. Second, the doctrine of prosperity is a gross example of the church's cultural accommodation to the worldly values of American materialism. It is a direct contradiction of the examples of the Lord Jesus, the Apostle Paul, and all the heroes of faith, who were "destitute, afflicted, ill-treated, men of whom the world was not worthy" (Heb. 11:37, 38). The doctrine of prosperity is not worthy of such men.

Notes

1. Harrell, *All Things Are Possible*, p. 229.
2. Copeland, *The Laws of Prosperity*, pp. 18–20.
3. Gloria Copeland, *God's Will Is Prosperity* (Tulsa: Harrison House, 1978), p. 54.
4. K. Hagin, "The Law of Faith," *Word of Faith* (Nov., 1974), pp. 2–3.
5. Charles Fillmore, *Prosperity* (Unity Village: Unity School of Christianity, 1981), p. 33.
6. Ibid., p. 72.
7. Ibid., pp. 50, 51.
8. Trine, *In Tune*, p. 135.
9. Ibid., p. 141.
10. Copeland, *The Laws of Prosperity*, pp. 98, 101.
11. Trine, *In Tune*, p. 138.
12. Ibid., p. 137.
13. Ibid., pp. 138, 139.

14. Kenyon, *Jesus the Healer*, p. 67.

15. Hagin, *Authority*, p. 22.

16. E. W. Kenyon, *Advanced Bible Course: Studies in the Deeper Life* (Seattle: Kenyon's Gospel Publishing Society, 1970), p. 59.

17. Ibid.

18. Hagin, *New Thresholds*, pp. 54–55.

19. Price, *Faith, Foolishness or Presumption?* p. 34.

20. Ibid., p. 28.

21. Ibid., pp. 25, 26.

22. Ibid., p. 28.

23. Ibid.

24. Bauer, Arndt, & Gingrich, *A Greek-English Lexicon of the New Testament and Other Early Christian Literature* (Chicago: Univ. of Chicago, 1957), p. 893.

25. Gordon D. Fee, "The New Testament View of Wealth and Possessions," *New Oxford Review* (May, 1981), p. 8.

11 Summary and Conclusion

This analysis of the Faith movement has characterized the Faith theology as "a different gospel." In the context of the divine anathema pronounced by the Apostle Paul on those who preach different gospels (Gal. 1:6–9), it is a charge that is not made for the sake of mere literary metaphor or theological polemic. The issues at stake are considerably more than theological hairsplitting about biblical minutiae. Only those theologi cal systems that syncretize foreign bodies of religious belief—thereby jeopardizing the central core of biblical doctrine, ethics, and practice—should be characterized as different gospels. Using this criterion, is the charge justified that the Faith theology constitutes a different gospel? I think that it is, for three reasons: (1) its historical origins; (2) its heretical doctrines; and (3) its cultic practices. Let us summarize our findings in each of these areas.

Summary

Historical Origins

The Faith teachers are not, as commonly believed, the progeny of wild-fire healing revivalism. There are two historical streams of divine healing in American church history: (1) the Holiness/Pentecostal stream; and (2) the New Thought/ Christian Science stream. The Faith movement comes from the latter, not the former. It has often been misplaced in the Holiness/Pentecostal stream because researchers usually assume that because Kenneth Hagin was a post-World War II healing revivalist and charismatic, the Faith movement must also be a recent charismatic phenomenon. Bruce Barron is correct that Kenneth Hagin may be classified as a charismatic healing revivalist, but Hagin is not, as commonly believed, the father of the Faith movement. Hagin plagiarized in word and content the bulk of his theology from E. W. Kenyon. All of the Faith teachers, including Kenneth Hagin and Kenneth Copeland, whether they admit it or not, are the spiritual sons and grandsons of E. W. Kenyon. It was Kenyon, not Hagin, who formulated every major doctrine of the modern Faith movement. Hagin did incorporate theological bits and pieces from his background in classical Pentecostalism and healing revivalism. But the guts of the Faith theology— its five major doctrines of Revelation Knowledge, Identification, Faith, Healing, and Prosperity—were taken from the writings of Kenyon.

To understand the historical origins of the Faith movement, one must begin with its patriarch, E. W. Kenyon. Barron's depiction of the Faith movement as being in the lineage of classical Pentecostalism and healing revivalism is thus found to be false, because Kenyon belonged to neither. The post-World War II Healing Revival did not begin until 1946, far past the prime of the elderly Kenyon, who died in 1948. In his heyday (c. 1921–41), Kenyon was on friendly terms with many classical Pentecostals and ministered often in their circles, but he specifically rejected the hallmark of Pentecostal theology: Spirit-baptism as a second, subsequent work of grace, of which tongues is the definitive initial evidence. It is highly doubtful that Kenyon himself ever spoke in tongues; if he did, it is clear that he later renounced his experience. Kenyon preached healing and prosperity, but he did so as a non-Pentecostal. Hence, the historical origins of the Faith theology must lie somewhere in Kenyon's life other than in his superficial contact with classical Pentecostals.

The roots of Kenyon's theology may be traced to his personal background in the metaphysical cults, specifically New Thought and Christian Science. Kenyon's education exposed him to a wide variety of non-Christian ideologies. In 1891, he attended the Emerson School of Oratory, an institution that has been described by its own historians as permeated with New Thought metaphysics, and whose founder, Charles Emerson, died a member of the Christian Science mother church in Boston. During his own time in Boston, Kenyon also attended the services of Minot J. Savage, a prominent Unitarian preacher, author, and leader. Kenyon's friends verify that he was well-read in metaphysics, in the writings of Ralph Waldo Emerson, and in New England Transcendentalism.

His friends also verify that Kenyon openly confessed the influence of metaphysical thought upon his own theology. We earlier quoted John Kennington, who said that Kenyon was "very conversant with Christian Science concepts" and that "he admitted that he freely drew the water of his thinking from this well." We also quoted Ern Baxter, who stated that Kenyon told him that "there was a lot that could be gotten from Mary Baker Eddy" and that he was undoubtedly influenced by her. Kenyon's motives for incorporating metaphysical thought into his theology are less clear, but the evidence would indicate that, if they were conscious on his part, his motives were probably benign. Sensing the amazing growth and overt presence of the supernatural in the metaphysical cults, and the lack of the same in traditional churches, Kenyon attempted to forge a synthesis of metaphysical and evangelical thought in order to help the traditional church provide for its members the missing supernatural element that caused many to defect to the cults. The resultant Faith theology is a strange mixture of biblical fundamentalism and New Thought metaphysics.

Heretical Doctrines

It is also heretical. Historically, the term "heresy" is best reserved for major departures from Christian orthodoxy, especially the doctrines of God, Christ, revelation, and salvation. There are many peculiar ideas and practices in the Faith theology, but what merits it the label of heresy are the following: (1) its deistic view of God, who must dance to men's attempts to manipulate the spiritual laws of the universe; (2) its demonic view of Christ, who is filled with "the satanic nature" and must be "born-again" in hell; (3) its gnostic view of revelation, which demands denial of the physical senses and classifies Christians by their willingness to do so; and (4) its metaphysical view of salvation, which deifies man and spiritualizes the atonement, locating it in hell rather than on the cross, thereby subverting the crucial biblical belief that it is Christ's physical death and shed blood which alone atone for sin. All four of these heresies may be accounted for by Kenyon's syncretism of metaphysical thought with traditional biblical doctrine.

Cultic Practices

Many of the eccentric and dangerous practices of the Faith movement may also be accounted for by this association. These practices may not directly challenge Christian orthodoxy (right belief), but they do violate the church's orthopraxy (right practice), and, thus, pose a serious threat to the spiritual, psychological, and physical safety of God's people. The following cultic practices of the Faith theology are mentioned in this regard.

(1) PMA/Positive Confession. Many regard this as a healthy practice, emphasizing the psychological benefits of positive thinking and speaking. What this fails to consider is the historical fact that those who first taught PMA/positive confession—the New Thought metaphysicians— attributed its power to cosmic principles and occultic deities. Though the Bible does emphasize the importance of a pure mind and holy speech, it nowhere states that a person can alter physical reality through mental means, and it certainly does not encourage verbal confession of the divine Name and Word as means of manipulating God's will. In fact, the Scriptures strictly prohibit both.

(2) Sensory Denial. Like the metaphysical cults, the Faith movement teaches believers to deny sensory reality, particularly when it indicates the physical symptoms of illness. This practice has led to numerous tragic deaths in both movements.

(3) Implicit Rejection of Medical Science. These deaths were all the more tragic because with prompt medical care, many could have been easily avoided. The Faith teachers do not, like Christian Science practitioners, explicitly forbid the use of medical science; like the less radical New Thought teachers, their rejection of medicine and doctors is implicit. By virtue of their own example, the Faith teachers insist that believers can, and should, grow in their faith to the point where they no longer need medical science. Only those in the Faith movement who are immature in their faith guiltily seek medical care.

(4) Prosperity. This practice, which has become both the drawing card and holy grail of the Faith movement, may also be traced to the metaphysical cults. The doctrine of prosperity instills greed for material things, it teaches the egocentric notion that one should give to get, and it has bankrolled the unbridled ambitions of more than a few charismatic ministers and televangelists.

Where Do We Go from Here?

An Appeal to the Faith Movement

Although many have claimed that the Faith teachers have moderated of late and moved toward the center, this moderation has not found its way into their writings and tapes, which continue to be produced and distributed without revision on a massive scale. The Faith teachers may have toned down their rhetoric and altered some of their jargon, but their cultic theological system is the same one that engendered the Faith controversy of the early 1980s. Like the Shepherding-Discipleship controversy, the Faith controversy has never been resolved at the doctrinal level, nor will it be until the Faith teachers recant the above doctrines and practices. Cultic and heretical doctrine cannot be "moderated," as if all that is necessary are a few cosmetic alterations and word changes. The Faith theology is based upon cultic presuppositions, and until these presuppositions are recanted, any pseudomoderation will only make it a bigger threat. Moderated heresy is still heresy. I would appeal to the pastors and lay people of the Faith movement to recognize the following: (1) the cultic historical origins of their movement; (2) the degree to which these origins have influenced their doctrines and practices; and (3) the need to recant these cultic doctrines and practices and reconstruct their theology upon a more solid biblical foundation.

A Question for the Independent Charismatic Movement

Having grown up in a liberal Protestant denomination that participated heavily in the ecumenical movement, I am particularly sensitive to appeals for unity that do not include biblical doctrine as a basis of Christian unity. Although the efforts of organizations such as the Network to promote unity in the independent charismatic movement are noble, their agenda sounds quite similar to that of the World Council of Churches, which charismatics have long, and probably correctly, castigated as the epitome of liberalism. The Network does have sound doctrinal standards, but either these standards do not really determine its membership, or the Network is unaware of the degree to which the Faith theology violates these standards through its cultic doctrines and practices. My question for the independent charismatic movement is this: when are the two major historical controversies of our movement—the Shepherding controversy and the Faith controversy—going to be resolved, *really* resolved, at the *doctrinal* level? However sympathetic many of us might be to the noble goals of organizations such as the Network, until these doctrinal issues are addressed and their controversies resolved, there can be no real unity.

A Warning to the Pentecostal and Evangelical Movements

Those who are in evangelical and classical Pentecostal churches should not suppose that because they are not direct participants in the independent charismatic movement, they will be left unscathed by its more extremist elements, such as the Faith movement. The ability of charismatic doctrines and practices to infiltrate denominational churches is too well documented from the past to be ignored in the future. The Faith teachers have a far broader sphere of influence than their own in the independent charismatic movement. Their metaphysical concepts have spread to numerous believers who do not count themselves part of the Faith movement, including many in Pentecostal and Evangelical churches. This contagion cannot be allowed to continue. The Faith theology must be identified and shunned for what it is: a different gospel.

A Concluding Observation and Prediction

It would be wonderful to think that, if the Faith (and Shepherding) controversy were suddenly resolved, the independent charismatic movement would then return to sound standards of doctrine and practice. This is, indeed, an attractive prospect, but it is not a realistic one. Even if these past controversies were magically to disappear, it would probably only be a matter of time before the independent charismatic movement would be taken captive by yet another biblically unsound and theologically aberrant teaching. History dictates that before long, one more "prophet" will arise among us, proclaiming the latest "Now" word for charismatics, who will then be gathered up into the next movement to sweep through our ranks.

The main cause for these chronic doctrinal tangents is readily apparent. *From its inception to the present, the independent charismatic movement has had a defective doctrine of revelation.* We charismatics are not adequately committed to the principle that the Bible is the only infallible rule of faith and practice. Correct doctrine comes from one source: apostolic teaching as it is expressed and preserved in the Holy Scriptures. The revelatory gifts of the Spirit—prophecy, words of wisdom and knowledge—can and should have their place in the church, but these gifts were never intended to become an alternative source of doctrine, thereby subverting the teaching of the Lord Jesus and his apostles. Until we become seriously committed to the principle that all doctrine and practice must be derived from the hermeneutically sound exegesis of God's Word, our movement will remain vulnerable to an endless series of prophetic revelators and their bizarre teachings.

What then must be done to prevent this from happening again in the charismatic movement? We need a doctrinal reformation based on the principles of *the* Reformation. We must reconstruct our doctrine of revelation in such a manner as to allow for the revelatory gifts of the Spirit that are our charismatic heritage, but also clearly insist upon the Reformation principle of *sola Scriptura*. As the Reformers knew so well, the Scriptures alone must rule the faith, doctrine, and practice of the church. As we charismatics have come to recognize, however, those same Scriptures teach that the revelatory gifts of the Spirit also have their sphere in life of the church, something the Reformers did not admit. This special insight may enable charismatics to say more than the Reformers said about the doctrine of revelation, but it does not allow us to say less.

Afterword:
The Faith Movement Today

To prepare for writing this afterword I recently read a five-inch thick file containing the hundreds of letters, reviews, and newspaper articles from all over the world sent to me in Holland since *A Different Gospel* was published in 1988. I moved to Amsterdam that same year to pursue missionary church-planting in Europe, and for the last five years, I have served as the senior pastor of the Crossroads International Church of Amsterdam, a growing interdenominational congregation of over 400 people from more than 15 nations. My life has changed considerably from the days when as a graduate student and adjunct instructor of theology at Oral Roberts University I wrote *A Different Gospel*. And it is precisely because of my present work as a pastor and my travels in Europe and the former Soviet Union as a missionary church planter, that I continue to affirm what I first wrote.

A Movement that Shoots its Wounded

As a pastor, I grieve for those who have been victimized by Faith theology. Before me, I have from my file a letter about Bob (not his real name), who rejected Christianity because the Faith promises of prosperity did not work for him as advertised. Then I see the letter from a woman we'll call Mary, who suffered brain damage when the symptoms of her headache—that she was by faith "confessing" were not real—turned out to be advanced rheumatic fever. Her case reminds me of a couple that I once pastored who in their previous Faith church had let their newborn baby die of a medically treatable condition. And next I came across a letter from a lady whose story for obvious reasons must remain anonymous. Let me share it with you:

> Dear Mr. McConnell:
>
> I have just completed the first part of your book *A Different Gospel*. I just wanted you to know that I truly appreciate all the work and

research you put into this book. I also felt that you might want to know a little about my story. . . .

I just disconnected myself from a church pastored by Rhema graduates eleven months ago. I had been a member for seven years. I began attending in 1981 and was married in 1983. I married a wonderful Christian man who had been born again 14 years at the time, myself only four. He had read Hagin's books, however, he had never attended a "Faith" church until our marriage.

He passed away in September . . . leaving me a two year old son and three months pregnant. You see, he had suffered from colitus[sic] for several years. Doctors would say he should have his colon removed by age 30 to avoid the risk of cancer. (He had seen physicians in the military when the colitus[sic] started).

During our marriage, he would assure me he was healed because of the teachings he had received and was denying the symptoms as a lie. He died at age 30 from liver cancer. The cancer was only one month in his body. It had started in his colon.

I see now that doctors are truly our friends, not enemies reporting lies. Still I am left alone with two small children ages one and three. My hope is now resting in Rom. 8:28 that surely God will work out all things for our good.

I sincerely thought we were following Jesus for those years. I now cry when I think of my friends left behind. When I first left the church in February, I was quote, "blacklisted." You see, the devil is dividing their church. It is a very sad situation.

I hope my story will help your research in some way.

Respectfully,[1]

Thankfully, this dear woman has picked up the fragments of her life and is still serving the Lord. She is one of thousands of people who have been victimized by Faith theology and subsequently told it was their own fault. Their "testimonies" will never appear in charismatic publications. They are "the dark side" of the Faith movement, the Orwellian "un-people" many charismatic leaders are not willing to acknowledge even exist.

All of these people are quite different, but one thing that many have in common is that after their losses they were, to use their terminology, "blacklisted" by the leaders of their Faith churches. Some were told that they lacked faith. Others were accused of having hidden sins in their lives. All were told that they had not applied Faith teachings correctly. But ironically the problem really was that they followed Faith theology all too well, and paid dearly for it. Amazingly, many have clung to their faith in Christ despite their losses, while others have left the church, never to return. I find it incredible that in all of the various critiques of *A Different Gospel*, not one has expressed serious concern for these people. Apparently, we in the charismatic army still shoot our wounded. It is to these wounded ones that I dedicate this afterword.

The Walking Wounded throughout the World

Not only do I stand behind *A Different Gospel* for pastoral reasons, but my experience as a missionary has only increased my conviction that the Faith movement is a divisive element of the charismatic renewal. Several people have tried to tell me that the Faith movement in America has moderated of late and has moved away from its more radical beliefs and practices. Having lived out-side of America since 1988, I am not in a position to evaluate this claim and can only hope it is true. I find it difficult, however, to see how a movement can claim to have moderated when none of its major doctrines have ever been retracted, nor any of its hundreds of publications reedited. The books and pamphlets of the Faith move-ment, especially those of Kenneth Hagin, have been translated and published throughout the world in their original form. This is the very same literature that divided the charismatic renewal in America in the '70s and '80s. It is now cutting the same divisive swath in many other parts of the world.

I have personally talked to or received correspondence from church leaders concerning the schismatic effects of Faith theology on churches in Sweden, Norway, Holland, Belgium, Germany, Rus-sia, Latvia, Estonia, Bulgaria, England, South Africa, Kenya, Canada, and Mexico. The problems caused by Faith theology are particularly acute in the countries of the former Soviet Union and the Eastern bloc. A bishop from Latvia, for example, shared with me how mis-sionaries from a radical Faith church in Sweden are taking over entire churches. Their *modus operandi* is to ship the Latvian pastor back to Stockholm for free indoctrination, while in his absence they catechize his church in Faith theology. I have received requests from church leaders in Russia, Bulgaria, and the former Yugoslavia to have *A Different Gospel* translated because of the spiritual havoc created by the Faith movement. Recently, Pentecostal leaders from Holland have contacted me about a translation into Dutch because they just do not know how to deal with the Faith teachers' claims of a superior revelation of healing and prosperity.

And so it is throughout the world, especially among poorer nations. The outrageous promises of Faith theology naturally sound attractive to citizens of developing countries who often lack adequate food, housing, and basic health care. When the countries of the former Soviet Union first opened their doors to the West, for example, virtually anything from America—any product, idea, or theology—found instant acceptance with the culturally and spiritually starved masses. The Faith teachers did, indeed, make many converts in these countries; but then again, so did every other Christian missionary (or for that matter, the cultists and the pornographers, as well). The problem is that, like many Western products, Faith theology promises far more than it delivers. Much of it often does not translate well into non-Western cultures, and what does translate creates expectations of health and wealth that cannot possibly be sustained in their underdeveloped economies.

Wherever it goes in the world, Faith theology has what people in the medical profession call a "placebo effect." A placebo is a substance having no medicinal value administered by doctors merely to reassure a patient. The patients often believe the substance will make them better, and for a while it does. But sooner or later, the effects of the placebo wear off, and patients are no better for having taken it. So it is with Faith theology in underdeveloped countries. At first, the Faith placebo is received with enthusiasm by nationals as the panacea for all that is wrong in their countries. But eventually (and inevitably), the Faith theology does not heal all diseases, right all wrongs, fill all pockets, or suddenly cause supply to meet demand. People in the former Soviet Union, for example, are discovering that the Western gospel of prosperity does not cure their economic woes any better than Western capitalism. When the Faith gospel does not perform as advertised, many people reject not only it, but Western Christianity as well. Having been innoculated with an injection of the Faith gospel, these walking wounded become spiritually resistant to the true gospel, not only from other Westerners, but also from their fellow nationals. As one Latvian pastor who is trying to help these spiritual drop-outs reported, "When I try to minister to my backslidden countrymen, they say to me, 'If the Americano preacher cannot help me, how can you?' "

I am not saying that the impact of the Faith movement on world missions is all negative. Quite the contrary, Faith missionaries are aggressive evangelists and resourceful church planters. Many Faith churches are making a big difference in the world for Christ, both spiritually and socially. Pastor Ray McCauley's enormous church in South Africa, for instance, has done an incredible work of racial reconciliation in a country struggling to throw off the vestiges of apartheid.[2] The Manna movement in Portugal has almost single-handedly brought that country its first real evangelistic revival. Many other Faith success stories on the mission field could and should be cited. To the degree that Faith pastors stick to preaching the gospel and planting churches, they are a real force for God and effective on the mission field. Let the record show that I enthusiastically acknowledge the contribution of the Faith movement to world missions.

But let the record also show that I am saying that the price tag of the Faith movement's missionary successes in divided churches and spiritual drop-outs is far too high. Just as in America, the Faith theology has had a mixed impact on the mission field. That is always true of syncretism: a mixed message produces a mixed movement that has mixed impact. The cultic elements of Faith theology are like tares among the wheat in the Faith movement's missionary harvest. Granted, every movement in the history of the church has had its spiritual casualty list. The Reformation certainly did, as did the Wesleyan and Pentecostal movements. But the huge number of spiritually "missing-in-action" and "missing-and-presumed-dead" in the Faith movement is completely unacceptable. It is not considered good form in the present charismatic renewal to keep mentioning this price in shattered faiths, divided churches, and even human lives. Many have justified Faith extremism by quoting the well-worn proverb, "It's easier to restrain a fanatic than resurrect a corpse." But when those fanatics start leaving corpses, both spiritual and physical, then it is time to speak, and speak loudly. Much to my chagrin, however, I have discovered that in the charismatic renewal, this is easier said than done.

On Being "Spiritually Correct"

One of the things that I found both fascinating and disturbing was how important it is to be "spiritually correct" in some charismatic media circles. It is as important to be spiritually correct to receive a fair hearing from the charismatic press as it is to be politically correct with the secular press. In its first year of publication,

A Different Gospel received very favorable reviews from both Pentecostal and Evangelical periodicals.[3] But in Charismatic circles, it was
a completely different story.[4] For example, after *A Different Gospel*
was first released, it was advertised in the September/October 1988
issue of *Ministries Today* magazine, a charismatic periodical from
Strang Publications aimed at Christian leaders. In the January/
February 1989 edition of this same magazine, a Faith pastor objected to the ad, and *Ministries Today* promptly canceled it with this
comment:

> We regret carrying the advertisement for a book that seems designed
> to discredit and undermine the ministry of Kenneth Hagin and many
> other sincere ministers of the gospel. . . . As soon as the book came into
> our hands, we knew it was not a volume that we could endorse, so we
> canceled any further advertisements for it.

Reader reaction was immediate. Over the next two issues of
Ministries Today, numerous letters to the editor protested the ad's
cancellation, calling it "selective censorship." One pastor wrote this:

> I'm deeply disappointed in the lack of journalistic guts this turn of
> events demonstrates. Will such extremes in theology ever be allowed
> to balance out when the theological institutions and periodicals, such
> as yours, take such a defensive position? A better approach is to listen
> to the author's major points and permit the truth to win out in the
> forum of public debate.

In response, the late Jamie Buckingham then promised that the
magazine would provide "an objective review" of the book, which
followed in the September/October 1989 issue. Although I found the
subsequent review something less than objective,[5] *Ministries Today*
did at least provide some public forum by summarizing the book's
conclusions and by publishing a brief interview with me clarifying
some of my views.

Unfortunately, the debate that followed in the charismatic periodicals was extremely short-lived and one-sided. Only those who
supported Faith theology were allowed to write for *Minstries Today*
or Strang Publications' more popularly aimed magazine, *Charisma*.
Why were not some respected Pentecostal-charismatic theologians
on the other side of the Faith issue, such as Gordon Fee, Charles
Farah, or William Menzies, asked to express their views? Or why
wasn't Bruce Barron, whose book *The Health and Wealth Gospel* was
considered by many a model of theological diplomacy, invited to
contribute an article to the debate?[6] Reader reaction to *Ministries
Today*'s attempt at censorship should have suggested to its editorial

staff that their audience wanted to hear from voices on *both sides* of the Faith controversy.

My own experience suggests that the charismatic press is even more selective and biased than the secular press. I was interviewed by many religion reporters from secular newspapers and found most of them to be polite and fair. Their reviews were journalistically balanced, they sought comments from both me and local Faith teachers, and even defended the Faith movement on some points.[7] The charismatic press, however, continued to fire one-sided broadsides at *A Different Gospel* and never again solicited any response from me. With one exception, I never answered any of my critics at Strang Publications. The one exception was William DeArteaga.[8]

Quenching the Spirit

Of all the critiques of *A Different Gospel*, the most formidable is William DeArteaga's *Quenching the Spirit.*[9] The central thesis of his book is that throughout the history of the church, the ministry and gifts of the Spirit have been supressed by those committed to "consensus orthodoxy," a form of orthodoxy that prioritizes historical tradition over biblical revelation. Philosophically, consensus orthodoxy is characterized by what DeArteaga calls a "materialist-realist" view of the world that functionally excludes the supernatural from the church. DeArteaga believes that the heretic plays an essential role in the church by challenging the deficiencies of consensus orthodoxy, thereby forcing the church to open itself to new beliefs and practices that the Spirit wants to restore, or even add, to the church. When it comes to heresy, DeArteaga believes that there are two "perennial" heresies attested in the Bible that resurface in various forms throughout church history: (1) Gnosticism—a philosophy based on radical dualism and idealism; and (2) Pharisaism—"a religious attitude and heresy that so affirms the role of tradition that a new move of the Holy Spirit is often identified as demonic."[10] As a *via media* to these two heresies, DeArteaga advocates what he calls "faith-idealism," a supposedly biblical form of idealism that prioritizes the unseen over the seen, and the supernatural over the natural.

Some of the differences between DeArteaga and myself are more apparent than real. Actually, we seem to agree on some major points about Faith theology. DeArteaga concedes the following historical conclusions of *A Different Gospel* with very little qualification. (1) Kenneth Hagin drew the major points of his theology from

E.W. Kenyon. His plagiarism of Kenyon was "unintentional," however, and according to DeArteaga, reflects only the "informal bor-
rowing" of preachers whose standards of documentation are below
that of the publishing industry.[11] (2) Kenyon is the theological and
historical founder of the Faith movement[12] and also greatly influenced the charismatic movement at large.[13] (3) Both Christian Science and New Thought metaphysics are cultic heresies, each
expressing various degrees of gnostic idealism.[14] (4) Kenyon incorporated cultic elements of New Thought metaphysics into his personal theology.[15] DeArteaga readily admits that Kenyon "obviously
adopted the idealist perspective for interpreting Scripture and living
the Christian life of faith from New Thought sources."[16] (5) Kenyon
was not himself a Pentecostal, either by theology or experience.[17]
(6) Kenyon's doctrine of "identification", which interprets the atonement as an exclusively spiritual event taking place in hell, not on the
cross, is "theological error."[18] (7) Kenyon's practice of rejecting
medication in favor of healing prayer and positive confession was,
and is, a "dangerous practice."[19]

If I am interpreting him correctly, DeArteaga and I appear to
agree on the above points. The main difference between us is how
these historical facts are to be understood. De Arteaga criticizes my
interpretation of the history and theology of the Faith movement on
the following points. He contends: (1) Despite their gnostic and
cultic beliefs, certain New Thought writers salvaged elements of
biblical truths about the supernatural and restored them to the
church. Chief among these was Charles Fillmore of the Unity School
of Christianity.[20] (2) Several Christians who began in New Thought
rejected its gnostic and cultic beliefs, filtered them into a form consistent with what the Bible taught about faith-idealism, and then
introduced the purified form of New Thought into the mainstream
of the Pentecostal and charismatic movements. According to
DeArteaga, chief among these individuals was Kenyon.[21] (3) Kenyon's critical remarks about New Thought and Christian Science are
adequate proof for DeArteaga that the founder of the Faith movement thoroughly broke with his cultic background and after 1916
was no longer influenced by it in any significant way.[22] (4) DeArteaga
argues that heretics play a vital role in the church. He claims that I
do not recognize that the church has discovered some theological
truths only in response to certain heretics preaching half-truths.[23]
Thus, the fact that Kenyon formulated his faith-idealism drawing
upon the metaphysical cults in no way impugns his theology in

DeArteaga's mind. (5) Kenyon's distinction between Sense Knowledge and Revelation Knowledge is the key to his theology, but it comes from Paul's writings, not those of the metaphysical cults.[24] (6) Kenyon limited his use of positive confession to the promises of the Bible; and he learned this theological restraint from Ralph Waldo Trine, chief exponent of New Thought metaphysics.[25] (7) Doctrinal innovations are part of the Protestant tradition and, therefore, it is absurd to reject the Faith theology simply because it is new.[26] (8) Only the Bible can be used to measure orthodoxy. Historical orthodoxy and the theological tradition of the church are of no value in determining heresy.[27]

Before I respond to *Quenching the Spirit* and offer a defense of my own work, let me say that DeArteaga has written an interesting polemic against cessationist theology. I found myself agreeing with him on many points. DeArteaga is a serious student of history and has scrupulously documented his sources. He is generally accurate in his summaries of my own work and asks some legitimate, penetrating questions. If only all of my critics had done their homework to the degree which DeArteaga obviously has. Although I may disagree radically with his conclusions, I must concede that DeArteaga has read my work closely, something I cannot affirm of most of my critics. And although DeArteaga and I are obviously far apart on most issues of the Faith controversy, let me say that I regard him as a worthy opponent, whose intellectual integrity is apparent at numerous points in his work.

A Response to William DeArteaga

DeArteaga sees a progression from Charles Farah's critique of the Faith movement, *From the Pinnacle of the Temple*, of which he wholeheartedly approves,[28] to Dave Hunt's *Seduction* and *Beyond Seduction*, of which he decidedly does not approve. According to De Arteaga, *A Different Gospel* is a "polemic" that stands somewhere between Farah and Hunt, both in chronology and content. This appraisal is only partially accurate. It is true that Charles Farah was my theological mentor while I was a student at Oral Roberts University (a fact in which I take great pride). It is true that while I was writing my M.A. thesis on the Faith movement, "The Kenyon Connection," Farah pointed me in the direction of Kenyon as the historical founder of Faith theology. It is true that Hunt drew heavily upon my thesis as the basis of his critique of the Faith movement, especially in *Beyond Seduction*. Finally, it is true that I have gone on record as saying that Hunt did far more good than harm in raising legitimate questions about the origins and content of many charismatic practices. I still believe this to be the case.

But that is where the historical connection between Hunt's work and my own ends. Anybody who has even cursorily read our respective books would be aware of the differences. First, Hunt comments on a broad range of charismatic theologies and practices, while my work is limited strictly to the Faith movement. Second, Hunt's documentation is light at points, and focuses primarily on the earlier, less mature works of the people he is critiquing. *A Different Gospel* is replete with primary source quotations from the full corpus of the writings of Kenyon, Hagin, Price, Copeland and many other Faith teachers. Third, Hunt repeatedly implies that the points of charismatic theology which he condemns are also some kind of Last Days indicator of the church's End Times spiritual apostasy.[29] My work contains no such eschatological rhetoric. Moreover, I agree with those who claim that Hunt often uses "a satanic conspiracy motif," villifying his opponents in a manner that should have no place in healthy theological debate.[30] The subject matter of counter-cult research is difficult enough without using inflammatory language and techniques.[31] DeArteaga is quite right in challenging Hunt on both methodology and phraseology, as well as many other matters of interpretation. I found myself agreeing with DeArteaga's critique of Hunt on numerous points.[32]

Hunt-in-Reverse

Unfortunately, DeArteaga utilizes many of the same techniques for which he rightly criticizes Dave Hunt. On some points, DeArteaga is "Hunt-in-reverse." This is apparent on several fronts. For instance, DeArteaga assumes a degree of theological unity in the charismatic renewal even greater than that assumed by Dave Hunt or John MacArthur. This fails to consider the deeply rooted theological pluralism that has characterized the charismatic renewal from the beginning. Despite his abhorrence of the term, DeArteaga tacitly implies a charismatic version of "consensus orthodoxy" and then labels anyone within the movement who questions it a closet Pharisee. He concedes that I am a charismatic, but then proceeds to paint me with the same brush and in the same basic colors as the cessationist anti–charismatics Dave Hunt and John MacArthur. For the record, I have never opposed or tried to "quench the Spirit" of the charismatic renewal, nor am I, as DeArteaga claims in his preface, seeking to "offer a formidable challenge to the integrity of the charismatic renewal."[33] "My challenge was to the Faith movement only. In the introduction of this book, I stated unapologetically that I am an active participant in charismatic renewal and have been so for twenty years. In that same introductory paragraph, I made it clear that "those who interpret this book as a rejection of charismatic renewal interpret it wrongly."[34] My research targeted just one limited stream of the charismatic renewal, yet I am interpreted by DeArteaga as a historical precursor to cessationist anti-charismatics who have attempted a full frontal assault on the entire movement.

DeArteaga's objections notwithstanding, to confront the Faith movement is not synonymous with rejecting charismatic renewal. DeArteaga seems to assume that the charismatic renewal is a monolithic, theologically homogeneous movement, and that to reject one part of it is to reject the whole. But that simply is not the case: it never has been, and never will be. There are an estimated 332 million Pentecostal and charismatic believers worldwide, and in America alone the theological diversity is staggering.[35] The faith movement has no monopoly on the charismatic renewal, and actually comprises a relatively small percentage of the independent charismatics in America.[36] In defending the Faith movement, therefore, DeArteaga no more speaks for charismatics than I do in reproving the Faith preachers. I am quite certain that there are many charismatics who will agree with DeArteaga's assessment of the Faith movement, and I am equally certain that there are just as many charismatics who will agree with mine. Both sides are charismatics, and neither deserve the label "Pharisee" in the pejorative sense in which DeArteaga intends it.

DeArteaga also villifies his theological opponents in the same manner that Hunt does. He contends that *A Different Gospel* is a "polemic" from a charismatic of questionable motivation, a near-miss "Pharisee." His strategy is to isolate me as a charismatic dissident and extremist. But I am not the first charismatic, nor will I be the last, who considers the Faith movement a dangerous and aberrent expression of charismatic renewal. Either DeArteaga is unaware of the many others in the Pentecostal-charismatic camp who cannot accept Faith theology, or he has conveniently chosen to ignore them.[37] He also declines to respond to scholarly critics from the Evangelical world,[38] or to the Christian Research Institute, America's most reputable counter-cult organization,[39] or to the many other cult-watching groups that have taken on the Faith movement.[40] DeArteaga's silence about their concerns is deafening.

DeArteaga's use of the term "Pharisaism" betrays the same reductionist view of history and "satanic conspiracy motif" as Dave Hunt. Whereas Hunt paints his theological opponents as victims (or even agents) of an End Times "seduction," DeArteaga villifies those who would dare to criticize the charismatic movement in general— or the Faith movement in particular—as Pharisaism revisted.[41] In his opening chapter, DeArteaga claims that modern day Pharisees are from "a hellish spiritual inheritance,"[42] and are guilty of "the sin against the Holy Spirit," which is unforgiveable.[43] Both Hunt and DeArteaga portray a reductionist and conspiratorial view of history.[44] DeArteaga equivocates as to whether or not I personally am guilty of Pharisaism. On the one hand, he seems to say that I am a Pharisee because I reject the Faith movement solely on the basis of its historical origins, not its biblical content,[45] (which is not true, as anybody who has read the second half of this book can attest). On the other hand, in almost the last footnote of his final chapter, DeArteaga exonerates me of Pharsaism because I refused to write a sequel to *A Different Gospel*.[46] My only virtue appears to be that I said my piece and refrained from further comment (until now). This would seem to be an example of being "damned by faint praise."

DeArteaga's thinly veiled attempt to silence public debate through pejorative labels and emotional appeals to "the unity of the Body" has a long-standing precedent in the independent charismatic renewal. Similar rhetoric was used to intimidate dissenters within the "Shepherding-Discipleship" movement of the early '70s.[47] Appeals to the unity of the charismatic renewal were also common to silence the criticism of those outside Shepherding circles.[48] In the faith movement, suppression of questions and criticism is justified under the rubric of the "touch-not-the-Lord's anointed" rule.[49] Hagin's use of threats of divine judgment to intimidate his critics has been duly noted in this volume.[50] Consider the following recent threat of Faith evangelist Kenneth Copeland.

> There are people attempting to sit in judgment right today over the ministry that I'm responsible for, and the ministry Kenneth E. Hagin is responsible for. . . . Several people that I know had criticized and called that faith bunch out of Tulsa a cult. And some of 'em are dead right today in an early grave because of it, and there's more than one of them got cancer.[51]

DeArteaga is far more subtle and moderate in his use of spiritual threats, but his direct association between modern-day Pharisees and the unforgiveable sin would appear to have even more far-reaching ramifications than Copeland's threat of premature death. Such rhetoric is a formula for spiritual disaster! Many have documented that one of the chief characteristics of "spiritual abuse"— and spiritually abusive churches— is the use of fear tactics to quiet dissent within the ranks and render church leaders impervious to criticism and questioning.[52]

One of the real curiosities of DeArteaga's book is that he agrees with my central point as to the cultic origins of Kenyon's theology and his role as the founder of the Faith movement. Admittedly, he interprets the history of the Faith movement in a radically different way than I do. But I find it somewhat paradoxical that DeArteaga not only concedes the historical fact of Kenyon's background in the metaphysical cults, he also critiques Kenyon and Hagin on several of the very same theological points that I do. Apparently, he is free to confront the errors of the Faith teachers, but others are not. What DeArteaga really seems to be saying in *Quenching the Spirit* is that because of his personal background in the metaphysical cults, he is in a better position to discern the spiritual pros and cons of the Faith movement than others, myself included.[53] This claim, of course, begs the question as to DeArteaga's historical objectivity in evaluating the cultic background of Faith theology and the theological integrity of his own synthesis of the Bible and metaphysical literature.

DeArteaga on Kenyon

DeArteaga would have us understand Kenyon as the one who more than any other preserved and codified a biblical concept: "faith-idealism." He freely admits that Kenyon drew heavily upon the metaphysical cults, but claims that Kenyon's version was "grounded by biblical bounds and divested of Gnostic elements."[54] The question is: did Kenyon really break with New Thought in 1916, as DeArteaga claims, or did he unknowingly continue to preach and practice cultic ideas having no basis in the Bible? I firmly believe the latter to be the case.[55] Kenyon was a sincere, godly man, but many of his New Thought ideas were sincerely wrong. Unfortunately, it is precisely these cultic concepts that came to dominate Kenyon's later writings and that have been further radicalized in the modern Faith movement. It is these same cultic heresies that account for both its worldly triumphs and its spiritual tragedies.

The significance of Kenyon in DeArteaga's mind is that he filtered the metaphysical cults of their heretical elements and reinjected their much needed truths back into the life of a cessationist, anti-supernatural church. This is an interesting thesis that cannot bear up under the scrutiny of Kenyon's actual writings. DeArteaga believes that Kenyon was most strongly influenced by the cults during the days following his enrollment at the New Thought Emerson School of Oratory. If DeArteaga's interpretation of Kenyon as a cultic filter of heretical ideas is correct, one would expect that his earlier writings would demonstrate the strongest presence of New Thought concepts. They should show up in their purest form in Kenyon's periodical *Reality*, which he published during his days as superintendent of Bethel Bible Institute (1900–1923). But a careful examination of *Reality*—about which DeArteaga does not comment or even list in his footnotes and bibliogaphy—shows that Kenyon was far more orthodox in his early years than in his later ones. A chronological study of Kenyon's writings reveals that the cultic elements of his theology increased with every book that he published. Thus, DeArteaga's cultic-to-charismatic interpretation of Kenyon simply does not match the historical progression of his extant writings.

The above is not the only historical linchpin of *Quenching the Spirit* that falls to the ground upon examination. DeArteaga argues that not only did the church of Kenyon's day need his "new type of Christianity," it also needed the gnostic Christian Science and New Thought cults, upon which Kenyon drew heavily for his theology. Even though they were heretical, the metaphysical cults preserved biblical truths found nowhere else in the American church of the late nineteenth and early twentieth centuries. But surely this is a gross distortion of the historical record. As DeArteaga well knows, healing and the supernatual were very much alive in the nineteenth-century Faith-Cure movement led by Charles Cullis and spread by William Boardman, Andrew Murray, Adoniram Gordon, Carrie Judd Montgomery, and A. B. Simpson. Any of these pioneers in the American divine healing movement could have served nobly as a theological foundation for Kenyon's healing ministry.

DeArteaga counter-claims that the death of Cullis dealt a lethal blow to the Faith-Cure movement and that the polemical attacks of "Victorian Pharisees" James Buckley and B. B. Warfield finished it off.[56] As a result, Kenyon had no choice but to draw on cultic sources for his theology of healing. This is simply not true, and DeArteaga cites in his footnotes the very man who could have informed him otherwise. Paul G. Chappell, dean of the Oral Roberts Seminary and historical scholar of the nineteenth century healing movement in America, writes this about the enduring legacy of the Faith-Cure disciples of Charles Cullis.

> Perhaps their most significant contribution as a group was the fortify-
> ing of the foundation of the divine healing movement with the produc-
> tion of a permanent literature necessary to make this a legitimate
> movement in American Christian theology. . . . Their ministries en-
> compassed a balanced gospel and included diverse social concerns.
> The group as a whole was theologically acute and ecclesiastically well
> informed. . . . From its inception, the movement transcended denom-
> inational distinctions and drew supporters and practitioners from
> every background. . . . Theologically for the divine healing movement,
> this group of Cullis' disciples was to have lasting significance. . . . The
> generations which followed them had at their disposal a well-reasoned,
> biblical, theological, and practical approach to the practice of divine
> healing.[57]

The proof positive of Chappell's interpretation, and the fatal flaw of DeArteaga's, is the explosion of the Pentecostal movement in the first decade of the twentieth century. The Pentecostal movement was built upon the theological foundation of the Faith-Cure move-ment. But even as DeArteaga readily admits, Kenyon was no Pen-tecostal, either experientially or theologically, and he was openly hostile towards the movement until late in his life. He could have easily drawn upon Pentecostal or Faith-Cure sources for his theol-ogy, but he chose not to do so. The burden of proof is on DeArteaga to explain why. In any case, his idea that the church of Kenyon's day needed heretics to preserve biblical truth does not stand up to his-torical scrutiny. That was not true of early twentieth century or of any other church age.

Does Heresy create Orthodoxy?

DeArteaga believes that "historical orthodoxy cannot be the measure of heresy" because it has "been wounded by serious errors from the beginning."[58] He further claims that "the church in the past has discovered and affirmed theological truth in response to heret-ical movements containing half-truths."[59] Claiming that I should have been aware of this process, DeArteaga censures my belief that the church needs both the Bible and historical orthodoxy to determine what is and is not heretical. As a firm proponent of the Reformation principle of *sola Scriptura*, I agree wholeheartedly with DeArteaga that the Bible is the only sourcebook of faith and practice. Where we part company is concerning the role of the church over the centuries in determining what theologies and movements can legitimately claim to reside within the boundaries of biblical truth.

I categorically reject DeArteaga's claim that there is a cause-and-effect relationship between heresy and orthodoxy. Heresy does not create orthodoxy. Heresy is the perversion of orthodoxy. Heresy is to orthodoxy what a prostitute is to a woman. Heresy is a painted, sensuous, seductively dressed perversion of God's revelation that gives pleasure for a price, and pain in the end. In *Quenching the Spirit*, DeArteaga cites Harold O.J. Brown's book *Heresies* as supporting his idea that heresy predates and even creates orthodoxy.[60] This is a distortion both of Brown's position and of historical orthodoxy itself. In his opening chapter, Brown explicitly rejects what DeArteaga believes about the nature of heresy. According to Brown,

> Heresy . . . presupposes orthodoxy. . . . If we hope today that the orthodoxy we believe is the "faith once delivered to the saints" (Jude v. 3), then it is necessary to assume that it is older than heresy. But heresy appears on the historical record earlier, and it is better documented, than what most of the church came to call orthodoxy. How then can heresy be younger, orthodoxy more original? The answer is that orthodoxy was there from the beginning, and heresy reflected it. Sometimes one catches a glimpse of another person or object in a mirror or a lake before seeing the original. But the original preceded the reflection, and our perception of it. . . . The heresy we frequently see first, but orthodoxy preceded it.[61]

Brown then proves his thesis that orthodoxy precedes heresy, not vice versa, as DeArteaga claims. I agree with Brown that "the history of orthodoxy is the history of truth."[62] DeArteaga is quite correct in pointing out that the early church's struggle with Gnosticism, Montanism and Marcionism forced it to articulate its orthodox interpretation of biblical revelation. I would even concede that this resulted in an unfortunate transition in the early church from charismatic to excessively ecclesiastical authority.[63] DeArteaga's claim, however, that "heretics have forced the church into the discovery of its deepest truths"[64] is both historically misleading and theologically dangerous. The historical process of which DeArteaga should have been aware from his reading of Brown's *Heresies* is not that heresy creates orthodoxy, but that "century after century man's [*sic*] religious imagination leads him to re-create ancient heresies in re-action to the same orthodoxy, which has now been constant for long."[65] That is what Kenyon has done with Faith theology. That is what DeArteaga is in danger of doing with faith-idealism.

Faith in Who, not How

DeArteaga appeals to the philosophical categories of idealism to defend Kenyon and to realism to attack Kenyon's opponents. Biblical faith, however, does not fit neatly into the categories of either idealism or realism. In fact, DeArteaga's distinctions are a philosophical imposition on the Bible. Biblical faith is grounded in Christology, not epistemology. In other words, faith is not, as DeArteaga claims, primarily *what* you know, or *how* you know it. Faith is fundamentally *Who* you know. It is person-to-person, not person-to-principle. It is knowing God in and through Jesus Christ. Faith in the Bible is faith in the God of Israel and faith in Jesus, God's Messiah; it is faith in his person and work, his deity and his human-ity, his revelation and his redemption. In advocating faith-idealism, DeArteaga distorts the theocentric and christocentric focus of bibli-cal faith. Like Kenyon, his view of faith ultimately leads to a radical form of fideism, a form that not only denies the rational basis of belief, but also severes its connection to the sensory world.

In the end, faith for DeArteaga is New Thought epistemology, a radical and cultic way of knowing. His epistemology sets up a semi-dichotomy of idealism and realism and claims that those who would enter the supernatural realm must radically prioritize the former over the latter. But DeArteaga's dichotomy is far too close for my comfort to the spirit-matter dualism of the Gnostics. No, DeArteaga and Kenyon do not deny the reality of matter, as does Christian Science, but their radical prioritization of spirit over matter leads to the same bottom line as that of Mary Baker Eddy and most other New Thought cults: sensory denial. Debating the practice of sensory denial may seem to be an academic squabble for ivory tower types. But when you've pastored and talked and corresponded as I have with people who have lost loved ones to it, suddenly it does not appear so trivial or arcane.

DeArteaga commits the classic error of the overzealous apolo-gist: in denying one extreme he swings to another. The Bible holds the real and the ideal in dynamic tension, affirming both and deny-ing neither. Granted, Faith theology does not deny the reality of physical matter, but its doctrine of Revelation Knowledge does prioritize the ideal over the real in a way that leads to denial. In this, Faith epistemology reflects Kenyon's syncretism of New Thought, a fact which DeArteaga not only admits, but celebrates. But his cause for rejoicing should be tempered by those whose faiths and lives have been shipwrecked by the practice of sensory denial. It is my conviction that the Faith theology of Kenyon lies outside the boundaries of both biblical revelation and historical orthodoxy, and is, therefore, heretical. Prudence would demand reserving judgment on DeArteaga's faith-idealism. But if DeArteaga wants us to follow him up the stream of faith-idealism, he must first tell us where it is going.

The Now and Not Yet of Faith

DeArteaga's faith-idealism not only upsets the biblical balance between the ideal and the real, it does not even acknowledge the far more biblical tension between the "Now" and the "Not Yet." Besides its cultic dichotomy between the ideal and the real, the fundamental error of both faith-idealism and Faith theology is one of "eschatology." In many people's minds, eschatology deals only with events surrounding the end of the world (the return of Christ, the Antichrist, Armageddon, etc.). But actually, eschatology is far broader than this. It also delineates the balance between faith and hope, the historical stages of human redemption, and the present relationship of the believer to the future life. One of the most profound aspects of biblical faith and eschatology is the theological balance that it strikes and the historical tension that it preserves between the present and the future, between the "Now" and the "Not Yet."[66]

Faith in the Now. Neither DeArteaga's faith-idealism nor Kenyon's Faith theology preserves this tension and balance. The eschatology of the Faith movement states that "faith is always present tense, that "faith is now" and that "if it is not now it's not faith."[67] Hope, on the other hand, "is always future tense" and is depicted as an "enemy" and "hindrance" of faith, as "a beautiful delusion."[68] What the Faith teachers are saying is that true believers will refuse to accept illness or poverty as having any power over them in this life. God wants us to be healed *now*; God wants us to be rich *now*. Those who are not healthy and wealthy—the chronically ill or the Third World poor—those who can only hope for these things in the future life, are labeled as deceived, ignorant, and unbelieving. Hope for the future is the enemy of the faith in the now.

The Not Yet of Faith. The Faith eschatology greatly perverts biblical teaching about hope and the futuristic time frame of the believer's full redemption. Faith is not "always in the now," as the Faith teachers claim. Faith is also a conviction about the future life that dictates and empowers one's actions in the present. Little wonder is it that the Faith theology disparages the place of hope in the triad of Christian virtues which, according to Paul, are the most permanent and preeminent of all: "Now abide faith, hope, love, these three" (1 Cor. 13:13). Closely associating faith and hope, Paul describes Christians as those who are "called in one hope" (Eph. 4:4) and who "through the Spirit, by faith are waiting for the hope of righteousness" (Gal. 5:5). Faith is not the right to demand that God gives us everything that we want in this life. Many times, true faith demands that we patiently wait for that which we will never see. "In hope we have been saved," says Paul, "but hope that is seen is not hope; for why does one also hope for what he sees? But if we hope for what we do not see, with perseverance we wait eagerly for it" (Rom. 8:24, 25). That for which the believer waits in hope most eagerly is Christ Jesus himself, who is the "blessed hope" (Tit. 2:13) and "the hope of glory" (Col. 1:27).

Paul is not alone in his emphasis upon hope. Other biblical writers likewise advocate a theology of hope. DeArteaga's idealism emphasizes that "faith is being certain... of what we do not see," but he neglects the counter-balance of the first half of the verse from Hebrews: "faith is being sure of what we hope for" (Heb. 11:1). The writer to the Hebrews says that hope is our "anchor of the soul" (Heb. 6:19), our assurance that Christ will return to complete our salvation and impart our reward. Peter states that by his mercy, Christ "has caused us to be born again to a living hope" in order to "obtain an inheritance which is imperishable and undefiled and will not fade away, reserved in heaven for you, who are protected by the power of God through faith for a salvation ready to be revealed in the last time" (1 Pet. 1:3–5). Biblical salvation encompasses past, present, and future: "I have been saved; I am being saved; I will be saved." The Faith theology ignores Peter's exhortation to "fix your hope completely on the grace to be brought to you at the revelation of Jesus Christ" (1 Pet. 1:13).

The fundamental error of "Faith in the Now" is its failure to discern the relationship of the second coming of Christ to the salvation of humanity. According to the Faith theology, the work of Christ in atonement (identification) completed all that was necessary to redeem humanity from sin, sickness, poverty, and the devil. Next to nothing is said in Faith theology about the second coming of Christ as the completion of his victory over these evil forces. The Faith teachers contend that because Christ has already redeemed us, no evil should befall the believer who is truly exercising faith in the promises of God. Many of the promises claimed by Faith teachers are not promises intended by God to be fullfilled in this life; they are descriptions of the life to come, of life in the millennium. Before this millennial life is available, Christ must return to transform our mortal bodies (Phil. 3:21), to abolish all rule and authority (1 Cor. 15:24), to destroy the devil (Rev. 20:1–10), and to establish the new heaven and the new earth (Rev. 21:1–5).

"Kingdom Now" Theology

The Faith theology does not preserve "the mystery of the kingdom of God." This mystery is twofold. First, the mystery consists in the fact that the kingdom which many of the Jews of Jesus' day expected would come with the supernatural judgment and wrath of God upon his enemies actually came through the death and resurrection of Jesus the Nazarene. Second, the mystery consists in the fact that the kingdom inaugurated by Jesus in his first coming will not be consummated until his second. The kingdom was truly realized in the person and work of Christ, but among people, it is a kingdom "in process of realization." The process will not, and cannot, be completed until Christ returns. In the interim between Christ's first and second comings, the wheat grows together with the tares and the kingdom of God does warfare against the dominion of the devil. The Faith teachers deny that the kingdom of God is in the process of realization, claiming that it is present in the earth to the point that believers can be delivered from all sin, sickness, and poverty of the devil. They recognize that spiritual warfare must be waged by the Christian in order to be free from these things, but they also claim that the believer has absolute authority to conquer and eradicate these forces of evil completely from his life. The only process of realization is in the faith of the believer, not in the presence of God's kingdom.

In the jargon of biblical theology, the Faith interpretation of the kingdom of God could be labeled as a "hyper-realized" eschatology.[69] The Faith eschatology is "hyper-realized" because of its extreme promises to the believer of a life which is absolutely invulnerable to any type of evil. It claims that "the powers of the age to come" have *completely* come in this life and that these powers can be used *at will* by the believer with enough faith and knowledge of how to operate them. There is no process of realization of God's kingdom in Faith eschatology; the kingdom can be completely realized in the lives of those who exercise Faith principles. We see evidence of this hyper-realized eschatology in the Faith doctrines of healing, authority, prosperity, identification and deification. The overrealized nature of Faith eschatology emphasizes the "Now" of the kingdom of God to the exclusion of the "Not Yet."

The miraculous ministry of the Holy Spirit is in no way compromised by this "Now/Not Yet" view of the kingdom of God. Nobody has ever accused John Wimber of a deficit of signs and wonders, and he makes this understanding of the kingdom the basis of his "power evangelism."[70] Wimber also points to the eschatological tension between the "Now" and the "Not Yet" as a partial explanation of why not all are healed by prayer.[71] Many other "Third Wave" evangelicals support this understanding of the kingdom without giving place to cessationist theology.[72] In the incarnation of Jesus, the kingdom and its powers were truly present, were truly "now." Through the person of Jesus Christ and by the power of his Holy Spirit, the powers of the Age to Come can and do come to the church as the "first fruits" of its redemption. Nevertheless, the kingdom is "Not Yet" consummated until Jesus comes again. The powers of the kingdom are available only as the Holy Spirit *sovereignly* manifests them in God's time and place. The "Now/Not Yet" mystery of the kingdom and its powers is distorted by the hyper-realized eschatology of the Faith movement.

When Polemics are Worth It

DeArteaga takes me to task for writing a "polemic" against the Faith movement. Is *A Different Gospel* a polemic? In all honesty, I would have to answer "yes." The word "polemic," however, bears several definitions, not all of which are bad. It basically means "a controversy, or an argument intended to refute theological error." We certainly had plenty of that in Tulsa, Oklahoma, in the late '70s and early '80s, when as a graduate student I was writing the master's thesis at Oral Roberts University that would become *A Different Gospel*. Virtually the entire theological faculty in the ORU School of Theology at that time opposed the teachings of the Faith movement, and rightly so, in my opinion. The issues at stake, both theological and pastoral, were in those days enormous. They still are. Even apart from the question of theological orthodoxy, the cultic and heretical elements of Faith theology can breed a psychologically unhealthy state of mind, or what some Christian therapists of religious addiction call "toxic faith."[73] One prominent Christian psychologist believes that through the medium of Christian television, this religiously addictive faith is being spread all over the world.[74]

Yes, *A Different Gospel* is a polemic, and I offer no apologies for it. Polemics are worth it when lives are at stake, when faiths are being destroyed, and when churches are being divided. We are not just talking here about how many angels can fit on to the head of a pin. We are not just arguing about predestination versus free will, or inerrancy versus infallibility, or limited versus unlimited atonement, or any of those other complex arguments theologians have been debating for centuries, and upon which no one's life depends. When it comes to Faith theology, however, we are talking human lives. If just one life has been lost because of Faith theology, it is one too many. Even one life merits a polemic. But there has not been just been one life sacrificed to Faith theology. There have been hundreds of people, good people: people like the husband of the lady whose letter began this afterword; people like Wesley Parker,[75] or the 126 similar deaths of children whose parents refused them medical treatment in the name of prayer;[76] people like the ninety or so that we know that died in connection with Hobart Freeman's radical Faith church in Wilmot, Indiana. Please don't tell me that Freeman was a renegade Faith preacher not representative of the Faith movement at large. It is a matter of historical record that Freeman was "deeply influenced by healing evangelists like Kenneth Hagin, John Osteen, Kenneth Copeland, and T. L. Osborn, along with the writings of E. W. Kenyon."[77] Sure Freeman was a renegade! Of course, he was a Faith monster run amok from whom anybody would want to distance themselves publicly. But the Faith teachers wrote the books and pamphlets that helped to drive Freeman over the edge. And the same writings that produced him could produce others.

If the Faith movement has moderated as is being said by some, let it be demonstrated by a massive reediting of their printed materials, materials that are being translated and distributed all over the world in their original form. As far as I am concerned, the Faith controversy will never be over until that happens. This is not about politics, it is not about public relations, or being "spiritually correct." It is about doctrine, killer doctrine, doctrine that has taken hundreds of human lives and destroyed thousands of faiths and churches. Somebody must give an account for these lives. Some of us have been waiting for a long time for the top level leaders of the Faith movement to respond for themselves to their critics. We are still waiting.

D.R.M.
Amsterdam, the Netherlands
May, 1994

NOTES

1. With the exception of dates and ages that I have changed or omitted to protect further the woman's identity, this letter is reproduced exactly as she wrote it.

2. Stephen Strang, "A Pastor Dares to Face Apartheid, *Charisma* (June, 1988), 63–66.

3. William W. Menzies, "Will Charismatics Go Cultic?" *Christianity Today* (Mar. 3, 1989), pp. 59–60; see also Menzies' book review in the *Pentecostal Evangel* (Aug. 14, 1988), p. 30; and Donald Smeeton's review in *Bulletin of the European Pentecostal Theological Association*, 8 (1, 1989), pp. 34–36.

4. Jerry Horner, "Faith Teachers Under Siege," *Charisma & Christian Life* (Feb., 1989), p. 38. Horner contends that my case for Kenyon's background in the cults depends on "questionable hearsay and circumstantial evidence." But Horner never presents any evidence for his claim, and at times focuses on minutiae, like typographical errors. He criticizes my documentation, which almost all other reviewers have regarded as the strength of *A Different Gospel*.

5. "Another Gospel or Another Inquisition?" Ministries Today (Sept./Oct., 1989), pp. 84–89. This review had three parts: (1) a book summary consisting of extended excerpts; (2) a book analysis by editorial director Paul Thigpen; and (3) a brief personal interview. Thigpen's analysis concedes the historical connection between Hagin and Kenyon, but denies that Kenyon's background in the cults had any significant influence upon his theology. Calling my placement of Kenyon within the metaphysical movement "guilt by association," Thigpen claims that Kenyon could be rightly placed within the Wesleyean-Holiness movement, even though Kenyon steadfastly denied both sinless perfection and the second work of grace, the two hallmarks of Wesleyanism. Thigpen claims that Kenyon's view of atonement (Identification) is merely an example of the Ransom Theory. This fails to consider that all who have held this theory in church history do not deny, as Kenyon does, that Christ's atonement was a physical death taking place on the cross, not a spiritual one in hell. Thigpen censures me for not successfully reaching Hagin for a personal response, when it is common knowledge that he refuses

to dialogue with any of his critics. He believes that Hagin is guilty of "verbal irresponsibility rather than heresy" (p. 87), and that I am guilty of "fueling the fires of another inquistion" (p. 88).

6. Barron continued to take the battle to the Faith movement in his own gentle, but firm way. See, "Why Settle for Riches if You can be a God? Updating the Word-Faith Controversy," paper presented to the Society for Pentecostal Studies (Nov. 11, 1988), especially his excellent section on charismatic politics, pp. 27–28.

7. Richard Vara, "Charismatic Doctrines Criticized in New Book," *Houston Post* (Sept. 10, 1988), sec. E, p. 6; Dana Sterling, "Former Tulsan attacks Hagin's Teachings," *Tulsa Tribune* (Dec. 24, 1988), sec. A, p. 11; James D. Davis, "Author Says Prosperity Gospel is 'Heresy,' " *Tulsa World* (Nov. 20, 1988).

8. See my response to DeArteaga's critique, "Letters to the Editor," *Ministries Today* (Jan./Feb., 1992), p. 13.

9. William DeArteaga, *Quenching the Spirit: Examining Centuries of Opposition to the Moving of the Holy Spirit* (Altamonte Springs, Fla.: Creation House, 1992). It should be noted that Creation House is a subsidiary of Strang Communications, publisher of *Charisma* and *Ministries Today* magazines.

10. Ibid., p. 293.

11. Ibid., pp. 228–29.

12. Ibid., p. 200.

13. Ibid., p. 212.

14. Ibid., p. 153.

15. Ibid., p. 200.

16. Ibid., p. 204.

17. Ibid., p. 211.

18. Ibid., p. 227.

19. Ibid., p. 211.

20. Ibid., p. 160.

21. Ibid., pp. 163–64.

22. Ibid., pp. 203–4.

23. Ibid., p. 223.

24. Ibid., p. 207.

25. Ibid., p. 209.

26. Ibid., p. 222.

27. Ibid., p. 223.

28. DeArteaga has nothing but praise for my theological mentor Charles Farah's opposition to the Faith movement, and well he should. But he is rather selective in his interpretation of Farah. It is true that *From the Pinnacle of the Temple*, written for a popular audience, is a model of restraint. Farah was, however, quite capable of turning up the heat when needed, especially when addressing a more academic audience. In his address to the Society of Pentecostal Studies being held at ORU in 1980, "A Critical Analysis: The Roots and Fruits of Faith-Formula Theology," Farah named names and called Faith theology "charismatic humanism," "the new gnosticism," and "a burgeoning heresy." Those of us in attendance that day gave him a standing ovation. He deserved it (p. 80; p. 80, n. 21).

29. "The unbiblical and delusive penchant for new 'revelation knowledge' that comes apart from the words of Scripture has led many Pentecostal/charismatic splinter groups into gross heresy and even into full-blown occultism. This delusion seems to be growing today as part of the last-days apostasy which the Bible warns must come before Christ returns" (Hunt, *Beyond Seduction*, p. 239).

30. Kim Riddlebarger, "This Present Paranoia," *Power Religion: The Selling Out of the Evangelical Church?* (Chicago: Moody, 1992), p. 275–76.

31. My theological opponents have argued that my use of the terms "cultic" and "heretical" are equally inflammatory. I admit that both constitute serious charges that should not be made lightly or without substantive evidence, but I went to great lengths to describe what I did and did not mean by both terms. I took pains to explain that I used the term "cultic," not in the sensational sense, but in the theological and historical ones (pp. 16–18). Moreover, I was careful to state that I do not believe the Faith movement itself to be a "cult" (p. 19). My point was that certain key doctrines and practices—by no means, all or even most—were of cultic historical origin and theological content. I was similarly circumspect in my use of the term "heretical," granting that the Faith movement's heresy was "material" (unintentional) rather than "formal" (p. 20). I repeatedly granted the probability that Kenyon's incorporation of cultic doctrines into his theology was unconscious and that his preaching of heretical ideas was, no pun intended, in "good faith."

32. For further critique of Hunt's work, see *Seduction? A Biblical Response* by Thomas F. Reid, Mark Virkler, James A. Laine, and Alan Langstaff (New Wilmington, Pa: Son-Rise, 1986).

33. *Quenching*, p. 13.

34. *A Different Gospel*, p. xvi.

35. David K. Barrett, "The 20th Century Pentecostal/Charismatic Renewal in the Holy Spirit, with its Goal of World Evangelization," *International Bulletin of Missionary Research* (July 1988); taken from the *Dictionary of the Pentecostal and Charismatic Movements*, ed. Stanley M. Burgess, Gary B. McGee, and Patrick Alexander (Grand Rapids : Zondervan, 1988).

36. It is difficult to assess exactly how large the Faith movement is, especially in comparison to the charismatic renewal at large in America (see Barrett, ibid., p. 9). The only institutional organizations of the Faith movement are the International Fellowship of Faith Ministries (2000 churches), the International Convention of Faith Churches and Ministries (495 churches), Rhema Ministerial Association (525 churches), and Faith Christian Fellowship International (1000 ordained ministers, but my sources within the organization estimate that only 150 or so have churches). The problem with these figures is that many Faith churches and pastors have multiple memberships in the various Faith organizations, and many more have no membership at all. A very generous estimate in my view would be that there are around 5 to 6 thousand Faith churches in America. If we use the widely accepted and conservative estimate of 60 thousand white independent charismatic churches in America (Barrett, ibid.), that would mean that the Faith movement comprises only around 8 to 10 percent of the charismatic churches at large in the States. This estimate does not include

those charismatics in traditional Protestant and Catholic churches, Black charismatics, or Third Wave Evangelicals.

37. Besides the opposition of the Christian Research Institute mentioned below, there are many other radical opponents of the Faith movement noticeable for their absence in DeArteaga's footnotes and bibliography: Bruce Barron's *The Health and Wealth Gospel,* Gordon Fee's *The Disease of the Health and Wealth Gospel,* Judith Matta's *The Born Again Jesus of the Word-Faith Teaching,* Arnold Prater's *How Much Faith Does it Take?,* John Fickett's *Confess it, Possess It: Faith's Formulas?* (see bibliography for full references). In addition, DeArteaga neglects to mention the opposition of the Assemblies of God to the Faith theology, which was stated officially in "The Believer and Positive Confession," *Pentecostal Evangel* (Nov. 16, 1980). With the possible exception of Prater, all of the above are clearly in the Pentecostal-charismatic camp. Are these people also "Pharisees"?

38. DeArteaga cites, but does not engage Michael Horton, ed., *The Agony of Deceit: What Some TV Preachers are Really Teaching* (Chicago: Moody, 1990); especially relevant to the Faith controversy are R.C. Sproul's "A Serious Charge" (pp. 33–46), Henry Krabbendam's "Scripture Twisting" (pp. 63–67), and Walter Martin's "Ye shall Be as Gods" (pp. 89–105), described below. Appendix C on the Faith theology, "A Ready Reference Guide" (pp. 267–78) is excellent. See also, Jim Kinnebrew, "The Theology of Positive Confession" (Th.D. dissertation, Mid-America Baptist Seminary, 1988).

39. The able successor of Walter Martin, founder of the Christian Research Institute, is Hank Hanegraaff, whose latest book, *Christianity in Crisis* (Eugene, Ore.: Harvest House, 1993) continues the fight with the Faith movement begun by Martin. Hanegraaff's hard-hitting book came out too late for DeArteaga to respond to it in *Quenching the Spirit,* but Martin had been declaring his opposition to Faith theology for over a decade. Before he died, Martin stated that "for ten years I have warned . . . that we were heading into the kingdom of the cults with the Faith teachers. You are no longer heading there, baby, you're there (quoted in Hanegraaff, p. 360; citing Martin, "The Warnings of God, CRI audiotape #C-210, side 1). DeArteaga could and should have, however, dealt with Martin's claim that "those who propagate these erroneous views (the 'little gods,' the 'born-again Jesus'and so on) have sadly crossed over into the kingdom of the cults and stand in need of genuine repentance, lest they come under the inevitability of divine judgment" (Martin, "Ye Shall Be as Gods," *Agony of Deceit,* p. 104). In any case, DeArteaga will sooner or later have to respond to CRI and Hanegraaff, who considers the Faith leaders to be "false teachers" (p. 360).

40. Brian Onken, "The Atonement of Christ and the 'Faith' Message," *Forward,* 7 (1984)1, pp. 10–15; Robert M. Bowman, "Ye are Gods? Orthodox and Heretical Views of the Deification of Man," *Christian Research Journal,* 9 (Winter/Spring, 1987), pp. 18–22; "Trends toward the New Age Inside the Church," *Report from Concerned Christians* (Sept./Oct., 1987); "Creating Your Own Reality: 'Word of Faith' — Preparation for the Antichrist's Kingdom," *Report from Concerned Christians* (July/Aug., 1988).

41. *Quenching,* pp. 16–26.

42. For example, DeArteaga claims that Jesus taught a principle of "acquired spiritual inheritance" that "warns every generation that present

attitudes opposing the work of the Holy Spirit place a person in the hellish spiritual inheritance of the prophet murderers" (*Quenching*, p. 23).

43. DeArteaga writes that "spiritualism is a sin of discernment, a serious sin which must be confessed and can be forgiven. However, the opposite sin of discernment, claiming that the works of the Holy Spirit are really the product of demonic activity, calling something sorcery when it is in fact from God, is more than a serious sin; it is *unforgiveable* [emphasis in the original]. . . . This alone should make the accusation of sorcery or unusual spiritual phenomenon something that a Christian makes reluctantly" (Ibid., pp. 24, 25). DeArteaga seems to be saying that those who commit spiritualism can be forgiven, but those who criticize it wrongly cannot. This is yet another example of the fear tactics used by many charismatics to intimidate opposition and suppress a free exchange of theological dialogue.

44. Nowhere is DeArteaga's historical reductionism so painfully apparent as in his interpretation of heresy. He reduces the entire compex history of heresy to two "perennial" heresis: Gnosticism and Pharisaism. No credible church historian would support such a simplistic thesis, much less Harold O. J. Brown, whom DeArteaga cites (without giving a page number) as the source of his claim that "the Bible defines Pharisaism as a heresy" (p. 16). I read Brown's *Heresies* and could not find a single reference to Pharisaism in either the text or the index. His work certainly could not be legitimately cited as historical support of DeArteaga's curious claim that Pharisaism is a "perennial" heresy of the church. Quite the contrary, Brown extols the many contributions made by historical Judaism to early Christianity (Harold O. J. Brown, *Heresies : The Image of Christ in the Mirror of Heresy and Orthodoxy from the Apostles to the Present* [Garden City, N. Y. : Doubleday, 1984], pp. 14–17). What is clear is that DeArteaga has taken a historical movement within Judaism, invested it with his own polemical meaning, and used it as an inflammatory, pejorative label. Having lived in Europe the last six years and having seen firsthand the rise of neo-Nazism, I am shocked that DeArteaga would use historical Judaism in such a manner. Given the historical tensions in Judeo-Christian interrelations, using a Jewish sect as the source of a conspiratorial view of history is just plain irresponsible. I am certain that DeArteaga had no anti–Semitic intentions, but that does not mean others who will read his work don't. Granted, DeArteaga is not the first to use the Pharisees as theological boogeymen, but that does not mean that he should not be the last. Yes, Jesus confronted the Pharisees, but Jesus was a Jew. In a post–Holocaust age, we Gentiles should no longer use historical Judaism as a negative literary metaphor.

45. *Quenching*, p. 230.

46. *Quenching*, p. 290, n. 28.

47. Patrick K. Caspary, "Nationwide Reports of Abuse in the Shepherding Cult: Written by Ex–Leaders and Followers who Tell of Hurt, Brainwashing, and Control" (unpublished paper on file in the Holy Spirit Research Center, Oral Roberts University), p. 1; Wayne Fast, "Sheep, Shepherd, and Submission" (signed affadavit on file in the Holy Spirit Research Center, Oral Roberts University).

48. On March 8–12, 1976, for example, charismatic leaders met in Oklahoma City to attempt to reconcile the Shepherding controversy. It was

agreed by those present that compliance with Matt. 18:15–17 demanded that they refrain from challenging each other's ministry on either a personal or doctrinal basis ("Report on the 1976 Charismatic Leaders Conference," unpublished document on file at the Holy Spirit Research Center, Oral Roberts University). Commenting on the "Statement of Ethics" published by this conference, Howard Ervin, professor theology at Oral Roberts University, wrote that "doctrine is . . . not a matter of private judgment, but to be judged by a Church judicatory." Ervin felt that the inclusion of doctrine in this statement constituted "a gag rule" on theological dialogue in the charismatic renewal. For a summary of the doctrinal issues at stake in the Shepherding controversy, see Edward E. Plowman, "The Deepening Rift in the Charismatic Movement," *Christianity Today* (Sept., 1975), pp. 52–54; Stephen Strang, "The Discipleship Controversy Three Years Later," *Charisma* (Sept., 1978), p. 14; Vinson Synan, "Reconciling the Charismatics," *Christianity Today* (Apr. 9, 1976), p. 46; J. S. O'Malley, "Discipleship Movement," *Evangelical Dictionary of Theology*, ed. Walter A. Elwell (Grand Rapids: Baker, 1984), p. 320.

49. For a devastating critique of the "touch-not-God's-anointed" rule, see H. Hanegraaff, "Are God's Anointed Beyond Criticism?", *Christianity in Crisis*, appendix A, pp. 363–65.

50. See above, pp. 64–65.

51. Kenneth Copeland, "Why All are Not Healed" (Ft. Worth, Tex.: Kenneth Copeland Ministries, 1990), audiotape #01–4001; quoted in Hanegraaf, "God's Anointed," p. 363.

52. Ronald M. Enroth, *Churches That Abuse* (Grand Rapids: Zondervan, 1992), see especially pp. 93–108, 147–65; David Johnson, Jeff VanVonderen, *The Subtle Power of Spiritual Abuse: Recognizing and Escaping Spiritual Manipulation and False Spiritual Authority within the Church* (Minneapolis, Minn.: Bethany House, 1991), see especially, pp. 63–71, in which the authors discuss "power posturing," "unspoken rules," and "the 'can't talk' rule."

53. In the preface to *Quenching the Spirit*, DeArteaga writes, "I was uniquely equipped to approach this challenge because of my own spiritual life. In my search for God from 1974 to about 1980, I surveyed much of the metaphysical literature available. The grace of God led me out of that environment and enabled me to see that though elements of truth existed there, they were surrounded by and imbedded in Gnostic heresies. I am thankful that what little I wrote during that period was not widely distributed" (ibid., p. 13).

54. Ibid., p. 212.

55. See above, pp. 42–51.

56. *Quenching*, pp. 116–26.

57. Paul G. Chappell, "The Divine Healing Movement in America" (Ph.D. dissertation, Drew University, 1983), pp. 278–82.

58. *Quenching*, p. 223.

59. Ibid.

60. Ibid., pp. 150–51.

61. Brown, *Heresies*, p. 4.

62. Ibid., p. 5.

63. For an excellent overview of this process, see William C. Placher, *A History of Christian Theology* (Philadelphia, Pa.: Westminster, 1983), pp. 44–54.

64. *Quenching*, p. 150.

65. Brown, *Heresies;* Brown's position for the preexistence of orthodoxy over and against heresy finds support in Jaroslav Pelikan's *The Emergence of the Catholic Tradition (100–600,* vol. 1, *The Christian Tradition: A History of the Development of Doctrine* (Chicago: Univ. of Chicago Press, 1971), p. 69:

> The presupposition of [the orthodox theologians] was that the primitive deposit of Christian truth had been given by Christ to the apostles and by them in turn to the succession of orthodox bishops and teachers, while the heretics were those who forsook this succession and departed from this deposit. . . . With only a few latitudinarian exceptions, both the heretics and the orthodox . . . were agreed throughout the controversies from 100 to 600 that there was only one true doctrine, which each party claimed to possess. The truth was one, and there could be no pluralism in its confession; one's opponents were not merely espousing a different form of Christian obedience, they were teaching false doctrine. The heretics were no less implacable than the orthodox in claiming that only their position was the correct one. . . . At least as early as Irenaeus, therefore, 'heresy' came to be the term for a deviation from the standard of sound doctrine.

DeArteaga is correct in pointing out the sometimes symbiotic relationship of heresy to orthodoxy. But he drastically overstates this fact in his assertion that heresy predated and created orthodoxy. The early church was not nearly as ambiguous in its own delineation of heresy as DeArteaga claims.

66. I first became aware of this distinction after reading the works of the late professor of New Testament at Fuller Seminary, George Eldon Ladd, whose views of the kingdom are embodied in *The Presence of the Future* (Grand Rapids: Eerdmans, 1974), and *Theology of the New Testament* (Grand Rapids: Eerdmans, 1974).

67. K. Hagin, *What Faith Is*, p. 3.

68. Kenyon, *Two Kinds of Faith*, p. 32; K. Hagin, "The Secret of Faith," *Word of Faith* (March, 1968), p. 2.

69. This term comes from Gordon Fee's *The Disease of the Health and Wealth Gospel.*

70. John Wimber, *Power Evangelism: Signs and Wonders Today* (London: Hodder & Stoughton, 1985), pp. 18–27; see also, p. 175, n. 1, in which Wimber acknowledges his dependency on George Ladd and James Kallas for his understanding of the kingdom of God.

71. John Wimber with Kevin Springer, *Power Healing* (San Francisco: Harper & Row, 1987), p. 157.

72. See, C. Peter Wagner, *How to Have a Healing Ministry without Making Your Church Sick* (Ventura, Calif.: Regal Books, 1988), especially pp. 91–112, 237–60; see also, Don Williams, *Signs, Wonders and the Kingdom of God: A Biblical Guide for the Reluctant Skeptic* (Ann Arbor, Michigan: Servant Books, 1989).

73. Stephen Arterburn and Jack Felton, *Toxic Faith: Understanding and Overcoming Religious Addiction* (Nashville: Thomas Nelson, 1991), especially pp. 47–97. Of the 21 characteristcs they list of religiously addictive "toxic faith," the Faith movement demonstrates varying levels of ten of them: (1) Instance Peace: "when tragedy strikes, true believers should have imme-

diate peace," pp. 52ff.; (2) Guaranteed Healing, pp. 54ff.; (3) Irreproachable Clergy, pp. 58ff.; (4) Monetary Rewards: "material blessings are a sign of spiritual strength" pp. 60ff.; (5) Investment Tithing: "the more money you give to God, the more money he will give to you," pp. 62ff.; (6) Spiteful God: "problems in your life result from some particular sin," pp. 66ff.; (7) Biblical Exclusivity: "if it's not in the Bible, it isn't relevant," p. 76; (8) Bullet-Proof Faith: "a strong faith will protect me from problems and pain," pp. 83ff.; (9) Divinely Ordained Happiness: "more than anything else, God wants me to be happy," pp. 92ff.; (10) Possibility of Becoming God: "if you focus on all that you are, you will discover that you are God and in control of your fate," pp. 94ff. According to Arterburn and Felton, "possessing just one toxic belief can poison an entire relationship with God" (pp. 96–97). Many spiritual drop-outs of the Faith movement can attest to how true this is.

74. Archibald Hart, dean of the Graduate School of Psychology at Fuller Theological Seminary, writes that Christian televison can make "the 'wealth and success' gospel (designed to excite or reduce tension) an intimate temptation and create desires that can easily grow into addictions without some balancing influence. More and more Christians are being driven to believe that success is their birthright and that God promises all who follow him a 'flower-strewn pathway' free of all pain and problems. Such a Christianity is doomed to failure— as well as being unbiblical. The Christ of the Gospels never promised that sort of nirvana" (Archibald D. Hart, *Healing Life's Hidden Addictions* [Ann Arbor: Servant Publications, 1990], p. 58). In all fairness, however, it must be acknowledged that Hart also regards "heresy hunting" as a form of religious addiction (pp. 139–41), a warning to those whose sole ministry is being a doctrinal detective in the body of Christ.

75. Wesley's story is told in his father Larry Parker's book *We Let Our Son Die* (Irvine, Calif.: Harvest House, 1980).

76. Jack Kelly, "How Could Parents Let a Child Die?" *People* (May 16, 1988), pp. 136–38; "In the past 15 years at least 126 children in the U.S. have died because their parents . . . withheld medical treatment out of a doctrinal conviction that prayer is the only allowable treatment for illness."

77. John Davis, "Freeman: Mystic, Monk or Minister?" Warsaw [Indiana] *Times-Union* (Sept. 27, 1983), p. 1a.

Select Bibliography

Faith Movement and Controversy

Barron, Bruce. *The Health and Wealth Gospel.* Downers Grove, Illinois: Inter-
Varsity, 1987.

Baxter, J. Sidlow. *Divine Healing of the Body.* Grand Rapids: Zondervan, 1979.

Bosworth, F. F. *Christ the Healer.* Old Tappan, New Jersey: Fleming H. Revell,
1973.

Capps, Charles. *Authority in Three Worlds.* Tulsa: Harrison House, 1980.

_____. *Can Your Faith Fail?* Tulsa: Harrison House, 1976.

_____. *Changing the Seen and Shaping the Unseen.* Tulsa: Harrison House,
1980.

_____. *God's Creative Power Will Work for You.* Tulsa: Harrison House, 1976.

_____. *How to Have Faith in Your Faith.* Tulsa: Harrison House, 1986.

_____. *Paul's Thorn in the Flesh.* Dallas: Word of Faith Pub., 1983.

_____. *Releasing the Ability of God through Prayer.* Tulsa: Harrison House,
1978.

_____. *The Tongue: A Creative Force.* Tulsa: Harrison House, 1976.

Copeland, Gloria. *God's Will Is Prosperity.* Tulsa: Harrison House, 1978.

Copeland, Kenneth. *Believer's Voice of Victory.* Newsletter. Kenneth Copeland
Evangelistic Assoc., Ft. Worth, Texas.

_____. *The Force of Faith.* Ft. Worth: Kenneth Copeland Pub., 1983.

_____. *The Force of Righteousness.* Ft. Worth: Kenneth Copeland Pub., 1984.

_____. *The Laws of Prosperity.* Ft. Worth: Kenneth Copeland Pub., 1974.

Farah, Charles. *From the Pinnacle of the Temple.* Plainfield, New Jersey:
Logos, 1978.

_____. "The 'Roots and Fruits' of Faith Theology." Unpublished Paper,
Society for Pentecostal Studies, Nov., 1980.

Fee, Gordon. *The Disease of the Health and Wealth Gospels.* Costa Mesa,
California: The Word for Today, 1979.

Fickett, John. *Confess It, Possess It: Faith's Formulas?* Oklahoma City: Presby-
terian & Reformed Renewal Ministries, 1984.

Freeman, Hobart. *Did Jesus Die Spiritually?: Exposing the JDS Heresy.* Warsaw,
Indiana: Faith Ministries & Publications [n.d.].

Frodsham, Stanley Howard. *Smith Wigglesworth: Apostle of Faith.* Springfield, Missouri: Gospel Publishing House, 1973.

Gosset, Donald, ed. *The Power of the Positive Confession of God's Word.* Tulsa:
Custom Graphics, 1981.

Hacking, W. *Smith Wigglesworth Remembered*. Tulsa: Harrison House, 1972.

Hagin, Kenneth. *Authority of the Believer*. Tulsa: Faith Library, 1967.

_____. *The Believer's Authority*. Tulsa: Faith Library, 1985.

_____. *Bible Faith Study Course*. Tulsa: Faith Library, 1980.

_____. *Bible Prayer Study Course*. Tulsa: Faith Library, 1981.

_____. *Demons and How to Deal with Them*. Tulsa: Faith Library, 1980.

_____. *El Shaddai*. Tulsa: Faith Library, 1980.

_____. *Four Steps to Answered Prayer*. Tulsa: Faith Library, 1980.

_____. *The Gift of Prophecy*. Tulsa: Faith Library, 1984.

_____. *The God-Kind of Love*. Tulsa: Faith Library [n.d.].

_____. *God's Medicine*. Tulsa: Faith Library, 1977.

_____. *Godliness Is Profitable*. Tulsa: Faith Library, 1982.

_____. *Growing Up Spiritually*. Tulsa: Faith Library, 1976.

_____. *Having Faith in Your Faith*. Tulsa: Faith Library, 1980.

_____. *Healing Belongs to Us*. Tulsa: Faith Library, 1977.

_____. *How to Write Your Own Ticket with God*. Tulsa: Faith Library, 1979.

_____. *How You Can Be Led by the Spirit of God*. Tulsa: Faith Library, 1978.

_____. *How You Can Know the Will of God*. Tulsa: Faith Library, 1980.

_____. *The Human Spirit*. 3 Vols. Tulsa: Faith Library, 1980.

_____. *I Believe in Visions*. Old Tappan, New Jersey: Fleming H. Revell, 1972.

_____. *I Went to Hell*. Tulsa: Faith Library, 1982.

_____. *In Him*. Tulsa: Faith Library, 1975.

_____. *The Key to Scriptural Healing*. Tulsa: Faith Library, 1977.

_____. *The Ministry of a Prophet*. Tulsa: Faith Library, 1984.

_____. *Must Christians Suffer?* Tulsa: Faith Library, 1983.

_____. *The Name of Jesus*. Tulsa: Faith Library, 1981.

_____. *New Thresholds of Faith*. Tulsa: Faith Library, 1980.

_____. *The Origin and Operation of Demons*. Tulsa: Faith Library, 1981.

_____. *Paul's Revelation*. Tulsa: Faith Library, 1983.

_____. *The Precious Blood of Jesus*. Tulsa: Faith Library, 1984.

_____. *The Real Faith*. Tulsa: Faith Library, 1980.

_____. *Redeemed*. Tulsa: Faith Library, 1966.

_____. *Right and Wrong Thinking*. Tulsa: Faith Library, 1966.

_____. *Seven Things You Should Know about Divine Healing*. Tulsa: Faith Library, 1981.

_____. *Seven Vital Steps to Receiving the Holy Spirit*. Tulsa: Faith Library, 1980.

_____. *Three Big Words*. Tulsa: Faith Library, 1983.

_____. *Turning Hopeless Situations Around*. Tulsa: Faith Library, 1981.

_____. *Understanding Our Confession*. Tulsa: Faith Library [n.d..].

_____. *Understanding the Anointing*. Tulsa: Faith Library, 1985.

_____. *What Faith Is*. Tulsa: Faith Library, 1978.

_____. *Why Do People Fall under the Power?* Tulsa: Faith Library, 1980.

_____. *Word of Faith*. Newsletter. Kenneth Hagin Evangelistic Assoc., Broken Arrow, Oklahoma.

_____. *You Can Have What You Say*. Tulsa: Faith Library, 1980.

_____. *Zoe: The God-Kind of Life*. Tulsa: Faith Library, 1982.

Hagin, Kenneth Jr. *Kenneth Hagin's 50 Years in the Ministry: 1934–1984.* Tulsa: Faith Library, 1984.

Harrell, David. *All Things Are Possible: The Healing & Charismatic Revivals in Modern America.* Bloomington, Indiana: Indiana Univ. Press, 1975.

Hughes, Don. *What About Job?: The Truth.* Broken Arrow: Don Hughes Evangelistic Assoc., 1984.

Hunt, Dave. *Beyond Seduction.* Eugene, Oregon: Harvest House, 1987.

Hunt, Dave & T. A. McMahon. *The Seduction of Christianity.* Eugene, Oregon: Harvest House, 1985.

Kenyon, E. W. *Advanced Bible Course: Studies in the Deeper Life.* Seattle: Kenyon's Gospel Publishing Society, 1970.

————. *The Bible in the Light of Our Redemption.* Seattle: Kenyon's Gospel Publishing Society, 1969.

————. *The Blood Covenant.* Seattle: Kenyon's Gospel Publishing Society, 1969.

————. *The Father and His Family: The Story of Man's Redemption.* Seattle: Kenyon's Gospel Publishing Society, 1964.

————. *The Hidden Man: An Unveiling of the Subconscious Mind.* Seattle: Kenyon's Gospel Publishing Society, 1970.

————. *Identification: A Romance in Redemption.* Seattle: Kenyon's Gospel Publishing Society, 1968.

————. *In His Presence.* Seattle: Kenyon's Gospel Publishing Society, 1969.

————. *Jesus the Healer.* Seattle: Kenyon's Gospel Publishing Society, 1943.

————. *Kenyon's Herald of Life.* Newsletter. Kenyon's Gospel Publishing Society, Seattle, Washington.

————. *Kenyon's Living Poems.* Seattle: Kenyon's Gospel Publishing Society, 1935.

————. *New Creation Realities: A Revelation of Redemption.* Seattle: Kenyon's Gospel Publishing Society, 1945.

————. *The New Kind of Love.* Seattle: Kenyon's Gospel Publishing Society, 1969.

————. *Reality.* Periodical, Bethel Bible Institute, Spencer, Massachusetts.

————. *Sign Posts on the Road to Success.* Seattle: Kenyon's Gospel Publishing Society, 1938.

————. *The Two Kinds of Faith: Faith's Secrets Revealed.* Seattle: Kenyon's Gospel Publishing Society, 1942.

————. *The Two Kinds of Knowledge.* Seattle: Kenyon's Gospel Publishing Society, 1942.

————. *The Two Kinds of Life.* Seattle: Kenyon's Gospel Publishing Society, 1971.

————. *The Two Kinds of Righteousness.* Seattle: Kenyon's Gospel Publishing Society, 1942.

————. *What Happened from the Cross to the Throne.* Seattle: Kenyon's Gospel Publishing Society, 1945.

————. *The Wonderful Name of Jesus.* Seattle: Kenyon's Gospel Publishing Society, 1927.

Lindsay, Gordon. ed. *The John G. Lake Sermons.* Dallas: Voice of Healing, 1949.

MacMillan, John A. *The Authority of the Believer.* Harrisburg, Pennsylvania: Christian Publications, 1981.

_____. *Encounter with Darkness.* Harrisburg, Pennsylvania: Christian Publications, 1980.

Matta, Judith A. *The Born-Again Jesus of the Word-Faith Teaching.* Fullerton, California: Spirit of Truth Ministries, 1984.

McConnell, Daniel R. "The Kenyon Connection: A Theological and Historical Analysis of the Cultic Origins of the Faith Movement." Master's Thesis, Oral Roberts Univ., 1982.

McCrossan, T. J. *Bodily Healing and the Atonement.* Tulsa: Faith Library, 1982.

Miller, Elliot. *Healing: Does God Always Heal?* San Juan Capistrano, California: Christian Research Institute, 1979.

Neuman, H. Terris. "An Analysis of the Sources of the Charismatic Teaching of 'Positive Confession.' " Unpublished manuscript.

Parker, Larry. *We Let Our Son Die.* Irvine, California: Harvest House, 1980.

Prater, Arnold. *How Much Faith Does It Take?* Nashville: Thomas Nelson, 1982.

Price, Charles S. *The Real Faith.* Plainfield, New Jersey: Logos, 1972.

Price, Frederick K. C. *Ever Increasing Faith Messenger.* Newsletter. Crenshaw Christian Center, Inglewood, California.

_____. *Faith, Foolishness, or Presumption?* Tulsa: Harrison House, 1979.

_____. *How Faith Works.* Tulsa: Harrison House, 1976.

_____. *Is Healing for All?* Tulsa: Harrison House, 1976.

_____. *Thank God for Everything?* Tulsa: Harrison House, 1977.

Simmons, Dale Hawthorne. "A Theological and Historical Analysis of Kenneth E. Hagin's Claim to Be a Prophet." Master's Thesis, Oral Roberts University, 1985.

Swaggart, Jimmy. *The Evangelist.* Newsletter. Jimmy Swaggart Ministries, Baton Rouge, Louisiana.

_____. *Hyper-Faith: A New Gnosticism?* Baton Rouge, Louisiana: Jimmy Swaggart Ministries, 1982.

Synan, Vinson. *The Holiness-Pentecostal Movement in the United States.* Grand Rapids: Eerdmans, 1971.

White, John. *The Golden Cow: Materialism in the Twentieth Century Church.* Downers Grove, Illinois: InterVarsity, 1979.

Wigglesworth, Smith. *Ever-Increasing Faith.* Springfield, Missouri: Gospel Publishing House, 1924.

_____. *Faith That Prevails.* Springfield, Missouri: Gospel Publishing House, 1938.

Metaphysical Cults and Their Background

Ahlstrom, Sydney E. *A Religious History of the American People.* New Haven: Yale Univ. Press, 1972.

Braden, Charles. *Christian Science Today: Power, Policy, Practice.* Dallas: Southern Methodist Univ. Press, 1958.

_____. *Spirits in Rebellion: The Rise and Development of New Thought.* Dallas: Southern Methodist Univ. Press, 1966.

_____. *These Also Believe: A Study of Modern American Cults.* New York: Macmillan, 1960.

Cady, H. Emile. *How I Used Truth.* Lee's Summit, Missouri: Unity School of Christianity, 1957.

_____. *Lessons in Truth.* Lee's Summit, Missouri: Unity School of Christianity, 1955.

Coffee, John and Richard L. Wentworth. *A Century of Eloquence: The History of Emerson College, 1880–1980.* Boston: Alternative Pub., 1982.

Cooke, George Willis. *Unitarianism in America.* Boston: American Unitarian Assoc., 1902.

Dresser, Horatio. *The Quimby Manuscripts.* Secaucus, New Jersey: Citadel, 1980.

Eddy, Mary Baker. *Christian Healing and Other Writings.* Boston: Trustees, 1875.

_____. *No and Yes.* Boston: Christian Science Pub. Society, [n.d..].

_____. *Science and Health with a Key to the Scriptures.* Boston: Trustees, 1875.

Enroth, Ronald et al. *A Guide to Cults & New Religions.* Downers Grove, Illinois: InterVarsity, 1983.

Ferguson, Charles. *The New Books of Revelation: The Inside Story of America's Astounding Religious Cults.* New York: Doubleday Doran & Co., 1928.

Fillmore, Charles. *Christian Healing.* Unity Village, Missouri: Unity School of Christianity, [n.d..].

_____. *Jesus Christ Heals.* Lee's Summit, Missouri: Unity School of Christianity, 1966.

_____. *Mysteries of Genesis.* Kansas City, Missouri: Unity School of Christianity, 1944.

_____. *Prosperity.* Unity Village, Missouri: Unity School of Christianity, 1981.

_____. *Talks on Truth.* Unity Village, Missouri: Unity School of Christianity, [n.d..].

Fillmore, Charles and Cora. *Teach Us to Pray.* Kansas City, Missouri: Unity School of Christianity, 1944.

Haushalter, Walter M. *Mrs. Eddy Purloins from Hegel.* Boston: A. A. Beauchamp, 1936.

Hoekema, Anthony. *Christian Science.* Grand Rapids: Eerdmans, 1972.

Martin, Walter. *The Kingdom of the Cults.* Minneapolis: Bethany Fellowship Inc., 1977.

_____. *Unity.* Grand Rapids: Zondervan, 1962.

Martin, Walter R. and Norman Klann. *The Christian Science Myth.* Grand Rapids: Zondervan, 1955.

Savage, Minot J. *Belief in God.* Boston: Geo. H. Ellis, 1882.

_____. *Religion in Evolution.* Boston: Geo. H. Ellis, 1876.

Sire, James W. *Scripture Twisting: 20 Ways the Cults Misread the Bible.* Downers Grove, Illinois: InterVarsity, 1980.

Trine, Ralph Waldo. *In Tune With the Infinite.* New York: Bobbs-Merrill Co., 1970.

_____. *What All the World's A-Seeking.* New York: Dodd, Mead & Co., 1920.

_____. *The Winning of the Best.* Indianapolis, Indiana: Bobbs-Merrill Co., 1912.

Wood, Henry. *New Thought Simplified.* Boston: Lothrop, Lee & Shepard Co., 1903.